# SIMPLE MINDS

## SONG BY SONG

# SIMPLE MINDS
# SONG BY SONG

LARELLE READ

FONTHILL

First published in Great Britain in 2026 by
Fonthill
An imprint of
Pen & Sword Books Ltd
Yorkshire – Philadelphia



print ISBN: 978-1-03615-692-3
ePUB ISBN: 978-1-03615-693-0
ePDF ISBN: 978-1-03615-694-7



A CIP catalogue record for this book is available from the British Library.



Typeset by Simon and Sons ITES Services Pvt. Ltd., Chennai, India.
Printed and bound in the UK by CPI Group (UK) Ltd, Croydon, CR0 4YY

FSC
www.fsc.org
MIX
Paper | Supporting responsible forestry
FSC® C013604

The Publisher's authorised representative in the EU for product safety is
Authorised Rep Compliance Ltd., Ground Floor, 71 Lower Baggot Street, Dublin D02 P593, Ireland.
www.arccompliance.com

For a complete list of Pen & Sword titles please contact

PEN & SWORD BOOKS LIMITED
47 Church Street, Barnsley, South Yorkshire, S70 2AS, England
E-mail: enquiries@pen-and-sword.co.uk
Website: www.pen-and-sword.co.uk
or
PEN AND SWORD BOOKS
1950 Lawrence Road, Havertown, PA 19083, USA
E-mail: uspen-and-sword@casematepublishers.com
Website: www.penandswordbooks.com

# Preface

My journey into the Simple Minds back catalogue truly began in the British summer of 2014. Until then, my knowledge of their music had been limited to the bigger hit singles. I owned a copy of *Once Upon a Time* during my mid-teens, but I never owned anything else. I would occasionally borrow a compilation album from the local library. At this stage Simple Minds remained firmly on my musical periphery.

Fast forward to around 2006 and the early days of streaming services and my first attempted exploration of their back catalogue. At this point I still wasn't quite ready for it and so it took until 2014 for my part-time dalliances to turn into a deep dive. From then on, I was hooked and voraciously listened to their entire musical output and researched their history.

What follows is an extensive breakdown of the history of Simple Minds, cataloguing their musical evolution. It is a comprehensive list, from their earliest demo recordings and songs performed during regular live sets, to their most recent releases, broken up into relevant categories and in chronological order. Over the past five decades, the band has amassed an impressive collection of material, as well as achieving singles chart success with more than twenty UK top-forty hits, No. 1 singles on both sides of the Atlantic, as well as five UK No. 1 albums and a Billboard top-ten album. This book aims to shed light on a catalogue containing almost 250 songs, the majority of which are original compositions. This is the concise story of Simple Minds' musical catalogue.

# Acknowledgements

The biggest help with research into the history of the band has been through Simon Cornwell and the website *Dream Giver Redux*, without which I would never have learned half of what I know about Simple Minds. His tireless work in relation to the band's history is fundamental to this book and without it my job would have been almost impossible. Simon, I owe you the most overwhelming debt of gratitude.

I'd also like to extend my thanks to the many knowledgeable Simple Minds fans I have come to know over the years, in particular Gordon Machray, Ronnie McGhie, Ben Barclay, Martin Potappel and Michael 'Baggers' Lees. I also extend this gratitude to the YouTube channels created by 'TopTonyChick' and 'Art&Talk'. The content provided on both channels has been invaluable.

I have drawn on numerous other sources of information to compile this book, and I have made my bibliography as extensive as possible.

I'd like to thank my partner Em for putting up with my obsession and being my long-suffering Simple Minds 'widow'. You deserve a medal!

Thanks also to my many gig buddies including Ally, Gillian, Michelle, Yvonne, Ruth, Sue, Francesca, Gina, Martyn, Alison and Chris. This book is dedicated to Robert Gray, Jackie Macmillan-Hughes, Rita Mcintosh and Annelore Brantegem.

# Contents

# Introduction

In the late autumn of 1977 the UK music scene was under the influence of the punk movement. In Glasgow, a new band had just been formed. They called themselves Simple Minds, and they would go on to be, without question, Scotland's most successful musical export.

Just a few months prior, Jim Kerr and Charlie Burchill had been in a punk outfit called Johnny & the Self Abusers, along with fellow high-school friends Brian McGee and Tony Donald. Kerr and Burchill forged a friendship when their respective families moved to the suburb of Toryglen in 1967, when Jim and Charlie were just eight years old. They met McGee and Donald while attending Holyrood Secondary School in the south side of Glasgow.

Johnny & the Self Abusers was the brainchild of the band's original singer Alan Cairnduff. The band had initially comprised friends John Milarky, Allan McNeill and Cairnduff. Kerr, Burchill, McGee and Donald joined a short while after. In true punk fashion, the band split on the day their one and only single was released on the Chiswick record label, featuring A-side 'Saints and Sinners' and B-side 'Dead Vandals'. Both songs were penned by Kerr and Burchill, although all the band members are given song-writing credits on the single label, except Cairnduff, who had left the band shortly before the final split. Milarky went on to join the Cuban Heels, while Kerr, Burchill, Donald and McGee formed what would become Simple Minds, bringing in a second guitarist, Duncan Barnwell, to join the band. In these early stages of Simple Minds, song-writing was handled by Kerr and Burchill.

The band's success was moderate; their rise to stardom began via word-of-mouth. On 17 January 1978 they played their first gig at local venue Satellite City (a discotheque located above the legendary local venue the Glasgow Apollo), before securing a weekly residency at the Mars Bar. Soon they had earned themselves a small but ardent following.

Towards the end of 1978 the band signed to Zoom records, an Edinburgh-based label run by Bruce Findlay, who would become the band's manager shortly afterwards. Findlay had struck a deal with major label Arista. Zoom would release records supported by Arista's funding. Initially creating Zoom to kickstart the musical output of local bands, Findlay had been releasing singles on the label until he signed Simple Minds. When the band joined the label, a new deal was struck with Arista. A three-album contract was signed between the band, Zoom and Arista. Simple Minds' debut album *Life in a Day* was released by Zoom in the spring of 1979.

The band by this point was a lean five-piece comprising Kerr on vocals (he was also the lyricist), Burchill on lead guitar and McGee on drums, with 1978 fresh recruits Mick MacNeil on keyboards and Derek Forbes on bass. Tony Donald had decided to leave the band during the summer of 1978, while the rest of the band had decided that Duncan Barnwell as second guitarist was surplus to requirements.

By 1979 the popularity of the band on the local live music scene was growing considerably, not only in Glasgow but also further afield throughout Scotland. They gained a support slot with Manchester group Magazine, who were touring the UK promoting their second album, *Secondhand Daylight*. Simple Minds were now able to promote *Life in a Day* beyond the Scottish border and as a result word started spreading across the UK. For such a new band they had gained themselves a good deal of exposure in the music press, as well as performing on television programmes such as the *Old Grey Whistle Test*. Minor chart successes were achieved with *Life in a Day*—both the lead single and the album. However, this was fleeting. The band then set their sights on mainland Europe.

In the meantime, they were back in the recording studio at Rockfield in Monmouthshire, laying down their second album, *Real to Real Cacophony*. The album is the epitome of a creative curveball and at the time Arista had trouble accepting the musical change of direction. Cracks began to appear in the Arista/Zoom partnership. Undeterred by the tensions with the label, the band set off for Europe and toured through Germany and Sweden in the autumn of 1979. A whistle-stop journey to New York, performing gigs at the end of October, including another recording for the *Old Grey Whistle Test*, broke up the German and Swedish tour dates.

The band continued their frenetic momentum into 1980 with more gigs on the European mainland as well as back home across the UK. Once again, they headed into the recording studio at Rockfield and produced their third album, *Empires and Dance*. If the chance to promote their debut album while supporting Magazine had seemed like a fantastic opportunity, it paled in comparison with the next support opportunity that came their way. This time they found themselves supporting Peter Gabriel on the European leg of his tour, fully financed by Gabriel. The lead single from *Empires and Dance*, 'I Travel', was their strongest single to date, but due to growing tensions with the Arista label, the release was fraught with distribution problems. Chart success continued to elude Simple Minds. The album stalled just outside the UK top forty, while 'I Travel' failed to break the chart.

By the end of 1980, Simple Minds' management was actively trying to get the band signed to an alternative record label. Bruce Findlay had knocked on the doors of CBS, Polydor and Virgin. Although Polydor offered more financial security, Findlay and the band decided to go with the Virgin deal as the label offered the band more creative control over their musical output. The band signed to the Virgin label in the spring of 1981.

More touring and recording in 1981 led to even broader horizons. The band toured the United States and Canada for the first time. They also travelled to Australia at the end of the year. Their twin album releases, *Sons and Fascination* and *Sister Feelings Call* saw them gain their first significant album chart success outside the UK. At the end of the recording of the album sessions, drummer Brian McGee left Simple Minds. He was replaced by Kenny Hyslop. The first single from *Sons and Fascination*, 'Love Song', broke into the top twenty singles chart in Australia. The tour of Australia and the overriding enthusiasm of the audiences there and in Canada propelled the band forward into recording what will be regarded by many as their breakthrough success, *New Gold Dream (81-82-83-84)*.

Simple Minds returned to the recording studio at the beginning of 1982 fresh with ideas from touring North America and Australia the previous year. They released 'Promised You a Miracle' in April and achieved their first UK singles chart success, reaching the top twenty. This only increased the momentum of the band during 1982. Tensions frayed with drummer Kenny Hyslop, however, and he was replaced by Mike Ogletree. The band toured Europe once again during the early months of 1982 and recorded *New Gold Dream* in the summer. The album was released in September. A couple of weeks later they were back in Australia and travelled on to New Zealand for the first time. They also returned to Canada and completed a final leg of the tour in the UK, with triumphant home gigs at Tiffany's in Glasgow on 18 and 19 November and again on 20 and 21 December. Drummer Mel Gaynor joined the band for this part of the tour.

The success of *New Gold Dream* was just a stepping stone for what was to come with Simple Minds. They continued to tour the album extensively through 1983. Where previous tours in North America had concentrated primarily on Canada, with just a smattering of dates taking them south of the border, the tail-end of the *New Gold Dream* tour saw the band play their most extensive list of dates in the United States yet. Another benchmark happened during August 1983 when Simple Minds were on the bill for the Phoenix Park Festival in Dublin. The band had started working on new material for the next album and one song had them so enthusiastic they decided to give it a live debut at Phoenix Park. The song was 'Waterfront' and from the testimony of fans present on the day, it went down a storm.

In the late summer of 1983 recording of *Sparkle in the Rain* began. The album was released in February 1984 and saw Simple Minds achieve their first of several UK chart-topping placements. The band now seemed more content to celebrate their roots and chose to record videos for both 'Waterfront' and 'Speed Your Love to Me' around Glasgow and the west coast of Scotland. The video for 'Waterfront' was recorded in locations that included the now world-famous Barrowland Ballroom in Glasgow's East End, as well as on the River Clyde, with the band members filmed aboard the Renfrew ferry. Scenes for 'Speed Your Love to Me' were also recorded at the ballroom, as well as under the M8 motorway underpass in Glasgow and around Loch Lomond.

Coinciding with the album's release came another gruelling touring schedule, starting out in Australia, hopping across the Tasman Sea to New Zealand, then back to Australia at the beginning of February. A string of UK and European dates followed through the spring and summer of 1984, turning the band into sold-out headliners and incorporating the summer festival circuit in Europe. In between, the various legs of the tour criss-crossed the Atlantic as Simple Minds performed headline dates, first with China Crisis as their support, and then later in the year Simple Minds were the support for The Pretenders. This was an opportunity for the newly wedded Jim Kerr and Chrissie Hynde to spend time together while simultaneously being out on the road. The final dates of the 'Tour du Monde' saw the band play in Japan.

By the end of 1984, Simple Minds were already in the early stages of writing material for their next album. When in the US touring with The Pretenders, producer Keith Forsey attended one of the shows and passed on a cassette to keyboard player Mick MacNeil, requesting that the band take a listen to a demo track he'd recorded with song-writing partner Steve Schiff. The song in question was 'Don't You (Forget About Me)'. MacNeil forgot about the tape. It was not until Forsey, along with film director John Hughes, contacted the band to enquire about their interest in the song that the rest of the band members were made aware of the tape. What happened next turned Simple Minds into a household name on both sides of the Atlantic.

Successes continued to rack up for Simple Minds. The exposure that they received from recording 'Don't You (Forget About Me)' and its propulsion up the Billboard chart brought about a string of hits. On the cusp of this, bassist Derek Forbes was asked to leave the band. He was replaced by John Giblin. Giblin's live debut just so happened to be at Live Aid in Philadelphia. Simple Minds had been asked to perform at the event, but not at Wembley Stadium (much to their consternation). The success of 'Don't You (Forget About Me)' led Live Aid organisers Bob Geldof and Harvey Goldsmith to insist that the band perform at the John F. Kennedy Stadium. They began their brief set with a freshly penned song, 'Ghost Dancing', before performing 'Don't You (Forget About Me)' and 'Promised You a Miracle' to the 90,000 strong crowd at the stadium and tens of millions of people watching live on television all around the world.

'Alive and Kicking', the lead single off their next album *Once Upon a Time*, reached the Billboard top ten, as did the album when released in October. In fact, the album produced an incredible four singles from its eight tracks, with three of them making the top forty singles chart on both sides of the pond ('Ghost Dancing' also made the UK top forty). From this, the next tour was the most extensive to date: a 150-date, twelve-month world tour, which began on 31 October 1985. Simple Minds were filling arenas and headlining festivals, playing to tens of thousands of fans across the globe.

A long-earned break from touring and recording spurred the release of the band's first live album, *Live in the City of Light*, in 1987. They performed at only a handful of concerts during the next two years, including two concerts in Brazil in January 1988, and the Nelson Mandela 70th Birthday Tribute held at Wembley Stadium in June 1988, during which they live debuted their tribute to the political prisoner with 'Mandela Day'.

Simple Minds chimed an end to the 1980s with the release of their ninth studio album, *Street Fighting Years*. Lead single 'Belfast Child' (released with 'Mandela Day' and 'Biko' as the *Ballad of the Streets* EP), took the No. 1 spot in the UK singles chart. It was Simple Minds' first and only UK No. 1 single (to date). *Street Fighting Years* became the band's fourth consecutive UK No. 1 album. The ensuing tour filled arenas and stadiums throughout Europe and the UK. The band also returned to Australia during the *Street Fighting Years* tour.

The 1980s was by far the most commercially successful decade for Simple Minds. They rose through the ranks by constantly touring and recording, starting with a firm local supportive following in their home city of Glasgow, then growing that audience outwards across the rest of the UK and into mainland Europe. Countries such as Germany, The Netherlands, Belgium, Italy, France, Denmark and Sweden took the band to their hearts. Further afield, they grew a strong fanbase on the back of early tours of Canada and Australia, the latter providing the band with their earliest singles chart success. This encouragement spurred them on to produce what is arguably their most revered album amongst their fans, *New Gold Dream (81-82-83-84)*. Although not their most commercially successful or highest selling album, it is deemed the touchstone of their early career. A turning point in the band's musical direction.

Prior to the release of *New Gold Dream*, Simple Minds had been considered an art rock/European electronic dance group. Their sound had industrial sensibilities with repetitious beats, hooks and riffs and Jim Kerr's lyrics during this period reflected those sounds with songs about dystopian European city life and travelling the world in the time of the Cold War freeze. Although the subject matter could be deep, yet fragmented and detached, the sound that cut through would always be joyous, uplifting and eerily danceable. There was no coldness to the music: it had heart and soul, and it won the praise of music critics and fans.

Simple Minds quickly evolved through the late 1970s and into the 1980s from post punk to art rock, from industrial dance music to New Wave synth pop-driven enlightenment, and on to become mainstream pop chart demigods and stadium-fillers with a political agenda. They were prolific with their musical output, releasing nine studio albums in the ten-year period from 1979–1989. It was inevitable that the 1990s would bring a paradigm shift. The most drastic change was the departure of Mick MacNeil from the band's line-up at the end of 1989. MacNeil reportedly went AWOL during the Australian leg of the *Street Fighting Years* tour. Touring had taken its toll on him, and he wanted a break from the relentless schedule. It was a request that largely fell upon deaf ears. Had MacNeil been heard or been allowed some time out, his departure might not have been inevitable. For Burchill and Kerr (in particular), a constant forward momentum was the driver of creativity. Until Kerr's own crisis of confidence drew him away to relative obscurity in contemplation of his own creative and musical future at the end of the 1990s, there was a constant forward thrust.

In 1990, Bruce Findlay left as the band's manager. This added to the turmoil that faced the duo left at the heart of Simple Minds, Jim Kerr and Charlie Burchill. In a creative world where two key players see forward propulsion as their creative spark, to have come full circle with song-writing entirely on the shoulders of Kerr and Burchill (as it had been during the formation of the band) must have made the two somewhat fearful of the future. Kerr would surely deny such a thing, even to this day. From the outside looking in, the duo did their best to appear unaffected by the upheaval. They just got on with it. MacNeil and Findlay were deemed further 'casualties of war'. Or perhaps, given Kerr's penchant for referring to Simple Minds' assault on the musical landscape as 'a crusade', MacNeil and Findlay's departures were due to them no longer wanting to 'fight the good fight'?

*Real Life* is the first album to contain original song compositions by Kerr and Burchill alone since their debut, *Life in a Day*. From second album *Real to Real Cacophony* onwards, other band members had been involved in the song-writing process, namely Mick MacNeil and Derek Forbes. When Forbes left in early 1985, John Giblin was also involved in writing compositions. The gap that had been left by MacNeil was to some extent filled by Stephen Lipson during the recording of *Real Life*. To my reckoning, it was this that helped *Real Life* continue the chart successes for Simple Minds. *Real Life* reached the top ten of the UK charts and produced four top forty hit singles. A tour of North America, Europe and the UK followed.

In 1992, Simple Minds released their first comprehensive compilation album, *Glittering Prize 81/92*. It was their fifth No. 1 album in the UK charts. The band was effectively on hiatus until the release of *Good News from the Next World* in early 1995. The fast sprints of album releases during the previous decade, involving the prolific creation of new material and culminating in commercial releases and almost ceaseless touring schedules, had slowed to a more manageable periodic cycle. Something which, when interviewed in 1995, Jim Kerr likened to, rather disparagingly (as far as the band itself was concerned), an Olympiad. In fact, he was concerned that the band would get stuck in this 'Olympiad-style' writing-recording-touring loop of a four-year period. The statement proved to be prescient, as from that time onwards Simple Minds have released a new studio album of original material roughly once every four years (with the odd exception).

The late 90s signalled the release of *Neapolis*, which was the first Simple Minds album in over 15 years not to make the top ten of the UK charts. During the short period from 1997–98, Derek Forbes returned to bass duties for Simple Minds. He was involved with the recording of *Neapolis* and toured with the band during this time.

The following year the band were recording again. The ensuing album failed to secure a commercial release.

Jim Kerr's creative flow was now beginning to dwindle. He found himself seriously contemplating bringing an end to Simple Minds, which in hindsight may have been news to Charlie Burchill. Kerr decided (at least part-time initially) to relocate to Sicily and invest in land, which would become the location for his hotel, Villa Angela, in Taormina. Working with a group of Italian DJs, Kerr slowly regained his creative passion and started song-writing again. This propelled Simple Minds on to the long road to recovery. A slow and steady rebuild began, which led to the releases of *Neon Lights* in 2001 and then *Cry* in 2002. While the creative momentum was again building in the studio, the band recommenced a regular touring schedule, which started off with the *Floating World* tour in the spring and summer of 2002. Although *Cry* was a chart failure, the resulting tour was a success, particularly among the ardent fanbase that had stuck with the band through what is now seen as Simple Minds' nadir. New members of the band during this period, bass player Eddy Duffy and keyboardist Andy Gillespie, were seen as welcome additions to the Simple Minds fold. In 2005 the Minds' musical output continued to achieve new chart success. Albums *Black and White 050505*, *Graffiti Soul* and *Big Music* all charted within the UK top forty, and 2018 release *Walk Between Worlds* gained the band their first top-five UK albums chart position in over 20 years—the previous being *Good News from the Next World* with a number two chart position in 1995.

In the flurry of musical output during 2009, Jim Kerr felt spurred into releasing his one and only solo album, *Lostboy! AKA Jim Kerr*, which debuted in 2010. This saw Kerr working on the album with several musical collaborators. Chief among them was Jez Coad, producer of Simple Minds' previous albums *Black and White 050505* and *Graffiti Soul*. Meanwhile, Charlie Burchill took a song-writing sabbatical. Coad, along with Kerr and Burchill, played an integral part in enabling the band to reach the higher echelons of commercial success once again. The same is also true of the producers who have been working with Simple Minds since the recording of *Big Music,* Andy Wright and Gavin Goldberg.

In case one is tempted to liken the song-writing partnership of Kerr and Burchill to either Lennon and McCartney or Richards and Jagger, there is one pivotal difference to consider. Jim Kerr has always stressed that he is not a musician—unlike Lennon, McCartney, Richards and Jagger. So the creative partnership between Kerr and Burchill is between musician and lyricist/singer. They obviously do bounce off each other creatively. What Kerr gives Burchill musically is a little unclear, but it may just be affirmation that Burchill's musical compositions are heading in the right direction. Within Simple Minds, Kerr seems to instinctively know what works and what doesn't as far as the band's overall musical direction is concerned. This acute insight has brought about much success for the band. In fact, one could say that Kerr not being a musician has been a strength rather than a hindrance. It could also be argued that, as a vocalist, Kerr does indeed perform with a musical instrument—though that may be seen (quite rightly) as hyperbolic. What he lacks in instrumental ability is more than made up for by an acute ear for melody and a talent for creating a lyrical canvas on which to paint the images he sees within the compositions he writes.

As for Charlie Burchill, not only has he been the band's lead guitarist from day one, but he has also played several other instruments on Simple Minds' recordings, as well as during live shows. In the past he has played saxophone and violin and has (over the years) also played and composed songs on keyboards. The likes of The Edge of U2 and Johnny Marr (formerly of The Smiths) have cited Burchill as a contemporary influence on their own guitar-playing style and technique.

Since 2014, Simple Minds have continued to produce new material and are still going out on the road touring, not only to showcase new material, but also to play live between new releases. The current fanbase is vast and ever-hungry for new material and opportunities to see the band play live. The fanbase is also diverse in age and demographic, from the die-hards who were there from the very earliest days seeing them perform at the Mars Bar in Glasgow in 1978, and were with them when they initially broke open the doors to commercial success with *New Gold Dream* in 1982, through to the more recent younger fans who attend gigs with their parents or other family members. A mixture of genders, creeds and nationalities is also evident. The band have fans everywhere, from mainland Europe, across to the Americas, into Africa, through Asia and down into the Antipodes. I personally know of fans based in Sweden, The Netherlands, Germany, Italy, France, Belgium, Spain, Kazakhstan, the United States, Canada, Mexico, Argentina, Brazil, Japan, Australia, New Zealand and South Africa.

Among their musical accolades, Simple Minds received the Q Inspiration Award in 2014, presented to them by James Dean Bradfield of Manic Street Preachers. In 2016, they were awarded the Ivor Novello Award for Outstanding Song Collection. The ceremony took place at the Grosvenor House Hotel in London. Singer-songwriter Steve Harley presented the award to founding band members Jim Kerr and Charlie Burchill, as well as to former member Mick MacNeil, with former member Derek Forbes receiving his award a short time later.

In 2022, Simple Minds recommenced the *40 Years of Hits* tour that had begun in February 2020 but was postponed indefinitely just ten dates in due to the Covid-19 pandemic. In October 2022 the band released their twenty-first studio album, *Direction of the Heart*, to positive acclaim.

At the time of writing, the band have just completed their *Global* tour 2024, with concerts taking place in Australia, New Zealand, Dubai, the United States, several European countries and the UK. Further touring is set for 2025, which includes dates for the Americas. To date, the band have performed an estimated 3,500 concerts during their career. Along with founding members Jim Kerr and Charlie Burchill (vocals and lead guitar respectively), the current line-up of Simple Minds consists of Sarah Brown on additional vocals, Gordy Goudie on additional guitars and keyboards, Ged Grimes on bass, Cherisse Osei on drums and percussion and Erik Ljunggren on keyboards.

1

# Early Compositions 1977–78

## Commercial releases, demo recordings, and significant live tracks by Johnny & the Self Abusers and Simple Minds

It was not until late 1978 that Simple Minds secured a record deal. That's not to say they languished waiting to be spotted. They rehearsed, performed, and wrote songs right from the start. Jim Kerr and Charlie Burchill started writing songs for Johnny & the Self Abusers in 1977 and continued when (along with McGee and Donald) they split from the Abusers and formed Simple Minds. Demo recordings were produced by Simple Minds, the first of which was in November 1977. Ostensibly still Johnny & the Self Abusers at the time, as Milarky and McNeill were involved in these first demo sessions, both left shortly after. The second set of demos were recorded once Donald had left, and MacNeil and Forbes had joined. Material from these recordings was eventually released on CD in 1998. Titled *The Early Years 1977–1978*, it was quickly withdrawn from sale. Also included here are songs featured on the Johnny & the Self Abusers single, as well as several songs that were performed live during Simple Minds' unsigned period. The songs featured have a level of significance in the band's embryonic development that warrants inclusion here.

### 'Saints and Sinners'

The A-side of the one and only Johnny & the Self Abusers single. The song is delivered in punk timing within a punchy one minute and fifty second duration. It's pithy but not particularly aggressive in style or intent. For a young man with a stutter, Jim Kerr shoots off an impressive rate of lyrics, keeping pace with the fast tempo of the song. Musically, it has a great guitar riff, with a nimble little solo halfway through. The pace keeps the listener on their toes. No time to get bored. Infamously, the single was released on the same day that the Abusers split, sometime during the first week of November 1977.

## 'Dead Vandals'

One of the earliest compositions involving Jim Kerr and Charlie Burchill as a song-writing unit. It has a driving, strumming beat. It has a more sophisticated twist than 'Saints and Sinners'. It is also twice as long, which also elevates it beyond the quick thrash of your standard punk song. Lyrically, Kerr stretches himself in having more to say. He more clearly articulates the words he sings when compared to 'Saints and Sinners', which at times ends up an incoherent jumble due to the frenetic pace. It's a song that conjures up the idea of 'wasted youth'. A gang of young people are just hanging about and wasting time in the city at night. It's a theme that Kerr would return to 35 years later when writing 'Broken Glass Park', but in antithesis as a celebration of an aspirational youth, dreaming of musical escape and translating those aspirations into action.

The protagonist in 'Dead Vandals' seems to lack direction, with the confessional declaration 'I just can't handle where to go and what to do.' In fact, it seems as if the song aims at a similar aspirational tone to 'Broken Glass Park'.

In a Facebook post from January 2022, Kerr quoted the opening lines to the song and declared it was: 'A juvenile attempt to describe in a three-minute rock song those times spent meandering among the centuries-old headstones of the Necropolis. I reckon it's one of our best tunes.' The song was officially released as a Johnny & the Self Abusers track as the B-side to 'Saints and Sinners'.

## '18-18'

A title that is a blatant nod to the similarly titled Alice Cooper track. Jim Kerr was a fan of early Alice Cooper and saw the band when they played the Green's Playhouse in Glasgow in the early 1970s. Much like 'Saints and Sinners', it has a fast punk tempo with a quick, punchy guitar riff and solo, as well as a saxophone solo towards the end of its speedy two minutes. Kerr's lyrics at this point describe or contextualise teen life in the late 1970s, expressing observations of attitude, dress, style (or lack thereof), and the individual teenager's place within it all. It's exciting but scary—particularly in a city such as Glasgow, as expressed in these lines: 'You want to go out/But there's danger about' and 'I see confusion ahead/You could be mixed-up or dead when you're 18'.

## 'Tonight'

This has a mid-range tempo, somewhere between that of 'Dead Vandals,' 'Saints and Sinners' and '18-18'. There's an attempt to be a little more sophisticated with the lyrics this time. Kerr is almost promoting the band with the lines of the chorus: 'We're gonna get it on tonight/Forget the rest/We're gonna do our best'. It's not the most ardent of punk songs, summed up with the lines 'Because they wanna make us fight/But we're staying close together'. Perhaps this is more of a statement on the idea that punk was seen as polarising to the rest of the population? Along with the stigma of punks being anarchists for the sake of it, when there was a stronger drive for creative freedom at play. I think this is what Kerr is trying to convey. Punks are—in a sense—freedom fighters rather than the terrorists they're being portrayed as by the city authorities and media.

## 'Little Bitch'

The song leans heavily into the rock 'n' roll feel musically. It's certainly influenced lyrically, if not musically, by The Velvet Underground, perhaps with a hint of T-Rex and Marc Bolan in there for good measure. Kerr is trying out his best Lou Reed as a lyricist, if not necessarily as a performer (as much as he tries). Thumping bass, great floor tom drums, lots of high chord guitars, some saxophone. It's a stand-out and quite the shame that it never went beyond being recorded as a demo for the purposes of seeking a recording contract.

## 'Pablo Picasso' (J. Milarky)

I felt this song should be included in this list of early Simple Minds material primarily because it featured so heavily in their live set during the late 1970s. It continued to be performed in the live sets until early 1980. It's not strictly a Simple Minds song and it should probably be classified as a cover, having been written by John Milarky. However, it was recorded as a demo track for the unsigned and newly named Simple Minds in November 1977, featuring Milarky on vocals. Punk enough in terms of the expletives used in the lyrics, it features lines directed at someone who is not thought of favourably. Although the title is a direct take from the Modern Lovers song, rather than a direct namecheck of the Spanish artist, its musical styling leans more to The Velvet Underground. With that said, Jonathan Richman (founder of the Modern Lovers) was also very heavily influenced by The Velvet Underground, to the point of following the band around as they toured the United States during the late 1960s. The main protagonist of the song is said to have been influenced by Milarky's brother.

## 'Subway Sex'

Possibly one of the weaker tracks of the early songs penned by Kerr and Burchill. Musically it is a blend of punk and classic rock, with a tinge of prog. The verses are quite wordy, and the chorus is repetitive and catchy, but ultimately one can understand why this track didn't go anywhere after its demo recording.

## 'Lies'

Back to fast-tempo punk, the song opens with a wailing sax followed by Kerr's scatter-gun delivery of lyrics. The lines come in such a torrent it's not an easy job to decipher all that's been said. The gist of the song's meaning can be discovered in its chorus: 'Lies/Make it up, come on give us your view/So how can I tell, how can I tell if it's true?' It's all done and dusted within two minutes. Short and to the point.

### 'European Son'

This is the second track from *Early Years 1977–1978,* performed by the first authentic incarnation of Simple Minds, comprising Jim Kerr, Charlie Burchill, Derek Forbes, Mick MacNeil and Brian McGee. The first track, 'Act of Love', will be discussed further during the chapter on *Direction of the Heart*. The band's progression is discernible on a track like 'European Son'. Musically they were coming on in leaps and bounds. The addition of Forbes and MacNeil was already proving to be worth its weight in gold. MacNeil's keyboard breaks, especially during the middle eight, are fabulous. Burchill's guitar is being played in a way that becomes his eventual signature style. Kerr expands his lyrical reach, but vocally he's still finding his feet, still searching for his voice. They are still giving more than just cursory nods to their influences, but they are slowly coming into their own. I also detect a couple of lines in the lyrics being used elsewhere. There is the use of 'I see the psychopath/I hear the silent laugh', which isn't a million miles away from the lines in 'Special View' (see *Life in a Day* additional tracks), 'I feel the aftermath/I see the madman's laugh'.

### 'Did You Ever?/Doo Be Doo'

Musically it's a fast tempo affair. Again, it's made all the richer for its progression with the addition of MacNeil and Forbes to the band. The lyrics are not easy to decipher but the chorus/chant of 'Doo be doo/Doo be doo/Doo be doo woah oh', is easily heard and irresistibly catchy. It featured in the band's live set during 1978 but was eventually dropped.

### 'Rosemary's Baby'

The track wears several influences on its sleeve. It's up tempo and has a lot of keyboard flourishes reminiscent of The Stranglers' Dave Greenfield or Magazine's Dave Formula. The song is a blend of elements of Magazine, The Stranglers, and The Boomtown Rats. A more traditionally structured verse/chorus/verse affair from Jim Kerr lyrically, it's not easy to decipher all the words, but it's obvious from the song's title what the subject matter of it could be, namely the Ira Levin novel turned into a film by director Roman Polanski starring Mia Farrow. There's more on Levin to come later. The song was performed during the live set in the latter part of 1978. There is a bootleg of the band performing at Grangemouth Town Hall in December 1978 and the song is reputed to feature on it. It was also recorded for the demo of *Life in a Day* in December 1978. However, it didn't make it to the later recording sessions for the album.

### 'You Better Watch Out'

Only one recording of this song exists, from a bootleg of their gig at the Mars Bar, Glasgow, on 30 July 1978—the first known bootleg of the band to have been recorded. It starts out with a rocking riff, as most of the tracks from the unsigned Simple Minds repertoire tended to do. Mick MacNeil's honky-tonk playing on this track exposes just how skilled he is as a player and what an asset he will be to the band for many years to come. It's hard to decipher many lyrics, but Jim Kerr's voice is sounding good, and the chorus is deathly catchy. Aspects of the song's musical structure are reminiscent of 'Gimme Some Loving' by the Spencer Davis Group. At three and a half minutes, it was the perfect length to keep the crowd going nicely through mid-set.

## 'Caught in a Dream'

A slow tempo song that contains elements of rock, prog and blues. It has a musical structure reminiscent of Iggy Pop's 'Turn Blue', a track from 1977's *Lust for Life*. I can even detect the use of the line 'I shot myself down' in the lyrics Kerr sings. The chorus is catchy enough, and the staccato drum fills add a musical intrigue, but the song does stretch on a bit at 6:30 duration. It's another early piece of original material that had the briefest life on the constantly evolving and ever-expanding Simple Minds set. I asked Jim Kerr via Facebook in November 2017 about what happened to the song:

> Nothing happened to it—that's what happened to it! It was one of a number of songs that we first wrote, played a few times and then stopped playing. Why did we stop? I can't remember with that one really. Either we got bored, or we just came to the conclusion that we didn't like it very much. We were writing one or two new songs most weeks during that period. With every new one we added, one would get dropped to make room. I don't recall anyone missing it too much when we dropped it. We certainly wouldn't go back to it.

## 'Take Me to the Angels'

This is a curious beast, in so far as Jim Kerr would go on to say in an interview in 1983 that he disliked 'The obvious rock 'n' roll language. "Don't You Want Me Baby" for instance or even "Great Balls of Fire" and things. I've always liked ambiguities and fragments and things with a bit more mystery to them.' Each line in the verses begins with 'Oh baby' and other than the chorus of 'Take me to the angels' and the first line of the song 'Oh baby, do you want to take me to the angels', no other words can be heard clearly on the two bootleg recordings that exist of the song. Despite what Kerr had said in 1983, he obviously wasn't averse to using clichéd rock 'n' roll language himself. As for the song's musical make-up? It leans heavily on the glam period of the early 1970s. Dare I say it is Bolanesque in style? It's a catchy tune and has a fantastic guitar solo in the middle. It was another song that fell victim to the prolific rate of creativity during Simple Minds' early development.

# 2

# *Life in a Day*

| | |
|---|---|
| UK: | 20 April 1979 |
| Personnel: | Backing vocals: Burchill, Forbes, McGee, MacNeil<br>Bass: Derek Forbes<br>Drums, percussion: Brian McGee<br>Guitars: Charlie Burchill<br>Keyboards: Michael MacNeil<br>Violin: Charlie Burchill<br>Vocals: Jim Kerr |
| Duration: | 43 minutes |
| Produced by: | John Leckie |
| Chart position: | UK: 30; US: - |

Simple Minds began recording *Life in a Day* in December 1978. Most of the recording took place through the winter inside the sub-zero ice box that was the Rolling Stones Mobile Studio. This is reflected in the sleeve notes on the album, handwritten by Jim Kerr, stating: 'Album recorded at a very low temperature'. The final touches were recorded at the prestigious Abbey Road Studios in London, and in recent times Kerr has recounted this as an event that made him nervous. The history of the studio got the better of him and made him feel physically ill at the prospect of being there. Conversely, bass player Derek Forbes was in his element and lapping up the time the band was given at Abbey Road.

Members of the band were big Velvet Underground fans, so their initial choice of producer for the album was John Cale. Arista felt he was too expensive and declined. Thus, production duties were given to John Leckie.

Most of the songs on the album had been written over the previous twelve months and performed live many times. This also caused consternation for Kerr, who felt disappointment about the reproduction of the band's sound in the studio once the album had been released. This feeling was a major driving force in the band returning to the recording studio just months after the release of *Life in a Day* to record follow-up *Real to Real Cacophony* at Rockfield Studios in Wales.

Musically, the album is steeped in post-punk sentiment. Kerr, when reflecting on his disappointment in the album, declared: 'We sound like The Boomtown Rats!' It is a worthy point. Several tracks have saxophones on them, not an instrument you would usually associate with the sound of Simple Minds were you to come across their music from 1981 onwards. Nor is the violin an instrument that you would usually think of as synonymous with their sound (at least not until the release of *Street Fighting Years* a decade after *Life in a Day*), but it does appear on arguably the most avant-garde track on the album, the eerie 'Pleasantly Disturbed'. Elsewhere on the album songs have a more traditional power pop/post-punk style. Fans attending their gigs at the time lauded 'Chelsea Girl', 'Pleasantly Disturbed' and 'Wasteland'. In fact, 'Chelsea Girl' was so loved by the fans at gigs that Kerr allegedly grew tired of performing the song, as it would invariably get an encore. It remained in the live set until early 1980. The prolific nature of the song-writing taking place in those early days meant that 'Chelsea Girl' was soon pushed out—at least for most of the 1980s.

Lyrics would undergo entire rewrites by Kerr and song titles would change as a result. For example, album track 'No Cure' had previously been titled 'Cocteau Twins', from which the Scottish band of the same name took their moniker, having seen Simple Minds perform at the Grangemouth Town Hall in 1978 supporting Ultravox. Another track, 'Destiny', had formerly been titled 'Sweet Things'. Prior to the album release the band appeared on the *Old Grey Whistle Test* performing what would be the album's lead single, the title track 'Life in a Day', as well the follow-up single 'Chelsea Girl'.

The album was released on 20 April 1979. Two weeks later it broke into the UK top forty at No. 37. The album peaked at No. 30. Of its two singles, 'Life in a Day' and 'Chelsea Girl', only the former had any (minor) chart success, making it into the top 100 in the UK singles chart but failing to break into the top forty.

## The songs

### 'Someone'

Duration: 3.40

It's an up-tempo opening track. It comes in with a great guitar and a quick keyboard flourish. A catchy riff and then it settles in with solo keyboards before that opening line of 'Ruby says she does not dream'. It's an intriguing way to begin a song; almost as if Jim Kerr is introducing us to a novel, and in a sense he is, if one were to use the simile of an album being akin to a novel and the opening track being its first chapter. What is up-tempo musically is countered by the lyrics of the song. There's a depressing air to it, with talk of the evening outside being 'cold and wet' and not being able to see sunlight. The young people want escape. Those that are left, anyway, as the second verse declares 'Streets more empty every day'. The protagonist of the song seems to be being pursued—'Someone's coming for me'—but then informs us that they're out of reach: 'I've got some feelings so distant no one else can see'.

As a pacey opening track, it made its way into the live set during the *Life in a Day* tour of 1979. It was a song that lived long in Kerr's mind as one that the band should revisit during subsequent tours. In an interview with journalist Billy Sloan in March 1984, Kerr mentioned 'Someone' as a track he'd have liked to include on the *Tour du Monde* of 1984, but time constraints for the setlist didn't make that possible. The song finally returned to the Simple Minds live set during the *5x5 Live* tour of 2012. The track was released as a B-side for the German issue of the 'Life in a Day' single in 1979.

## 'Life in a Day'

Duration: 4.00

The lead single off the album. It made a minor appearance in the UK singles chart, lower down the rankings outside of the top forty, peaking at No. 62 in mid-May, several weeks after its release. A hypnotic two-chord guitar/bass rhythm opens the song. Mick MacNeil's keyboard melody exudes an eeriness that foreshadows the paranoia and fear expressed in Kerr's lyrics, describing a protagonist running away from or being chased by ... a gang? Or perhaps it's a case of espionage. It doesn't sound like it's going to end well if we take note of the lyrical declaration of it being a 'fatal event'. Has the protagonist witnessed something they shouldn't have? The telling point of the whole song hinges on the line 'Some say it takes two to know/But could it all just be me?' For reasons that remain questionable, it was decided by Arista that 'Life in a Day' should be the album's lead single. The more obvious choice was 'Chelsea Girl'. This was the first in a series of dubious decisions that meant the record deal with Arista would be—in relation to the longevity of the band—a very short-lived affair.

## 'Sad Affair'

Duration: 2.45

I feel that this is one of the songs on the album that led Jim Kerr to likening the sound produced on *Life in a Day* to that of The Boomtown Rats. There is a prominent saxophone on this track, and it has elements that replicate the sound of 'Rat Trap'. It does feel like a 1970s throwback and seems off-kilter for a band that had been steadfastly looking forward. In fact, there is almost a rockabilly feel to the sound of the song, with the hand claps delivered throughout the tune between the song's lines of verse. Lyrically, the title denotes the subject matter perfectly. A soured relationship, one that the protagonist doesn't seem particularly phased about.

## 'All For You'

Duration: 2.50

This is one of the first songs that personally lured me into being an ardent Simple Minds fan. The song begins with a great rock riff from Burchill, with a high key two-note organ underpinning it. Overall, the song is more classic, catchy pop with some strange quirks. The middle eight with the piano is there due to then-manager Bruce Findlay having a play around in the studio one night. Producer John Leckie liked the result of the jarring notes Findlay had played so much that he mixed it into the recording of the track. Kerr's lyrics describe an encounter with a dramatic outcome. A knife attack has seemingly taken place. The narrator seems to suggest they've witnessed the attack, or perhaps been the perpetrator of it? And they made the attack 'All for you'. An act of protection or defence? A motivation or an alibi?

## 'Pleasantly Disturbed'

Duration: 8.00

A glorious epic. The jarring, slightly reverb guitar that intros it, as well the drums and bass that are present throughout, are heavily influenced by The Velvet Underground. The violin could well have been played by John Cale himself, but it wasn't. It was played by an orchestra recorded at Abbey Road Studios. It is this track that best reveals why the band were so keen to have Cale as the producer of their debut album. Jim Kerr is no Lou Reed when it comes to writing about the dark side of city life. I don't say this disparagingly. Kerr was very much finding his feet as a lyricist at this time, and his strength has always been bringing light to his subjects, not darkness. Drug addiction is the main theme of the track. At this point in the late 1970s, Glasgow was falling under the spell of heroin. The song was the dramatic finale to the band's first gig at Satellite City in January 1978. It was a show-stopping number in the set throughout 1978 and remained a firm favourite through subsequent tours until the latter months of 1980. The song was then performed as one of the highlights of the set during the *5x5 Live* tour of 2012.

## 'No Cure'

Duration: 3.38

This track started life under the name 'Cocteau Twins' and was responsible for the name of the band formed by Robin Guthrie and Will Heggie in 1979 in the Scottish town of Grangemouth. Kerr did some rewriting of the lyrics, mostly in the chorus as the verses are largely the same as they were when originally written in 1978. The tempo of the song gets altered and slowed from the previous 'Cocteau Twins' version. After going through its transformation, it was dropped from the live set, forever to remain as an item of trivia, for giving the band Cocteau Twins their name.

## 'Chelsea Girl'

Duration: 4.33

One of the earliest compositions penned by Kerr and Burchill as a song-writing duo. On several occasions Jim Kerr has told the story of a song-writing session with Burchill that took place in Kerr's parents' flat in Toryglen. When his mother came home from work (Irene Kerr was a shop assistant at the local Gregg's bakery) weighed down by a tray of strawberry tarts, both he and Burchill had been so deeply entrenched in the song-writing session they'd become famished and devoured the whole tray. The song was a live favourite of the audiences that saw the band perform during 1978. By the time it was recorded for *Life in a Day* in early 1979, Kerr was getting bored with performing it, but it was a 'hit' in all but chart success. Unlike its predecessor 'Life in a Day', it never bothered the UK singles chart. One could argue that the first mistake record company Arista made was not releasing the song as the lead single, instead holding on to it for the album's second single release. Arista believed that doing so would result in a greater chart success for 'Chelsea Girl', but the decision backfired.

## 'Wasteland'

Duration: 3.44

The song was one of the earliest Simple Minds compositions. In fact, it started life as a Johnny & the Self Abusers track and was one of the songs recorded as a demo in November 1977. Burchill plays a great riff on this song. There is a subtle change to the composition by the time it's recorded for *Life in a Day* some fifteen months later. The closing lines to the final verse were originally 'I've been wrong/ You've been unkind/Could it be your simple minds'. By the time the track was recorded for the album, Kerr had altered the end part of the line to 'There's so much more that I can't find'.

## 'Destiny'

Duration: 3.36

The track started out as a song called 'Sweet Things', originally penned by Kerr and Burchill in 1978. The only line that seems to remain from the original lyrics is 'I think you'd rather be alone'. This reveals how quickly Kerr's writing skills were advancing and how astute he was at putting his observations across with clarity in his lyrics. Not everything he writes is oblique and ambiguous. A bootleg recording was made of 'Destiny' when the band performed at Grangemouth Town Hall in late December 1978. The lyrics are not easily decipherable, but it's clear they were different from the version recorded for the album.

## 'Murder Story'

Duration: 6.18

First comes the death knell strike of a note of piano that signals this song is going to be dark. It has always reminded me of the canter of a horse with the way that the guitar riff and hi-hat cymbal tempo begins. Paranoia reigns supreme in this tale of deceit. Is our protagonist a witness to a murder? The chorus is delivered by Kerr in quite a matter-of-fact way, with a flurry of playful keyboard flair from Mick MacNeil, akin to an old bar honky-tonk. The second verse builds on the protagonist's paranoia with growing detail that makes you start to question whether he is the witness to a murder or the murderer himself. There is a clever irony in being informed by the line that 'The children from the street call out my name', with the backing vocal yell of 'Hey you'. Mid-song a change of tempo comes, signalled by a Burchill solo riff. A ramping up of the tension comes, with both verses repeated with more a sense of indignation than paranoia. There's a denial of guilt with 'It wasn't me/She said she was my sister'. Layers of Kerr's voice with differing backing vocal lines seem to denote the murder scene, all the while ramping up the tension with the increasing pace and now screeching guitar and heightened scale of piano keys. There's a repetition of innocence, then finally a clear declaration of 'It was me!' Then the song abruptly ends. It's perfect.

## Additional tracks

### 'Special View'

Duration: 4.14

The B-side to 'Life in a Day'. It was initially recorded as a demo in late 1978. It was then recorded during the album sessions, which would suggest it was a contender for inclusion on the album, but it was ultimately relegated to the B-side of the album's lead single. Musically, it's a rather eerie ballad, but is filled with a menacing kind of sensuality. I've always felt that it was a break-up song about a meeting of young lovers at a seaside location. A final meeting before the couple split.

### 'Garden of Hate'

Duration: 4.27

B-side to 'Chelsea Girl'. Another song title that harks back to a time when Simple Minds had a much more 'out and proud' darker edge to them, at least lyrically and with song titles. Once Simple Minds reach the New Wave of the early 1980s, Jim Kerr's lyrics are essentially uplifting in nature. Even when touching on more harrowing subjects like sectarian violence ('Belfast Child') and drug addiction ('Dolphins'), there is something positive to take away from them. But when the band started out, there was a definite darker edge present in songs such as 'Pleasantly Disturbed', 'Murder Story' and 'Garden of Hate'. The song begins with an eerie MacNeil synth waltz which quickly fades out, replaced by a catchy, rocking Burchill riff. It's another song that ratchets up the tension, with a mocking and snide repetition of the title with calls of 'Ha-ha/Ha-ha-ha' with a final crescendo and stop.

3

# *Real to Real Cacophony*

| | |
|---|---|
| UK: | 23 November 1979 |
| Personnel: | Bass: Derek Forbes |
| | Drums, percussion: Brian McGee |
| | Guitars: Charlie Burchill |
| | Keyboards: Michael MacNeil |
| | Saxophone: Charlie Burchill |
| | Violin: Charlie Burchill |
| | Vocals: Jim Kerr |
| Duration: | 41 minutes |
| Produced by: | John Leckie |
| Chart position: | UK: -; US: - |

There was a strong desire to get back to the drawing board when it came to the recording of *Real to Real Cacophony*. The band, largely collective in this feeling through the influence of Jim Kerr, wanted to shake off the disappointment of *Life in a Day*. Soon after the end of their first UK-wide tour supporting Magazine, they decamped to Rockfield Studios in Monmouthshire. It was a hedonistic time for the band and that transmogrified their sound and the musical output on *Real to Real Cacophony*. It was obvious that Simple Minds were feeling the pull towards the art rock influences that underpinned their existence, while simultaneously wanting to forge their own sonic future. Those summer days at Rockfield recording their follow-up album paved the way for Simple Minds to eventually foster and develop their own sound. It was the true start of them finding their way. They were taking baby steps but the baby in question was already as big as Finn MacCool.

There were also musical dalliances while recording as the band encountered their musical heroes. During the sessions at Rockfield, none other than Iggy Pop was recording in the adjacent studio, working on his *Soldier* album. Among his company during recording was David Bowie, the man responsible for giving Simple Minds their name, so heavy was his influence on them. All the band members were roped in to record backing vocals on the track 'Play It Safe'. For many years I believed that Bowie had overdubbed his own backing vocals for the song. It wasn't until recently that it dawned on me that I was hearing Kerr's vocals mirroring Bowie's.

The A&R team at Arista were dumbfounded by what the band delivered to them. To this day I find it incredible that acts such as Iggy Pop, Lou Reed and Patti Smith were on the label and seemingly had *carte blanche* to do what they wanted, whereas Simple Minds' output on *Real to Real Cacophony* was somehow deemed 'commercially unviable'. As former manager Bruce Findlay said to me when I interviewed him in 2019, the label just 'didn't know how to market them'. Unfortunately, this was reflected in the sales of the album, which were initially poor. As a result, Arista felt vindicated by their wishy-washy marketing of the album. The visual anonymity of the album artwork did not help. Although the title and band name were printed on the cover, the font was small and easily overlooked. Arista released just one single from the album, 'Changeling'. Although a great song, it can be argued it was not the strongest track on the album. Greater consideration should have been given to 'Factory' or 'Premonition' for single release, with the other offered up as a follow-up single.

## The songs

### 'Real to Real'

Duration: 2.47

Lyrically, it's like a work of science fiction. This was something that seemed to intrigue or at least entertain Jim Kerr in his younger life, but he ended up confessing that he was not much of a fan in his later years. The synths that Mick MacNeil uses on this song feel very akin to the 'knob-twiddling' of Brian Eno in his early Roxy Music days. It's certainly not a tune you can dance to easily. There is a buried talking voice accompanying the music after the first verse. A voice lost in a radio signal? It has a beautiful ethereal tone thanks to MacNeil's keys. The scales climb, and the final delivery of the verse is delivered with a key change, a rarity in a Simple Minds song. The track ends at a halt of instruments and an echoing vocal fade of 'No'.

### 'Naked Eye'

Duration: 2.21

I love the snare drum splashes on this track. There is a rather juvenile misheard lyric that ripples through the fanbase, misquoting Jim Kerr's first line as, 'Charlie was farting again'. In fact, it's quite a dark and fragmented piece. It feels like a song resulting from an experiment with the William Burroughs cut-up method of writing, where sentences (or in this case lines of song lyrics) are laid out in an original order to then be mixed up and rearranged. While usually abstract as a result, some songs can still make linear sense. David Bowie employed this technique, particularly through the early to mid-1970s. The lyrics read quite 'trippy'—as if the result of an acid trip—with lines like 'So high/Going up on the wall'. The song was performed live for a radio session at local Manchester station Piccadilly Radio 261. The session included performances of 'Chelsea Girl' and 'Garden of Hate', as well as a professionally recorded version of 'Here Comes the Fool'.

## 'Citizen (Dance of Youth)'

Duration: 2.53

A very politically fuelled song, this is an observation of a hypothetical eastern European country under either a Fascist or Communist regime. The song also acts lyrically as a precursor to the theme that would dominate the next album, namely the experience of being a visitor to such a country, and more broadly speaking travelling through central Europe during the Cold War of the late 1970s and early 1980s. The closing lines to the song give a picture of a journalist placed there for reportage, with a camera that 'takes a picture'. It was part of the band's live set during the *Real to Real Cacophony* tour of 1979–80. A live version of the song was recorded for the John Peel Sessions for BBC Radio 1 on 19 December 1979.

## 'Carnival (Shelter in a Suitcase)'

Duration: 2.49

This sounds like a frivolous piece in the way its timing alternates, but it does have some heavy undertones to its lyrics. Another potential tale of espionage with a tongue-in-cheek tone, it does feel like it has all the hallmarks of a 'filler' track. Perhaps it was an attempt by the band not to make all the subject matter on the album too weighty? It's never featured in any of the band's live sets and has largely faded into obscurity.

## 'Factory'

Duration: 4.13

To my ears, 'Factory' is the aural representation of an L.S. Lowry painting. I see within Kerr's lyrics a visualisation of Lowry's *Going to Work*, which depicts the industrial landscape around Manchester. Glasgow would no doubt have seemed similar in the childhood eyes of Jim Kerr during the late 1960s and 1970s. 'Going up, going down, going round 'til we drown again'. It's a kaleidoscopic clocking-on-and-off race of a bipedal stampede. There are even percussive sounds that tap into this idea of a bell tolling for the start and end of the working day. Kerr uses the phrase 'imitation of life', suggesting that life in the latter stages of the industrial revolution is a replication of how our lives play out in the wider world. Kerr has often had a tendency to self-plagiarise by reusing lyrics or turning the lyrics of one song into the title of another. The first evident example of the latter is 'Factory', in which Kerr mentions the 'Glittering Prize'. A theme he returned to in 1982.

## 'Cacophony'

Duration: 1.40

Simple Minds' first instrumental—at least purely in terms of chronology and track listing, if not also in composition. It's driven along by a short, punchy Burchill riff. At 100 seconds in length, it fades out to welcome the even more experimental instrumental offering of 'Veldt'.

## 'Veldt'

Duration: 3.20

This song sees the band express themselves in the most avant-garde and 'out there' way imaginable. Musically, it is heavily laced with a low bass and plonking piano keys. The vocals are mostly unintelligible noises, with Derek Forbes responsible for providing primate posturings. The only words I can decipher are Jim Kerr repeating the words 'go on'. Yet despite all this, the song conjures up within me a dark, dank jungle scene. That low bass and those chimp noises create a kind of claustrophobic atmosphere, of a lush and dense jungle that is impenetrable without wielding a machete to cut through the vast foliage. I can feel the sweat from the humidity of the tropical landscape pouring off me.

In my discussions with the fanbase about the track, I have put forward the idea that fans are either 'team "Veldt"' or not. It's the Simple Minds Marmite song. There appears to be no middle ground. Fans either love it and absolutely enjoy it for the sonic absurdity that it is, or loathe it with a passion and think it should be hidden away in the vaults forever. I am very much 'team "Veldt"'. If you could sum up the whole of the recording sessions of *Real to Real Cacophony* with just one track, 'Veldt' would give you everything you need to know.

## 'Premonition'

Duration: 5.29

Starting with a wonderful interplay between the bassline and a rim shot tap of snare that is soon accompanied by staccato guitar notes and a light flush of keys, the keyboard notes then sustain with a guitar that now expands and shrieks notes while simultaneously riding into a fabulous riff. It's like scenes from a war. The lyrics mention a 'brave little world' and 'a sound of machines' and 'sound of the shells'. The protagonist tells us of a 'Hole in my head/Where the creature has crawled'. It's very dark and menacing and is not a typical Simple Minds song in the sense that nothing appears to be hopeful or uplifting about it. This was a recurring theme that ran through earlier Simple Minds compositions, but even within a song like 'Pleasantly Disturbed' there is something remotely tangible to grasp in terms of trying to get light to permeate through the darkness. Where that is in relation to 'Premonition'? I find it hard to unearth. The protagonist ends the song by informing us with a single proclamation of its title that he could see it coming all along.

The song is a firm favourite of former manager, Bruce Findlay. The band were recorded performing the track in New York on 24 October 1979 and the footage was aired on the *Old Grey Whistle Test* television programme on 27 November 1979. The song was performed live regularly during tours through to the end of the *New Gold Dream* tour in 1983. It dropped out of the set thereafter, only to return in 2003. It has subsequently made several live appearances, most recently and surprisingly during the band's *Global* tour in 2024.

## 'Changeling'

Duration: 4.11

The lone single release from the album. Both band and management had high hopes that this track would chart well. The intro has a great catchy guitar riff with an accompanying synth. It has a groove and a great tempo with a fun back-beat drum. Perhaps the one thing that lets it down are the somewhat questionable opening lines, that result in it forever being synonymous with 'wombling free'. It's not really something that a burgeoning post-punk New Wave Scottish rock band would want to be associated with, is it? Of course, one could argue there were stronger contenders for the album's single; both 'Factory' and 'Premonition' could have fared better, but the decision for lead single was ultimately down to record company Arista. They decided that 'Changeling' had the strongest potential, believing they knew better. Another factor that hindered the record's success was the release date. It did not pre-date the album and was released in January 1980, several weeks after the album. The late release enabled the live recording of 'Premonition' from the Hurrah Club in New York City to be the B-side. Sadly, the single failed to chart.

## 'Film Theme'

Duration: 2.27

A short instrumental with a *film noir* feeling to it. One imagines two men walking along shadowy, dimly lit streets, trilby hats hiding their faces. Are they being pursued, or are they in pursuit of other seemingly clandestine characters? The band had early ambitions to have some of their musical output used in film scores and there was talk of tracks from the album appearing in a French documentary. The title of this track certainly confirmed the intent, but it would be 1985 before Simple Minds would achieve an unprecedented level of success through appearing on a film soundtrack.

## 'Calling Your Name'

Duration: 5.05

The song sounds a little more like those on their debut album. It first appeared when the band were touring as headliners for the later leg of the *Life in a Day* tour in 1979. A recording of the gig at Fforde Grene in Leeds features the song with only sparse lyrics that Jim Kerr had written. By the time of the recording sessions for *Real to Real Cacophony*, the lyrics were fully formed. Musically, the song was largely complete at the Fforde Grene gig. The track has a fantastic synth intro with a fine melody from Mick MacNeil. Lyrically the song is filled with fragments and flashbacks: an assassin in one scene, the victim of the assassin in the next. Kerr pieces snapshots into another tale of gloomy underworld angst.

### 'Scar'

Duration: 3.31

This track, lyrically, has always felt to me like Kerr's attempt at re-imagining JG Ballard's novel *Crash*, or The Normal's 'Warm Leatherette', which was inspired by the novel although it was a much softer and romantic affair, and not so steeped in sexual fetish. The line 'People in love talk far too much' brings a lasting resonance. Musically, the opening guitar chord works like the striking of a death knell. A beautiful synth melody follows, one of MacNeil's sweetest. A deep, growling bass contrasts the shimmering synth keys. Kerr's images are free-verse and fragmented. It plays out exactly like the flashbacks described in the second line of the song. Glimpses of a car crash scene. Dazzling glare from the sun, the lights—scars in the memory. The song was composed before recording sessions began at Rockfield for the album. It started out with a different set of lyrics, which Kerr rewrote during the recording sessions.

## Additional tracks

### 'Here Comes the Fool'

Duration: 4.45 (*Silver Box* version)

A song from the early period of the band's existence that never made it on to any official commercial recording at the time. Why this happened with this track is baffling. It was a firm favourite of the band members, and it was performed live and featured in the set from mid-1979 until spring 1980. A commercial recording of it was made when Simple Minds had a radio session for local Manchester station Piccadilly Radio on 7 June 1979. The song also featured on several bootlegs, including another performance for radio—the *In Concert* series for the BBC—which was recorded at the Paris Theatre in London on 8 August 1979. This recording was chosen as a track on the *Silver Box* compilation released in 2004. The song essentially remained the same throughout, except the Piccadilly Radio session version. In that first radio recording, the keyboards are more traditionally melodic in sound, the chorus had more harmony-driven backing vocals from Derek Forbes, and Kerr's lyrics in the verses were different. From the bootleg recordings that exist from Fforde Grene in Leeds on 29 July, there is a more eerie off-key sound to the keyboard opening, the harmonies of the chorus are gone, and the verse lyrics alter little. This is the version that remained consistent until the song dropped from the set. A catchy chorus, a great riff shared between guitar and bass, a rocking middle-eight guitar solo: the song was as much a crowd favourite as it was the band's own to perform. Why it never made it on to *Real to Real Cacophony* as a track remains perplexing.

# 4

# *Empires and Dance*

| | |
|---|---|
| UK: | 12 September 1980 |
| Personnel: | Bass: Derek Forbes<br>Drums, percussion: Brian McGee<br>Guitars: Charlie Burchill<br>Keyboards: Michael MacNeil<br>Saxophone: Charlie Burchill<br>Vocals: Jim Kerr |
| Duration: | 45 minutes |
| Produced by: | John Leckie |
| Chart position: | UK: 41; US: |

Much like the trio of albums that became known as the 'Berlin trilogy' for David Bowie, which he worked on with Brian Eno and producer Tony Visconti in the mid-to-late 1970s (*Low*, *Heroes* and *Lodger*), Simple Minds were once again working with John Leckie as producer for their third album, *Empires and Dance*. With the band now spreading their touring wings to incorporate Europe, the songs on *Empires and Dance* started a 'European travelogue' theme and a loose concept for the album. *Empires and Dance* reflected the Europe of the late 1970s/early 1980s that the band were experiencing. The stranglehold of the Communist block over central Europe, as expressed in 'I Travel': 'In central Europe men are marching', was evident during the period.

Recording started midway through 1980 when the band again decamped to Rockfield. When recording sessions for the album commenced in the summer, several songs had already been written and were being performed live during the latter stages of the *Real to Real Cacophony* tour. 'Capital City', 'I Travel' and 'Room' were the first of these to get debut live airings during the spring of 1980. A concert at the Lyceum in London in June included a set that almost exclusively featured songs from *Empires and Dance*. This indicated that the majority of songs for the album had already been penned prior to recording at Rockfield. The concert in question lists 'Kant-Kino', 'Capital City', 'Thirty Frames a Second', 'I Travel', 'Constantinople Line', 'Today I Died Again', 'Celebrate' and 'This Fear of Gods' as being performed. In fact this was the entire *Empires and Dance* album save for 'Twist/Run/Repulsion' and 'Room'.

There was also a dilemma over the date of release for the album. Arista wanted to try and make the most of the fact that Simple Minds would be touring Europe as support for Peter Gabriel starting at the beginning of September. The album was released on 12 September 1980, just two weeks into the European leg of the Peter Gabriel tour. Arista's reluctance to sanction a larger pressing run for the album led to sales stalling: 15,000 copies were pressed for the first run, with a delay before another 15,000 were pressed when the first run sold out. The album eventually made it onto the chart two weeks later, peaking at 41, before disappearing entirely three weeks after that. This lacklustre drive in promoting the album by Arista was one of the leading factors that eventually led to the split between record company and band.

## The songs

### 'I Travel'

Duration: 3.56

With a sequencer pulse that is heavily influenced by the similar sounding pulse on the Giorgio Moroder produced 'I Feel Love' by Donna Summer, but altering slightly with the inclusion of a more German-influenced *motorik* beat, 'I Travel' is an opening track that is explicit in its intent of forward propulsion, both in terms of the stylistic momentum for the band as well as the musical progression. At this time Simple Minds continued to be influenced by the artists that were their musical heroes, but conversely were also making headway in finding their own unique sound. 'I Travel' slots into that midway point, juxtaposed between pastiche of the Moroder influence and the burgeoning Simple Minds signature cinematic sound. Kerr described the track as a 'postcard' documenting the band striding out on to the European mainland, honing their craft and expanding their live audience. Mainland Europe in the late 1970s/early 1980s was polarised by the divide between the consumerist *bourgeoisie* and Communist agendas. The chorus of 'I Travel' highlights that divide lyrically, contrasting 'decadence and pleasure towns' with 'tragedies, luxuries, statutes, parks and galleries'.

'I Travel' was the album's first single, released on 16 October 1980. The single was packaged as a special limited edition with an added flexi-disc featuring a previously unreleased track from the *Real to Real Cacophony* recording sessions, 'Kaleidoscope', as well as a remixed version of 'Film Theme' titled 'Film Theme Dub'. Despite the packaging and the release of the single coinciding with the opening night of the band's headline tour to promote the album, the single failed to chart. The song has been a mainstay of the band's live set since 1980, with only one extended break between the mid-1980s and late 1990s. Its most recent inclusion on the setlist was during the *Global* tour 2024.

### 'Today I Died Again'

Duration: 4.39

Real industrial grit pervades this song. For me it has always conjured up the image of a painting by German artist Erich Heckel titled *Self-portrait with Model*, painted in 1916. I'm not sure why other than that it seems to embody the way the characters in the lyrics emerge in the mind's eye. There is the glint of irony for Kerr in using the line 'The clothes he wears/Date back to the war'. It's both downtrodden in the imagery it conveys, and also conjures the memory of a Monty Python sketch. It's minimalist in sound. A slow drum beat and whining, whirring synths, while an underpinning bass rhythm with those bending notes gives a dystopia-fuelled bliss. Where previously Jim Kerr had sung with a higher tenor voice, now he's beginning to dip into that baritone. At this point it may be pushed and forced, but it is still incredibly effective. The effects applied to his voice as he repeats the lines of the chorus in that protracted way with those drum fills rolling on behind, bringing forward the build in tempo towards the end of the track, are fabulous.

### 'Celebrate'

Duration: 5.03

A song about escape; namely from the oppression that Jim Kerr saw reflected in the people in certain parts of Europe—some areas of which the band travelled through. Our narrator in the song singles out another man for scrutiny, informing us of his apparel: 'The suit he wears belongs to me'. In fact, the line is not dissimilar to a line in the previous track. There's a long, hard road ahead to travel but life doesn't have to be all about work and just getting by. There can be escape and freedom. A life worth celebrating: 'Go west, young man'. Although steeped once again in that central European Cold War imagery, the title alone harbours the promise of something uplifting. Its metric beat is at times not unlike the sound of marching feet. Belatedly released as a 7-inch and 12-inch single after the band had parted from Arista in February 1981, producer John Leckie created an extended mix for the 12-inch single, as well as producing an edited version for the 7-inch. As a live song, it has been a lasting inclusion in the Simple Minds live set, being a regular until 1985 when it was given a break for over fifteen years, only to return as a regular from 2011 onwards. It also provided the name of the band's compilation album released in 2013.

### 'This Fear of Gods'

Duration: 7.00

A single note from a synth. Then the hook starts. Then the sound of a reel-to-reel tape building to a crescendo, which signals the arrival of the rhythm section. Fabulous drums and a bassline only Derek Forbes can deliver, all funk with bends and slides. Also, something of the Eastern in the way the saxophone is played and given echo and effects. It adds to the mystique. Like the most futuristic and industrial soundscapes Simple Minds conjured up during this period, the overall vibe of the song comes from continual repetitive hooks and loops, right down to repetitions in Jim Kerr's abstract and ambiguous lyrics. Personally, I think it is a seven-minute masterpiece. And I am obviously not alone in this thinking. The band have regularly added the song to the setlist over the past fifteen years after a thirty-year absence. There are several references to Kerr being inspired to write the lyrics after reading a short story written by Jorge Louis Borges in his collective work *Labyrinths*. My own investigations and research cannot find any conclusive proof of the existence of a parallel between the lyrics and anything in Borges' collections of writing. Perhaps the connection is so abstract it's not easily spotted? In any case, as with the thematic scheme of the music of Simple Minds during the period, it is a danceable dystopian drama.

### 'Capital City'

Duration: 6.14

A low, slow, brooding number. Its immediate strength comes from the guttural bassline of Derek Forbes, quickly accompanied by a drum beat that's only struck on every fourth bar. Burchill's guitar and MacNeil's choral melody add brightness to an otherwise menacing tune. The legato notes of guitar contrast the staccato notes of bass and synths. The song arrived on the scene as part of the live set before the album was recorded. At this point, it had the working title of 'Pulse'. Lyrically, I have always been intrigued by Jim Kerr's use of the line 'A city that they/we live on'—*on* rather than *in*. It's a strange one.

### 'Constantinople Line'

Duration: 4.44

There were several demos recorded for the album. Most likely at the insistence of Arista, after what they would consider to be the *Real to Real Cacophony* 'debacle'. 'Constantinople Line' was one of these recorded demos. It was ostensibly the same tune, but with a mostly different set of lyrics by Kerr—although it still has the 'hey waiter!' calls and retains the lines 'These stations are useful/These stations we love them'. The words relate more to a scene of general unease in train travel, whereas the final lyrics are more like the claustrophobic menace of *Strangers on a Train* and allude to a web of espionage and Communist Cold War uncertainty: 'Red/Red star/Red'. The track fades with a guitar emulating a passing train, reminiscent of the faded-up Earl Slick guitar opening on David Bowie's 'Station to Station'.

## 'Twist/Run/Repulsion'

Duration: 4.38

Another track that was demoed before recording sessions for the album commenced. Also, another track where the bare bones of the demo version can still be heard: it is ostensibly the same tune, right down to the reciting of the passage of the book in the background, only ceasing when the lyrics kick in. The demo had a slightly slower pace. The album version has the addition of some jarring warped, elongated and bent saxophone notes. The lyrics on the demo were sparse, with a bold declaration of 'STOP!' after each couplet of lines, as well as the notable point of the album title being contained in the lyric of the demo. The track's title chorus line takes the centre in the demo but is relegated to a backing vocal on the album version. The album version begins with a fade-in of an eerie reversed and warped voice. The lyrics are now a single verse that is repeated through the song three times at a pace that is admirable, given that Jim Kerr still had a detectable stutter when talking at this point. The lyrics tell the fragmented fear-mongering tale of a narrator's nightmare. A prisoner-of-war held captive? A civilian feeling trapped under a military regime? You decide.

## 'Thirty Frames a Second'

Duration: 5.14

A wonderful musical dance entwines itself between the synths and bass on this track. MacNeil's keys and Forbes's bass at times play a merry dance with each other, balanced by McGee's fine drumming. The rhythm section keeps to a hypnotic repetition. In contrast to the demo that was made (which musically is the most 'untouched' in shape from the other demo versions) is the change in Jim Kerr's vocal style within just a few months. Lyrically, the song is possibly the clearest in terms of subject matter. These are Kerr's least ambiguous lyrics, other than perhaps the opening track. The song recounts the story of a man in middle-age who appears to be experiencing an existential crisis which propels him backwards to a much younger and more youthful look. This in turn makes him a stranger to his nearest and dearest and his world starts to fall apart as a result.

## 'Kant-Kino'

Duration: 1.50

Named after a club that had once been a cinema in Berlin, where the band played in early 1980 on the *Real to Real Cacophony* tour, the underlying tone of the track is provided by the sound of a reel-to-reel tape machine. Along with the bass, it provides the rhythm for Charlie Burchill to loop a sweet guitar riff over it. As the track moves along there is a sequencer pulse woven through. A brief hush of some vocal effects is evident too. It's a short track segued to the end fade of '30 Frames a Second'. The tracks merge from one to the other seamlessly. Its fade-out then paves the way for the Morricone Western soundtrack styling of 'Room'. Its understated pulse and drive and repetitive loops make it a wonderfully hypnotic tune. This track is my favourite Simple Minds instrumental. Short, mysteriously uplifting and ethereal. It often moves me to tears for reasons I am at a loss to truly comprehend.

### 'Room'

Duration: 2.30

The song first appeared within the live set during the *Real to Real Cacophony* tour of 1979–80. However, there is some confusion among the band members as they recall the song being written specifically for a John Peel radio session that aired in early 1980. A bootleg of their gig at Stirling University on 15 November 1979 includes a recording of 'Room' played as an encore. At any rate, the song continued to be played live and then made the list for inclusion on the album. Driven by one of Derek Forbes' signature basslines, it is a brooding beast of a tune.

The lyrics have always had a sparsity to them and retained an *ad lib* quality. Along with instrumentals, this song has no lyrics printed on the lyric sheet that accompanied the album. During live performances, Jim Kerr would veer away from the lyrics that were recorded on the album version, returning to the earlier, more Iggy Pop 'Sister Midnight'-laced homage. One could appreciate why the two songs were performed back-to-back during their show at the Melkweg in Amsterdam on 23 March 1980. Perhaps there were other times on the tour that this took place? There is also something tantamount to a blend of The Doors and The Velvet Underground in the style of the song, with hollow Mo Tucker-esque percussion and short blast guitar riffs. It gives off such a dark, oppressive atmosphere. A kind of claustrophobia that makes it feel as if the listener is in said 'room', not entirely sure of what exactly is taking place but feeling that it is something sinister.

## Additional tracks

### 'New Warm Skin'

Duration: 4.35

The B-side to 'I Travel,' this song gives an indication of where the band will go next in their continuing pursuit of finding their own truly unique sound. Sonically at least, it seemed the natural partner to 'I Travel' to the extent that it had a more electronic dance feel than the deeper dystopian offerings on *Empires and Dance*. With a softer drum and (unusually for this period) a slightly buried bass, the synthesisers are brought forward with just a short flare of guitar during each line of the monosyllabic chorus 'New/Warm/Skin'. The song is meant to be a commentary on plastic surgery, yet curiously it contains the lines, 'Is this a war?/ Is this a god?' What this has to do with plastic surgery remains a mystery. Perhaps it is meant to imply man's war on the perceived imperfections designed by God?

## 'Kaleidoscope'

Duration: 4.15

The release of 'I Travel' as a single resulted in there being a limited-edition bonus with the first 7,500 copies pressed. This first run included a flexi disc 7-inch which contained this track and a remix of the *Real to Real Cacophony* track, 'Film Theme.' 'Kaleidoscope' was recorded during the *Real to Real Cacophony* sessions, having been written and performed live during the *Life in a Day* tour in 1979. It must have been deemed a potential B-side, which is surprising given that Arista went on to release a solitary single from the *Real to Real Cacophony* album—'Changeling'—and only after the album itself had been released. As a record label that was indifferent to the band and their potential to produce commercially successful singles, such was their enthusiasm for this track that Arista placed it on the compilation album they released early in 1982 titled *Celebration*.

## 'Film Theme Dub'

Duration: 1.26

A remix that quickens the pace of the track to more than double speed. It contains various other sounds and sequencers, and something that sounds akin to water gurgling down the drain of a sink. It is a fast-paced trippy little instrumental that is all over in less than ninety seconds.

# 5

# *Sons and Fascination*

| | |
|---|---|
| UK: | 4 September 1981 |
| Personnel: | Bass: Derek Forbes |
| | Drums: Brian McGee |
| | Guitars: Charlie Burchill |
| | Keyboards: Michael MacNeil |
| | 'Next' chorus: Jacqui, Ken Lockie |
| | Vocals: Jim Kerr |
| Duration: | 44 minutes |
| Produced by: | Steve Hillage |
| Chart position: | Sweden: 4; UK: 11; US: - |

By the end of 1980, relations between the band and parent record label Arista were strained. Arista had been making decisions that were impeding the band's chart success. By December 1980, such was the discontent that the band sent an open letter to *Sounds* magazine, apologising to fans who had been unable to purchase the 12-inch of 'I Travel'. In the letter, Simple Minds said that the trouble was due to Arista only pressing an initial 3,000 copies and being reluctant to press any more. Arista's response to the open letter was that they would press a further 5,000 copies. It was the straw that broke the camel's back as far as manager Bruce Findlay was concerned, and he set out to end the partnership Zoom had with Arista. Findlay searched for a suitable record label for Simple Minds to move to.

In the spring of 1981, the band signed to Virgin Records. They wasted no time in capitalising on the change of label and quickly started working on a new album.

With a change of record label, a change of producer also seemed a natural step. 'A change for change's sake,' as Jim Kerr would describe it when being interviewed in 1981 around the time of the release of *Sons/Sister*. The band had worked with John Leckie for their first three albums. Virgin suggested Steve Hillage for the new album and they seemed—albeit a little surprisingly to many—keen on the suggestion. Kerr was asked about Hillage's involvement when interviewed and he had this to say: 'We knew we'd get a lot of snide remarks, but we weren't concerned with that; we wanted a sound and Steve, with his mutual interest in Krautrock, really impressed us with his treatments'.

The band toured for a brief spell in March, which saw them cross the Atlantic for dates in Canada and the United States.

Upon their return, recording continued. The band had already gone into the studio before heading out on tour and before the signing of contracts with Virgin had taken place. 'The American' and 'League of Nations' were recorded. 'The American' was released in late spring while the band and Hillage were working in the studio.

The production of material in 1981 signals a particularly prolific period for Simple Minds. Their cup overflowed with ideas. Nothing was purged—everything was used. As Jim Kerr would declare when interviewed for *Sounds* magazine in 1981, 'I just think it's this feeling that "now" is the end of the first stage for us. Of our first days. I think we're just clearing ourselves out'.

There were so many tracks being worked on all at once it was becoming apparent that either the band would need to cull songs, or a double album would need to be considered. The only problem was that Virgin wouldn't cough up the additional funds required for the extra studio time to work on a double album. This resulted in tension between the band and Hillage towards the end of production, with each blaming the other for the messy situation.

Along with the change in producer, Simple Minds forged a new relationship with album art designer Malcolm Garrett. Garrett was Virgin's in-house cover artist, having previously worked with bands Buzzcocks and Magazine, and had just started producing work for Duran Duran. His work with Simple Minds would continue through to the end of the 1980s. I was privileged to have several email exchanges with Garrett several years ago and we discussed his involvement in producing the cover art for Simple Minds in 1981, in particular the use of the 'marching men' as we came to call them. They featured on several covers, including the single sleeve for 'Sweat in Bullet', as well as for some overseas issues of the album. There was also a reissue of 'I Travel' released by Virgin in 1983, which also features an outline image of a 'marching man' placed over the top of a photo of Jim Kerr striking a similar pose.

In relation to both the albums and a criticism Kerr had felt that the band had received about their sound being 'hollow travel music', he gave this response: 'We're not sending postcards from exotic places; there's a lot more to us than that. If it was hollow travel music, we'd probably have hit singles; as it is, our singles don't get played enough for that to happen'.

When interviewed about the inherent theme of the album in 1981, Kerr spoke of the sounds he'd hear at night from his bedroom when he was growing up in Toryglen. 'For twelve years I used to lie awake at night listening to the trains going back and forth to London. Perhaps that's when I got interested in the sound of travel'.

As an indicator of what lay in store for the band next, Kerr offered this: 'Whatever we do next album-wise I'm sure it will be something radically different, because I think there's a big difference between the second and first albums, and the second and third, but with the third and this, the difference isn't that big'. The album was the first to crack the top forty since the release of *Life in a Day*, peaking at No. 11 during a seven-week run.

## The songs

### 'In Trance as Mission'

Duration: 6.50

Starting with a bassline from Derek Forbes that immediately conjures up the momentum of movement, akin to the rattle of train wheels on tracks, slowly the instrumentation builds. First drums, then guitar, then finally a simple two-chord synth melody. Then comes one of the best opening lines to a song that Jim Kerr has ever written, 'For just one moment in time/I hear the holy backbeat'.

When interviewed for *Melody Maker* early in 1982, Kerr said:

> A song like 'In Trance as Mission', we just did that. We were using a lot of these chords that kept happening, they're up chords, they make you feel up. We'd have the backing track and with 'Trance' I only had a rough skeleton for what I wanted to do with the vocal, and for the rest lines began to improvise themselves. I was starting to say things like 'my hands are grasping at air'. There's one line in it that always freaks me out when I hear it—'I hear the holy backbeat', ya know, it's like a godly sort of Catholic thing. I don't know... 'Seeing Out the Angel', 'This Earth That You Walk Upon', 'In Trance', I don't know if it's a sort of godly feeling or something. No one in the group practices (religion), but most of the band are Catholic. I think perhaps—I was thinking about it the other day—you get stamped with that when you're young and it's there forever, you can't really escape it.

Although the track might have been grouped with the other two songs mentioned by Kerr as having a 'godly feeling', when interviewed six months earlier, Kerr had this to say in relation to the song: 'We work with atmospheres and moods, yet our music has a spirit and a soul, a humanity, that's lacking elsewhere. One of the songs on our new album has the line "Encourage your dreams". I think that's one of the most positive lines that have come out this year.'

## 'Sweat in Bullet'

Duration: 4.29

Funk is the musical key to 'Sweat in Bullet'. It's a Jim Kerr special, lyrically. No traditional verse/chorus structure with his lines. The start of the track comprises a single word for each line of the song—the first two of which are completely fabricated words. 'Airmobility' and 'dressability'. What do they even mean? Do they need to mean anything?

When interviewed in 1981, Kerr had this to say in relation to his song-writing:

> I don't sit down and write songs and verses. I'm just constantly writing and adding things, taking lines that have been written over the period of a year and piecing them together. One line can be the image of a song, and the rest can be padding. If it came to a lyric sheet, I'd now rather take a line from each song. I'd think you'd get more focus. It's becoming more of a schizophrenic thing. Of course, the lyrics are very important, but in terms of values and that, I wouldn't care if no one at all paid any attention. They're all pictures in themselves; every line's a different picture. It's the atmosphere of words. It could be for the sound, or it could be for the meaning, or for the image of the word. They deal with a lot of images and ambiguities.

Certainly for 'Sweat in Bullet' this statement rings true. The second single from *Sons and Fascination* (or the third if you're a 'double album and not separate entities' stick-in-the-mud), it entered the UK singles chart on 7 November 1981 at No. 66 and peaked at No. 52 the following week.

Both the 7-inch and 12-inch singles contained remixes by Peter Walsh. The 7-inch was an edited cut of the album version, whereas the 12-inch was an extended version with added cowbell. Just when you think a song can't have enough cowbell, here comes the 12-inch of 'Sweat in Bullet' adding even more cowbell to the mix. Reviews in the music press from the time of its release were willing the band to break through, particularly reviews within *Smash Hits* and *Record Mirror*. *Smash Hits* felt that their breakthrough was imminent. How prescient that statement would be.

Although Virgin appeared reluctant to increase the budget for the recording of the album, they seemed only too happy to provide a decent budget for producing music videos. Along with 'Love Song', the band filmed a video for 'Sweat in Bullet', recorded at the Kensington Roof Garden which at the time was being rented by Virgin. Time for filming was limited to such a degree that Jim Kerr sports a very noticeable eye infection in both videos. A single frame image from the video would go on to be used for the picture sleeve art for the band's next single, 'Promised You a Miracle'. The video is seen among the fanbase as possibly their coolest video.

The song has featured periodically in the live set over the years. Most recently it was performed during the *Global* tour 2024.

## '70 Cities as Love Brings the Fall'

Duration: 4.48

Ambiguous and fragmented, there is a vague tangible subject to this song, but despite what the title suggests, it doesn't appear to be someone in search of love and stopping at 70 cities along the way. It's another travelogue piece. Much like David Bowie's *Aladdin Sane* was a kind of travelogue in that its theme was portrayed as 'Ziggy Stardust in America', '70 Cities' continued the theme that permeated through *Sons and Fascination*, that of movement, motion and travel with a focal point this time on America. It's driven home by the chorus of 'Going somewhere/Getting some place/Going somewhere', all delivered in Kerr's wonderfully nuanced Glaswegian accent. Within the fanbase is a somewhat cheeky in-joke pertaining to Burchill's guitar hook sounding for all the world like a mooing cow. It also contains one of the most perplexing lines I have ever heard in a song, in which a person's right eye sheds a tear before the other. It's such a strange notion and image. As for the subject of love in the song? Is Jim Kerr confusing pride with love? There is an old saying, 'Pride comes before a fall'. Has he just substituted pride for love? And if so, he must be implying that the 'love' is a love of adventure and travel, right? Love of the status of being in a touring band, of life on the road? If so, then he also talks about its potential perils. At times, even for an ardent adventure-loving man such as Kerr, it can get wearing. 'When the other side of midnight calls/Remind me I'm glad to be here'. Is it all a case of be careful what you wish for? Existential lines such as those become increasingly rare from this point on.

## 'Boys from Brazil'

Duration: 5.29

For me, this song is the most significant legacy of Brian McGee's contribution to the Simple Minds story. It is a drumming *tour de force*. It also just so happens to not only be my favourite track on the album, but also my favourite Simple Minds song of all time. Jim Kerr, when interviewed shortly after the release of the album, said this about the track:

> Last year we spent a full year in Europe and when we came back, we'd got a totally different picture of Britain; found the attitudes, in Glasgow especially, really kinda frightening. All these neo-Nazi movements and things, not really with depth but people getting involved from some romantic point-of-view. I'm sure that's where a lot of our lyrics come from. The verse at the end of that is so ambiguous; on one hand it's like a fairy story saying, 'Not just a boy that's crying wolf now/Someone else is screaming up at our door', on the other hand, if that isn't heavy imagery!

Kerr is right. The imagery is stark and a curious blend of a Bond-style aesthetic and reptilian fantastical realism: babies wrestling with crocodiles is really something for the mind to picture. Of course, the song also shares its title with a book written by Ira Levin, who also wrote *Rosemary's Baby*—Kerr was obviously a fan of the author. On the surface, the Levin novel is no direct inspiration for the song's lyrics. Kerr himself said, 'It isn't about the book, but that was a starting point'. The plot of the book involves the desired rekindling of a Nazi movement through an elaborate story based on the existence of Hitler clones. The 'not just a boy that's crying wolf' line could have pertained to the phone call received by the book's protagonist from a young man alerting him to the killings of specifically targeted men. The protagonist initially dismisses this as a prank call until his tentative investigation vindicates the caller's findings.

Of all the songs produced for both albums, this track, along with two tracks from *Sister Feelings Call*—'20th Century Promised Land' and 'Wonderful in Young Life'—has never been performed live. There have been rumours within the fanbase that 'Boys from Brazil' had been rehearsed and even been overheard played at soundchecks over the years, but it has never been officially performed live, despite many requests from fans.

## 'Love Song'

Duration: 5.03

When interviewed in early 1982, Jim Kerr spoke of the pervading negativity that he felt clouded peoples' ambition and said, 'We took the opposite end by sort of labelling "Love Song" as love with the possibility of ambition'. Asked to elaborate further, Kerr responded:

> I don't know... possibility of ambition really. I love success, I love to see winners. If I watch an athlete at the Olympic Games or anything, I see someone win... I get really moved by success, winners. I don't know if that's success or glory or whatever, but I think it's a love of that, ambition towards that.

So, what about the curious line of 'America's a boyfriend?' It can only be deduced that it's a take on the so-called 'special relationship' that the UK and America appear to have maintained since the end of World War Two.

The second single released during 1981, in the second week of August, and one month prior to the release of the album, 'Love Song' had a four-week run on the UK singles chart, peaking at No. 47 in its second week. The single fared better abroad, particularly in Australia where it made it to the top twenty of the singles chart. In Canada, the song broke into the top forty singles chart.

Back in 2019, I interviewed the band's original lighting operator, Jaine Henderson. She told me that the song had been offered to her by Jim Kerr to record. The band produced a demo of the song and Kerr had laid down a guide vocal on the track. Henderson attempted to record a vocal for the song but wasn't happy with the result and was in any case uninterested in pursuing a musical career. She preferred being involved behind the scenes and working in the visual arts. Kerr had then asked her if the band could go ahead and record the song themselves.

The video for the song is one that still bewilders fans. Recorded inside the bar adjacent to the Kensington Roof Garden which featured in the 'Sweat in Bullet' video, it features Kerr in the role of DJ, with the rest of the band getting up to all manner of questionable shenanigans, mostly involving some form of physical violence. Both videos feature interim drummer Kenny Hyslop, who passed away on 15 September 2024.

In 1992, the track was remixed by Gregg Jackman and released as a double A-side single with 'Alive and Kicking' to promote the release of the compilation album *Glittering Prize 81/92*. The single resulted in 'Love Song' achieving a top-ten entry into the UK singles chart in October 1992, peaking at No. 6 in its second week on the chart.

Given the frequency with which the song has gone on to feature in the band's live set, it could easily be Simple Minds' most performed song of their entire back catalogue. It has featured in almost every tour since March 1981 with the only exception being during the *Street Fighting Years* tour of 1989/90. Several live versions have featured on various singles and live albums. Several remixes of the song have also been released on 12-inch vinyl over the years.

## 'This Earth That You Walk Upon'

Duration: 5.26

This song first featured as an instrumental B-side to 'Love Song.' It was an edited version which faded out after Charlie Burchill's guitar solo on the 7-inch single. The 12-inch single features the full instrumental version on its B-side. In the latter stages of the recording sessions for the album, a vocal was added.

The track is in keeping with the 'trance' theme, with Kerr's opening lyrics posing questions one would presume he would ask when striking up conversation during the periods the band were touring: 'What's your name? What's your nation?' On a more personal level, the track jogs the memory of an online interaction I had with Kerr regarding the recording of the album. Kerr had posted on Facebook linking to an article about the perils of sitting for long periods and it being detrimental to one's health. He asked the fanbase what they listened to when out walking. I replied that I didn't listen to music when out walking, and that I preferred to listen to the sounds of nature. However, I did listen to music when travelling on various modes of transport, and that these albums (*Sons and Fascination* and *Sister Feelings Call*) were my 'go to'. Kerr replied, informing me that these albums' lyrics were formed mostly while he was out walking, listening to the tracks on a Sony Walkman. 'I walked through Glasgow for days on end listening to Michael MacNeil's demo of "Theme for Great Cities", Charlie Burchill's solo on "This Earth That You Walk Upon" etc. Lucky me! No birdsong could compete.'

It is a masterful coupling: the Burchill guitar solo, followed by the lines that I feel Kerr uses to perfectly encapsulate the sound of that guitar solo. 'Screaming edge of light/Shines so, shines so hard'. The guitar weeps in a kind of lament at the beauty of all earthly things. Along with the beautiful synth of MacNeil and subtle percussion, it is a piece of trip hop years before its time.

## 'Sons and Fascination'

Duration: 5.23

In a post on the Simple Minds Facebook page in May 2016, Jim Kerr asked fans which song they felt exemplified Derek Forbes' best bassline. Kerr himself said, 'Countless great ones in my opinion, but I still remember the first time he played this and the impact that it had'. Kerr had added a YouTube link to 'Sons and Fascination' to his comment.

I don't know if I could single out any one Forbes bassline on this album for scrutiny—they are all magnificent. The drum machine thwacks that open the song are very quickly accompanied by one of those incredible Forbes basslines. Then there is a colourful, towering wash of synths from MacNeil. Next come Kerr's bullet-point lyrics, of which he said in an interview at the time 'every line's a different picture'. It is a collage of all that flits through his traveller's eye and is painted for us as listeners to see. Inspiration comes from all angles. Finally, Burchill arrives to accompany what works for a chorus in the Kerr world. There are lines within it that will crop up again in future (see 'Book of Brilliant Things'). If 'In Trance as Mission' works to introduce the Simple Minds 'American travelogue' theme to the listener, then one could say 'Sons and Fascination'—as the title track—cements all that the album desires to convey, coming full circle.

The track has been included sporadically in the live set since its composition in the summer of 1981. It was recorded live for a radio session for John Peel on Radio 1 in 1982. After the end of the *Sons and Fascination* tour in the summer of 1982, the song was bumped off the list to make way for more tracks from *New Gold Dream*. It didn't return to the set until many years later in 2009. It appeared frequently from then until 2012 and the *5x5 Live* tour, but once again faded out of favour until the most recent *Global* tour. It was performed several times during 2024.

## 'Seeing Out the Angel'

Duration: 6.10

A song in which every instrument plays its part exceptionally, Kerr's voice on the backing vocals included. There's a marital bliss happening between Burchill's chiming guitar and MacNeil's beautifully structured synth melody. The band might have been strong on repetitive hooks and loops at this juncture, but there is something dazzlingly hypnotic about 'Seeing Out the Angel'.

In an interview with *Melody Maker* in March 1982, when Jim Kerr was asked what inspired the song, he said:

> Well… It's two things really. I read a short story in a book that Derek had, it's all these awful ... almost like ghost stories. And one was about the Angel of Death coming, coming to take someone away ... and it was really ... again, it was beauty. I think there's beauty in fear or something like that. Apart from that, when I was young, I reckon I had a vision. It could have been a daydream or something, I don't know, but I remember telling my mother and father and things like that, and I reckon I saw an angel. It stuck with me all the years, and I've been writing words ever since I can remember. I'm not exactly sure why, because I was never interested in poetry or nothing. So, I had that thing for years, and then when I read this little, short story it just provoked lots of things […] I thought Charlie's guitar on 'Angel' sounded like church bells.

A fellow fan has done some research to find out which book Kerr might have been referring to. A tenuous clue given by Kerr led to a Philip K. Dick collection of short stories entitled *A Handful of Darkness*. One story in the collection seemed the most likely source for inspiration, 'Upon the Dull Earth'. In it, the female protagonist encounters angelic celestial-type beings and desires to be with them. The 'angels' misinterpret her desire as an immediate wish and, when she accidentally cuts her finger, these beings see it as a call for them to come to take her with them to their world. But she's not ready and it's not what she desired. Her boyfriend wants her to be returned to the human world and so an attempt is made, at great risk, with disastrous results.

As the final track on the album, this feels like the song that gives the biggest musical indicator of where the band are headed next. An instrumental remix version of the song is used as a B-side track for the 12-inch release of 'Promised You a Miracle'.

In the *Melody Maker* article mentioned above, journalist Adam Sweeting shared a wonderful observation he witnessed when travelling with the band in France as preparations for the release of 'Promised You a Miracle' were underway. Sweeting writes that the band had not heard the remixed version of 'Angel' yet and were about to listen to it on the touring van's cassette player. He continues:

> Already a masterpiece, sadly beautiful like a private requiem for the loss of something terribly precious. The band members sit silently as the new version plays. It finishes, and Kerr stares ahead at the road and the rain—'I can't see the road for the tears'. He looks to Burchill. 'It's beautiful, Charlie ...'

# 6

# *Sister Feelings Call*

| | |
|---|---|
| UK: | 4 September 1981 |
| Personnel: | Bass: Derek Forbes |
| | Drums: Brian McGee |
| | Guitars: Charlie Burchill |
| | Keyboards: Michael MacNeil |
| | Vocals: Jim Kerr |
| Duration: | 35 minutes |
| Produced by: | Steve Hillage |
| Chart position: | UK: 11; US: - |

## The songs

### 'Theme For Great Cities'

Duration: 5.50

Possibly one of the greatest instrumental tracks recorded, and certainly one of the band's best. When writing about the track on the Simple Minds Facebook page in 2017, Jim Kerr described (at length) the decision he made in not writing lyrics or adding vocals to the track. In essence, he felt the music conjured up images strong enough that the song didn't require his input. This still left the conundrum of what to title the track. As Kerr explained:

> I still knew I would have to come up with a stand-out title, to befit solidly the futuristic style and atmosphere that I perceived even on the first listen to the demo idea […] For that I chose 'Theme for Great Cities'—and to me it seemed to fit perfectly. I now could never imagine it being called anything else.

Again, although the initial concept for the track came from Mick MacNeil, all the band members at the time of recording acted as one cohesive unit on the track. In real terms, this working unit was still in its infancy, and in fact would soon change forever with the departure of drummer and founding member Brian McGee.

If you require an example of just how accomplished the musicianship of the individual band members was, and require proof of the talents of Burchill, MacNeil, Forbes and McGee, you need only listen to this instrumental. And if you want proof of the lyrical credentials of Jim Kerr, there is plenty elsewhere. But even here, his application of the most befitting title to an exemplary piece of music is possibly all the proof required.

The Facebook post about 'Theme for Great Cities' was also the one that mentioned reading Philip K. Dick, which in turn led to the fan theory about the short story that inspired 'Seeing Out the Angel'. Whether the same collection of short stories (*A Handful of Darkness)* inspired the title of this track is known only by Kerr. There is only one story in the collection that has any similarity in tone for inspiration, called 'Planet for Transients.' All that is certain is that more than forty years on, the sound of 'Theme for Great Cities' remains as fresh as in 1981.

## 'The American'

Duration: 3.50

Depending on where you stand in the whole 'one double album' versus 'two separate albums' argument (I'm in the latter camp), 'The American' can be classified as either the first single off the album, or the one and only single from *Sister Feelings Call.* For the sake of pedantry, let's stick to the latter. One thing can be agreed: it was the first single the band released with their new record label, Virgin Records.

The song feels like a bullet-point description of industrial America: images of boiler-suit clad factory workers, oil fields and arid bomb-testing sites in Nevada and New Mexico, including an image that would crop up again on the next album—a boy falling out of the sky. This time, one gets a strong sense that the 'boy caught falling out of the sky' is in fact Little Boy—the name given to the bomb that was dropped on Hiroshima on 6 August 1945. I make this link as in the previous line in the song, the protagonist sees 'a man with an airfield plan'.

When interviewed around the time of the *Sons/Sister* release, Jim Kerr spoke of the influence of travelling through America on the album recordings. 'We were driving in America through a desert wasteland when suddenly we see this giant building, a multi-storey thing and it says "GIANT CAN CORPORATION" on the front. It looked really impressive; it had to be a front for something.' Perhaps that is one image that permeates on this track? The 'Ameri-CAN'?

The song entered the UK singles chart on 23 May 1981 at No. 75 and peaked at No. 59 the following week. Even though 'Sweat in Bullet' and 'Love Song' had already been introduced into the band's live set, it was 'The American' that was chosen to be the first single release under the band's new record label.

When asked in 2019 when Kerr and Burchill felt their sound was becoming truly their own, Kerr said: 'When Charlie and Mick came up with "The American". The noise of that. I thought, "This is it. This is a Simple Minds thing."'

The track would become an instant crowd favourite when it first appeared live in 1981. It continues to appear on the band's setlist. Apart from during the *Street Fighting Years* (1989–90), *Real Life* (1991), *Neapolis* (1997–98) and *Black and White* tours (2005–06), it has been performed regularly, and most recently during the *Global* tour 2024.

Along with the original single release in 1981, the song also appeared on the B-side for the release of 'Promised You a Miracle' by A&M in America in April 1983. It also went through the remix treatment during the late 1990s when the band released several remixed tracks for singles from the *Neapolis* album.

## '20th Century Promised Land'

Duration: 4.53

I'm not a musician and I do not claim to have a musician's ear, but the time signature of this song—its syncopation—has always fascinated me. This perhaps caused a problem when it came to the band performing the song live, as this track, along with 'Boys from Brazil' and 'Wonderful in Young Life', has never been performed. Given the period when the albums were released, usually only one song would not make the live set, and to have all three of these tracks omitted is rare. In fact, it was only when researching this book that I discovered that '20th Century Promised Land' had never been performed live. I had naively assumed it must have been at some point. Given the nature of the song's lyrics, and how in many ways they remain topical, I find this surprising. Other tracks with tricky time signatures have had live airings, including 'White Hot Day' from *Sparkle in the Rain*. The curiosity over its exclusion for live performance is compounded by its appearance as a B-side for the single release of 'Sweat in Bullet.'

Another curiosity in relation to this track is the repeated use of lines Jim Kerr had taken from the Bertolt Brecht play, *Life of Galileo*: 'Unhappy the land that has no heroes/No, unhappy the land that needs heroes'. He had used them in another composition from the period, a track titled 'Life in Oils'. He obviously felt very strongly about these words and was compelled to use them on a track destined for commercial release.

## 'Wonderful in Young Life'

Duration: 5.20

In 2018 while the band were touring North America, Jim Kerr posted on Facebook about Simple Minds' first tour of Canada in 1981 and his memories of that tour, particularly the long road journeys to the cities spread throughout the vastness of the Canadian countryside. I asked him if he recalled a specific song that had formed during those long journeys on that inaugural tour, and his reply was 'Wonderful in Young Life'. This made perfect sense.

I vividly remember my own experience hearing the track for the first time and the impact it had on me personally. I felt it was one of the most beautiful songs I had ever heard. The excited feeling the music expressed and the imagery the lyrics conveyed triggered a feeling in me of missing out on being a part of something truly wondrous. The world was yours for the taking, so why not grasp it and have the best time of your life? The song made such a strong impression on me that I had a tattoo of a line from the song along my right forearm. It reads 'I'm singing memories'.

Along with the blending of lines of words such as 'free wonder style' and 'little Egypt eyes', Kerr also quotes the title of the album's opening track, 'Loving the city/A theme for great cities'. Where other tracks from both albums revealed a world in angst, where political tensions and uncertain times were at the forefront, calling on a need for change through stark ambition, 'Wonderful in Young Life' was much more celebratory. It gleamed with a sentiment that said, 'we are having the time of our lives, and you can too—if you want it enough'.

Tour information on the website Dream Giver Redux suggests that the song was performed live just the once. However, there is doubt that this performance actually happened, as some fans present at the concert have no recollection of the song being performed. There is no bootleg of the concert either. It seems strange that the band would perform the song at one show, then never perform it again. I don't believe that has happened with any other song in the whole Simple Minds catalogue. Either a song is performed at least a handful of times before being dropped, or they simply never perform it at all.

## 'League of Nations'

Duration: 4.56

If there is one song that could be accused of being the weak link in the content of *Sons/Sister*, it's possibly this track. Although it was one of the earliest tracks recorded and released as the B-side for 'The American', it feels like it was discarded quickly. The single version (which becomes the album version) is both musically and lyrically sparse. The title and—if several online sources for the lyrics are to be believed—the word 'relief' are repeated throughout. For my part, I think Jim Kerr is singing 'repeat'. What is clear is that the live recording, taken from the Hammersmith Odeon concert on 25 September 1981, which appears on the gatefold double 7-inch single and 12-inch single releases of 'Sweat in Bullet', contains more lyrics. By that reckoning at least, Kerr seems to have written more lyrics for the song. I have heard other versions on bootlegs and if he had been merely ad-libbing at each gig, the words would differ each time. So I think the live recording from the Hammersmith Odeon gig is a better version of the song than the one recorded in the studio earlier in 1981. It was only performed once after the Hammersmith Odeon gig, and has never been performed live since then.

## 'Careful in Career'

Duration: 5.08

The song feels like it could be the sequel to 'Factory'. Whereas 'Factory' dealt with what appears to be one man's breakdown at work, the subject matter of 'Careful in Career' appears to offer a take on the fallout of what happens in 'Factory'. At least, that could be one interpretation. Another is that it has subtle autobiographical elements. Lines such as, 'Performance or ecstasy/I'm looking at you looking in through at me/I've come so far already' seem to allude to Jim Kerr as frontman. Even in these very early days of the band, and given the precarious nature of the music business, it was clear that Jim Kerr had a strong desire to make a career out of being a member of a commercially successful band. Like 'Wonderful in Young Life', the song was given only a solitary live performance. Unlike that track, a bootleg was recorded, so there is positive proof that it was performed live by the band at least once.

### 'Sound in 70 Cities'

Duration: 5.04
An instrumental or 'non-vocal' version of '70 Cities as Love Brings the Fall', this track could be accused of being 'filler' for the *Sister Feelings Call* album.

## Additional tracks

### 'Life in Oils'

Duration: 4.13
Demo recordings the band produced around the time of their departure from Arista and signing to Virgin in early 1981 reveal that 'Life in Oils' had been one of a collection of five songs recorded at Glasgow's CaVa studios. The rest of the demo tracks: 'The American', 'Twenty One' (later to be retitled 'Sweat in Bullet'), 'Check Out' (later to be retitled 'Careful in Career') and 'Love Song' were all recorded during later sessions and made it on to either *Sons and Fascination* or *Sister Feelings Call*. Only 'Life in Oils' was discarded. This was the track on which Jim Kerr first quoted the lines from Brecht's *Life of Galileo* (see '20th Century Promised Land'). The demo begins with a very breathy vocal from Kerr which adds a feeling of claustrophobia and a dark sensuality. Lines of 'Breathe in/Breathe out' with Kerr inhaling and exhaling deeply for effect. A repetition of 'life in oils' and what sounds like Kerr singing 'twenty-one' follow. Is Kerr giving us a description of a painting he has seen and is fascinated by?

Given that the band felt unable to discard anything that they had written once in the recording studio for both the albums, it's curious that 'Life in Oils' was left off. It is also a shame that the only element of the song that was repurposed was the lines from the Brecht play. In comparison to the demo of 'Careful in Career', 'Life in Oils' seems like a more rounded composition. The former doesn't alter much in musical construction, but Kerr's lyrics are still underdeveloped. Conversely, the latter has more strongly developed lyrical content. The song was finally included as a previously unreleased demo track on the *Silver Box* set released in 2004.

# 7

# *New Gold Dream (81-82-83-84)*

| | |
|---|---|
| UK: | 17 September 1982 |
| Personnel: | Bass: Derek Forbes<br>Drums: Mel Gaynor, Kenny Hyslop (track 3), Mike Ogletree (tracks 2, 5, 6)<br>Female vocals: Sharon Campbell (tracks 2, 7)<br>Guitars, effects: Charlie Burchill<br>Keyboards, effects: Michael MacNeil<br>Keyboard solo: Herbie Hancock (track 8)<br>Percussion: Mike Ogletree<br>Vocals: Jim Kerr |
| Duration: | 46 minutes |
| Produced by: | Peter Walsh |
| Chart position: | UK: 3; US: 69 |

The first recording sessions for the album began in January 1982. A tour that included a triumphant spell in Australia prior to Christmas 1981 had buoyed the band with a renewed enthusiasm. 'Love Song' made the Australian top twenty singles chart, and there was a feeling that commercial success at home was just around the corner. After one final homecoming show on 29 December, the band took a short break. They were soon back in the recording studio in the New Year, with new songs penned and one destined to become their new single.

In February, Simple Minds were back on the road, continuing to promote *Sons and Fascination/Sister Feelings Call* across Europe. Concerts were held regularly from mid-February until early April. The break in the touring schedule was by no means a break in workload for the band. They were writing and demoing songs as well as promoting 'Promised You a Miracle', and making several television and radio appearances, including their debut appearance on *Top of the Pops*, which aired on 15 April 1982. The single heralded a new sound. When interviewed by the music press in 1982, Jim Kerr explained:

> I think we felt that we wanted to mirror everything we saw and listened to, and after listening to our last couple of things I did think we were getting a bit typecast. I mean, I don't get up at half past ten and play Joy Division. I play Diana Ross. But nobody would associate her with me, and I thought it would be good to show our other side. After making that decision, things seemed to take care of themselves. Even halfway through the song, I thought 'Hey, hang on—this isn't us. We should have drums crashing away'. But then I thought, 'Well, what is us?'

Gigs continued sporadically during the summer, in between writing and recording sessions which took place at the Old Mill in Fife, Scotland, as well as at Rockfield Studios in Wales and the Townhouse Studios in London. During the summer, as the band continued to record and tour simultaneously, new songs were being road-tested in front of an ever-growing and appreciative crowd. New songs included 'King Is White and in the Crowd' and 'Summer Song', introduced to the crowd by Jim Kerr at a concert at Tiffany's in Glasgow on 14 July 1982. 'Summer Song' was the working title for 'Someone Somewhere in Summertime'. 'Festival Riff' (the working title for the album's title track) and 'Somebody Up There Likes You' had both been used as stage arrival music on several occasions.

The band had been touring with drummer Mike Ogletree since February. During the latter stages of the recording sessions, producer Peter Walsh sought out the extra impetus of session drummer Mel Gaynor. Both Ogletree and Gaynor recorded drum tracks for the album's title track. Vocal recordings for the album were the last to be worked on, with Jim Kerr leaving some of his lyrical content to be penned during the final stages. This is particularly true for the title track.

Recording for the album was completed in August, with the band back on the road immediately afterwards. A few evenings prior to the release of the album, Simple Minds appeared on the *Old Grey Whistle Test* performing 'Someone Somewhere in Summertime' and 'Hunter and the Hunted'. There were more *Top of the Pops* appearances during September, with two separately recorded (mimed) performances of 'Glittering Prize'.

At the end of September, the band jetted off to perform a string of concerts in Australia, New Zealand and Canada, before returning to the UK in mid-November. It was at this point that Mike Ogletree was replaced in the touring band by Mel Gaynor. The first leg of what would be the extensive *New Gold Dream* tour finished with two dates at Tiffany's in Glasgow on 20 and 21 December.

The album was released on 17 September 1982. It entered the UK chart at No. 6, peaking at No. 3 in its second week. It spent twenty-three consecutive weeks in the charts, twelve of those within the top forty. A further thirty weeks were spent dropping in and out of the chart between 1983 and 1987. The album also achieved a modicum of success on the Billboard 200 chart in America, entering in February 1983 and reaching a peak position of No. 69 on 4 April 1983. It spent a total of nineteen weeks on the Billboard chart.

The album received favourable reviews from the music press, including one gushing appraisal from Paul Morley, written for the *NME*, stating, 'My loyalty towards Simple Minds is known to be considerable, yet even I am jarred by the constant beauty of this music. Truly, all I need say is that *New Gold Dream* robs me of my breath—but let's continue. Be swept, be drained, believe me'. And that was just the beginning of the review!

In an interview after the album's release, Jim Kerr reflected on aspects of Simple Minds' change in musical direction:

> I found that last year I got obsessed with 'This Is The 80s. These Are Future Times'. There was a lot of talk about men and machines. But I found my values are much more earthier, I found myself thinking about things I hadn't thought of since I was a child. I'd become obsessed with modern times when in fact it was rubbish. I gained so much from touring, because purely and primarily we really do love it. It's the amount of knowledge gained that I just couldn't by staying at home... Last year we were in Australia, the cities are just modern, but outside... It struck me the world was an old place. We were driving through hundreds of miles of trees that went from white to silver. I was getting goosebumps. It was taking me back to my childhood when I was scared of the dark. Instead of thinking about men and machines, I started thinking about people and earth and bone and stones, and I knew it was going to be portrayed in whatever music we came up with next. As I said, we never plan much, but I knew from the days we started recording that the music was really warm this time, and a lot more genuine than the things we'd done before. I'm really pleased that we'd managed to break through and hadn't lost ourselves.

## The songs

### 'Someone Somewhere in Summertime'

Duration: 4.35

The third single to be released from the album, in November 1982. It was the third top-forty single from the album. The 12-inch extended version of the song has a solo guitar intro by Charlie Burchill. This intro was played live when the song was performed during the early tours. Lyrically, the song could be interpreted as either a love song or a song that gives an impression of closeness and wonderment. The imagery it provides is bright and warm. The effect of the rain is one of a sun shower offering the protagonist a way of cooling from that constant 'burning slow'.

During an interview in 2018, Derek Forbes stated that Jim Kerr had told him the lyrics were partly inspired by a visit to Glasgow by Pope John Paul II, which took place at Bellahouston Park on 1 June 1982. A break in the touring calendar at the time could have meant that Kerr was present on the day, albeit merely observing the event from the periphery. Kerr's lyrics for the song, although beautiful, are still ambiguous enough to give elasticity to the song's meaning. Its mid-tempo allows it to fall within power ballad criteria.

There is no escaping the immense joy and feeling of belonging that the music and lyrics of the song fill the soul with. Musically, every instrument is complimentary to its counterparts. Burchill's guitar does not overplay its spot, nor do MacNeil's keyboards get too buried. Forbes' bass is comparatively subtle. Mel Gaynor's drums are understated—certainly when taking into consideration what is to come later, both on this album and more so with the band's two follow-ups.

As 'Summer Song' the band begin to perform the track live in July. During only its second performance, Adam Sweeting, writing for *Melody Maker* and reviewing the inaugural WOMAD festival, wrote that the band were, 'Still perfecting the live version and didn't stretch it to the limit, but they pulled enough out of it to convince even the most belligerent sceptic that the word "epic" is in order'.

A version of the 7-inch single was released with a picture sleeve housed inside a plastic cover. The picture sleeve folded out into a large poster of the band on the reverse side. The single entered the UK chart on 13 November 1982 at No. 54 and would peak at No. 36 the following week, spending a total of five weeks on the chart. Along with the 12-inch extended version mentioned earlier, there was a 7-inch edited version made for US release by A&M. There also appears to be another edited version of the song on the Canadian 7-inch single distributed through the Polygram label.

## 'Colours Fly and Catherine Wheel'

Duration: 3.49

Jim Kerr introduced this track as 'a song about jealousy'. Personally, I have always viewed the song as an adult fairy-tale. The *leitmotif* style of the music exudes Disney-like imagery. MacNeil's keyboards and Burchill's guitar are both high and sweet and are underpinned by an incredibly rhythmic and funky bass from Derek Forbes. Mike Ogletree's drumming has a subtlety in playing style that differs from Gaynor's. There's a softer deftness of touch.

Of course, Kerr's use of the name Belle conjures up a connection to *Beauty and the Beast,* known as *La Belle et la Bête* in French. This fairytale was first adapted for the cinema by Jean Cocteau (who had previously inspired another Simple Minds song) in 1946. The lyrics also give off 'fantastic realism'—particularly in the chorus with the idea of catching a boy from the sky and falling in love. It's another reuse of lyrics by Kerr. On the previous album the protagonist in 'The American' declared that they had 'caught a boy fall out of the sky', but there was nothing romantic about that instance, as it suggests the name of the Hiroshima bomb, Little Boy. The protagonist in 'Colours Fly' also says that 'Poor girls cry/In the beauty of both worlds'. One wonders which two worlds they are. The real world and the imaginary world? The present world and the afterlife? The chorus is given a further fairy-tale effect by the soft, angelic backing vocals of Sharon Campbell.

The song was regularly performed live during the *New Gold Dream* tour of 1982–83, but was then placed on extended hiatus, only to return during the *Neapolis* tour of 1998. It has since made periodic appearances in the live set, most recently during the *Global* tour 2024.

## 'Promised You a Miracle'

Duration: 4.26

The first single from the album, released on 2 April 1982. In fact, the song was recorded and released before there was even a full quota of songs for the album recording. It was the only song the band recorded that featured drummer Brian McGee's replacement, Kenny Hyslop. Hyslop had inadvertently introduced the band to the song 'Too Through' by Bad Girls by playing it constantly as he toured with the band in 1981. When listening to the track it is not hard to hear the similarities between the songs, particularly the top melody, which Kerr and Burchill borrowed from heavily for the chorus both vocally and with guitar. It was the marker for a new phase in the sound of Simple Minds. Although it still played to the electronic dance sensibilities of the band, there was much more funk and R&B than the European synth-orientated dance music they'd been offering on the previous three albums.

It was also a conscious effort on Jim Kerr's part to write a hit single. When discussing the single with *Record Mirror* in 1982, Kerr gave this explanation:

> We went to rehearse at the end of January—we'd booked the studios for a few days, but I got this idea in less than 15 minutes. For the first time I felt bold enough to say we had a good single. Previously we'd simply do albums and people would say that track will make a good single. We just didn't think in terms of setting out specifically to record a single.

'Promised You a Miracle' entered the UK chart on 10 April 1982 at No. 59 and peaked at No. 13 in mid-May, spending a total of eleven weeks on the chart. When interviewed after its release and asked why he thought it had taken until now for the band to break into the UK top forty, Jim Kerr said:

> I don't know if it's fair for me to say. I wouldn't like to... A lot of people get angry at me not getting upset at this fact. It's just that these bands I mentioned (Roxy Music, Gabriel-fronted Genesis, The Velvet Underground, The Doors, Brian Eno, Robert Fripp, etc), most of them never had hit singles or daytime

> airplay, and we just presumed we would be of that ilk as well. About this time last year, we made a world tour, and I listened to the radio everywhere and I found that we were never on the damned thing. So, I thought it would be really nice to carry on doing what we were doing but bearing more in mind radio play. That took us to January. We started to write some new songs, the first of which was 'Promised You a Miracle' and the breakthrough just seemed to take care of itself. I'm not really sure why, but for the past two years people have been saying 'Oh, that single of yours, that should have been a hit, or that should have been a hit,' but we've never really had any grudge to bear [...] It's just really appealing to get across to as many people as possible.

The various editions of the single released in the UK and overseas spawned a variety of versions which are all available to listen to on the super deluxe box set of *New Gold Dream* from 2016. Versions include: a 7-inch edit, extended version, US remix, US dub, and US Special extended remix. If you love 'Promised You a Miracle', this box set is for you. Further to this, a live recording of the song captured during the *Once Upon a Time* tour of 1985–86 was chosen as a promotional single for Simple Minds' first commercially produced live album *Live in the City of Light* released in 1987. This live recording of 'Promised You a Miracle' was also a top-twenty hit.

## 'Big Sleep'

Duration: 4.59

Although Jim Kerr has never confirmed it, the song has been interpreted as being about death. 'Big sleep' is usually used as a metaphoric term for death and the afterlife. The song's lyrics offer an ambiguous dialogue on the loss of someone close to its narrator. 'So where did you go? Where do you go in the big sleep?' Other indicators are there with the elements of lost communication, a sense of leaving, the mention of a 'valuable' and 'immaculate' friend and 'for a lifetime I'm grateful'. There is something so haunting and desperately sad in the lyrics. For all the gossamer, ethereal beauty of it, there is sadness to be found in the tracks on *New Gold Dream*. A sadness that can also be uplifting.

In discussing the making of the album during its recording, Kerr spoke about the change in musical direction the band were going through and had this to say:

> It's a bit schizophrenic. In some ways there is the most lightweight things [on it] ever, and on the other, it's heady as hell. There's no shortage of melody. Before we used to be too subtle with melody, trying to arrange things and getting clever on technicalities. This isn't like that; there's much more melody.

The track was a regular feature in the live set and a live version featured as a B-side on the 'Kick It In' single in 1989. A slightly extended version of the song featured on the 2005 DVD-Audio release of *New Gold Dream*.

## 'Somebody Up There Likes You'

Duration: 4.58

An instrumental on the album that curiously seems to have had lyrics at one point, which ended up being discarded. There are conflicting sources on whether it was Burchill or MacNeil that came up with the track, but considering how closely the men worked together, it is probably safe to assume it was a joint effort. I had the opportunity to ask Jim Kerr about the title of the track several years ago when Jo Whiley on Radio 2 conducted an audience questions interview with Kerr and Burchill prior to the *Acoustic* concert at the Hackney Empire in November 2016. I had often wondered if the title was a nod to the band's musical hero, David Bowie, as Bowie had a track on *Young Americans* titled 'Somebody Up There Likes Me'. Kerr responded:

> I think it was a Paul Newman movie that maybe Bowie took his title from. I think it was more to do with… It's an instrumental track, for those people who don't know. So, therefore it's one of our best [laughs], without doubt… and it's in tune. It's kind of a cosmic thing. It was our version of Pink Floyd. It's all a bit 'astral,' so ... hence the title.

Light-hearted anecdotes aside, Simple Minds were starting to gain a reputation for atmospheric instrumentals on their albums. Previously, the wonderful 'Theme for Great Cities' was a stand-out on *Sister Feelings Call*. When discussing why a particular song would remain an instrumental, Kerr offered this reasoning:

> With most songs, I usually have an idea pretty soon about the direction in which the text should develop. But in the case of instrumentals no textual ideas ever came up. Because everything was already there! I've never thought, that's a strong song; it needs a strong text. Never! They had to stay instrumental, no doubt about it. You hear voices, you see images in those songs. Why give them an identity when they already have one? They express as much as the songs I did write lyrics for. Conclusion: they make me superfluous.

## 'New Gold Dream (81-82-83-84)'

Duration: 5.40

The track had been developing under the working title of 'Festival Riff'. It was first heard by audiences in June 1982 when it was being used as intro music prior to the band arriving on stage. It was one of the last songs to have lyrics written for it. The story goes that Jim Kerr had been struggling to pull together lyrics that conveyed the imagery he was seeing when listening to the music. He felt that nothing was working. There were just a few days of recording time left. Inside the booklet included in the 2016 super-deluxe edition box set of the album, Kerr tells the story of how—with time running out to bring the lyrics together—the band were committed to fulfilling a festival appearance in Sweden during the final days of recording the album in mid-August. I can find no evidence of any Swedish dates for this period. They played a festival in Sweden towards the end of July, many miles away from where Kerr states he came up with the lyrics for the song in Örebro. The only festival dates that correlate to the end of the recording of the album are two concerts in Belgium on 15/16 August. So either Kerr had written the lyrics earlier than he thought, or they were written in Belgium rather than Sweden.

Another contentious issue is exactly how the lyrics were written. In the 2016 booklet, Kerr stated it was while he was listening to the music while having a bath in his hotel room. More recently, when writing about the album on Facebook for its fortieth anniversary in 2022, Kerr refuted his previous account by saying: 'Somewhere along the way, the details of that event seem to have been distorted. And so, for the sake of clarity. No! I have never written songs in the bath. Shower. Jacuzzi. Sauna. Or swimming pool. Most likely never will. But then again ...who knows?' So the song's lyrical formation remains steeped in mystery ... it was somewhere in northern Europe, either in a bath or not, around the middle of August 1982.

What is certain is that both Mike Ogletree and Mel Gaynor play drums on the track. Percussion is included, with one of the best examples of cowbell deployment on record. I cannot praise Derek Forbes' basslines enough during this period. Jim Kerr's lyrics speak of a sunset but I have always felt the way the song begins, with the fade-up of percussion and the synth melody, the bass riff and the legato guitar chords, evokes a sunrise—with the rays of the rising sun filtering out through billowing clouds that partially conceal the rising sun. One awakes to the 'New Gold Dream'. Long before Jim Kerr made the most of being stuck for words during the recording of 'Don't You (Forget About Me)' by adding some guide vocal 'la la la las', he used them at the beginning of 'New Gold Dream' to subtler effect.

The track has been a mainstay of the band's live set since its initial use as an instrumental intro in 1982. Since around the early 2000s, a regular inclusion in the lyrics has been the line 'Give me the truth/I want to hear it some more'. The song was released as a single in Italy to coincide with the band's arrival there on tour in March 1983. It was released as both a 7-inch edited version (which coincidentally was the version used for the American A&M release of the album) and a 12-inch, which used what would confusingly be titled the 'German 12-inch Remix'. The outro to this mix would give me goosebumps whenever I played it. I couldn't identify how the sound was produced: which instruments are responsible? Guitar, keyboards, a combination of both? I decided to ask the question on the Simple Minds Facebook page. To my delight, I received this response from Jim Kerr: 'That sound? Metaphorically you are listening to the transmute of base metals into the noble metals (gold or silver); the development of an elixir of life that can, in certain circumstances, confer youth and longevity. So, there you have it!'

## 'Glittering Prize'

Duration: 4.33

The second single released from the album. The track entered the UK chart at No. 61 on 28 August 1982. It peaked at No. 16 on 9 October during its eighth week on the chart. The song begins with a wail of Burchill guitar along with the strike of drums by Mel Gaynor. There's a backdrop of keyboards and bass and Jim Kerr's opening line is an optimistic call to 'shine the light on me'. It's soon followed by an elaborate bassline from Derek Forbes, with a lovely two-note melody from Mick MacNeil.

The song is as glittering as its title suggests. Brightly optimistic, with a story of the desire for success. When Jim Kerr introduced the song during early concerts, he described it as a 'song of ambition and courage'. It embodies notions of friendship and 'the attraction of fame' and the 'glittering prize is the price of lost loves'. It's almost a self-fulfilling prophecy for the band itself. Their breath about to be taken away by their success. A line that has been used twice before also features again, the 'act of love'. Firstly, a song with that exact title that was a Kerr/Burchill composition from 1978. Then it was in the opening line of 'Celebrate': 'Act of love/Is a luxury'.

When asked what the song was about when he was interviewed at the time of its release, Jim Kerr said: 'It's about getting a glimpse of something and going out on a chase for it against all the odds. If you're after something, or something is really beckoning, just go for it'. Much like the other singles from the album, 'Glittering Prize' was edited and remixed to produce several versions, including a club mix and extended theme (ostensibly an instrumental version of the club mix) for 12-inch copies and an edited version and an instrumental version subtitled 'Theme' for 7-inch copies.

## 'Hunter and the Hunted'

Duration: 5.54

Jim Kerr introduced the track when performing it live during early tours as 'a tale of two'. If 'Colours Fly' was one portrayal of a relationship and 'Promised You a Miracle' another—and within those songs lay trials and tribulations pertaining to relationships between couples—then 'Hunter and the Hunted' offers yet another spin on the complexities of an intimate relationship. This time, it almost comes across as if the male protagonist is the victim, or at least conflicted about how much he wants to surrender himself to love over lust. It seems as if he tells a tale of being 'cocooned up in Badlands'. The 'Badlands' is perhaps a metaphor for that thin line between love and lust. He suffers the 'side effects of living in temptation'. Where 'Promised You a Miracle' seemed purely fictional, and 'Colours Fly' had slightly suggestive autobiographical elements, 'Hunter and the Hunted' leans even more into the autobiographical. A 'young, brave, honest set'—the band and their friends? 'The greatest show on earth is here tonight, love'—the band? Jim addressing a potential lover watching in the crowd? Life was moving so fast for the band at this point. It was a constant schedule of touring, writing and recording on loop. All of this is expressed in the lines of 'Hunter and the Hunted'. Constant temptation placed in one's path, be it drink, drugs, women: all manner of excesses. The penultimate lines of 'Hunter and the Hunted', in which the protagonist of the song pleads, 'When you hear me screaming/I'll be seeing through the eyes of love', seem to be a nod to similar lines used by Lou Reed in the song 'Oh Jim'. Perhaps it was sheer coincidence, but given Kerr's unswerving admiration of Lou Reed, I doubt it. Reed's lyrics in 'Oh Jim' refer to the titular character as 'looking through the eyes of hate'.

'Hunter and the Hunted' reaches a level of sophistication that slowly builds through each track of *New Gold Dream*. All the band play their parts exceptionally, from Gaynor's subtle drumming, Forbes' two-chord bass intro, MacNeil's mellifluously melodic keyboard flourishes, Burchill's delicate guitar riffs and finally Kerr's soft and yearning vocal performance. It is Simple Minds *par excellence*. And the *pièce de resistance*? A cameo on keyboards by none other than Herbie Hancock. Many fans view this track as the album's pinnacle.

## 'King is White and in the Crowd'

Duration: 6.57

One of the earliest tracks to be written for the album. It was introduced into the live set in the summer of 1982, although its debut airing was earlier than that. The song had been recorded when the band performed in session for David 'Kid' Jensen on Radio 1 in February, along with 'Promised You a Miracle' and 'In Trance as Mission'.

In interviews with the music press just prior to the release of the album, Jim Kerr explained that their previous albums were 'all on one level, all the songs with the same pace and intensity'. In contrast he described the tracks on *New Gold Dream* as 'much more on a balance'. That balance gave a greater sense of light and shade in their musical output. A song such as 'King is White and in the Crowd' exemplifies this. That it doesn't feel misplaced on the album and manages to stand cheek-by-jowl with 'lighter' tracks like 'Colours Fly and Catherine Wheel', 'Promised You a Miracle' and 'Glittering Prize', is the point I believe Kerr was trying to get across with these statements.

The album ends with possibly the darkest subject matter imaginable, the aftermath of an assassination. It wasn't the first time Kerr had written about an assassin, and it wasn't the last. In an interview from 1981, Kerr talks about his fascination with assassins. 'Assassins really intrigue me. He's really alone for the moment that he's pulling the trigger. He's stepped completely outside the norm and for that moment he's seized a kind of power, he's stopped being ordinary.' The true focal point of the song is the victim's widow. The legend of the song is that Kerr was inspired in part by viewing news footage of the assassination of Anwar Sadat on television. The imagery of the song is like a montage of different scenes, with an underlying Eastern tone coming through the percussion and synthesiser elements. These add light to the darker shades of Kerr's lyrics.

At a running time of seven minutes, the song is the longest track on the album and is part of a growing Simple Minds tradition of extended-play album epics, with previous album tracks 'Pleasantly Disturbed', 'This Fear of Gods' and 'In Trance as Mission' all of similar duration. Usually, an album closer will give some indication of where a band or artist is headed to next musically, but 'King is White' offers up little other than that Mel Gaynor will assert himself as a powerhouse on the albums to come.

## Additional tracks

### 'In Every Heaven/Soundtrack for Every Heaven'

Duration: 4.27/4.55

The song was recorded during the sessions for *New Gold Dream* and was possibly considered as a B-side, but only the instrumental version titled 'Soundtrack for Every Heaven' was used on the B-side of the 12-inch single of 'Someone Somewhere in Summertime'. The vocal version of the song was kept in the vaults for many years until a DVD-Audio version of the album was released in 2005.

In a post on the Simple Minds website in October 2010, news was shared about the completion of a recording of the track the band had made that was produced by Andy Wright and Gavin Goldberg. Other new songs recorded during these sessions would appear on future Simple Minds releases. One mentioned, titled 'Broken Glass Park', had been on the live set of Kerr's solo project, *Lostboy! AKA Jim Kerr*. There was no mention on the post that Kerr had also been performing 'In Every Heaven' during a promotional tour of his one and only solo album to date. The 2010 recording of 'In Every Heaven' has never been officially released.

The original vocal recording of 'In Every Heaven' was officially released as a bonus track on the *X5* box set in 2012. A full extended version of the song was released as part of the super-deluxe box set of *New Gold Dream* released in 2016. This package also included an 'Early Version' (as titled) of the song, which has a basic drum track, intricate melodic synth and basic guitar riff. Kerr's vocal on this version is more like a guide vocal, in which he repeats the title of the song in varying vocal styles. It plays almost like a different song entirely. Sparse, repetitive, yet somehow hypnotically beautiful. The full composition has an ambitious air to it and a dream theme that is in keeping with the dominant concept of *New Gold Dream*. It also contains the curious line of 'kissing yourself goodbye'.

# 8

# *Sparkle in the Rain*

| | |
|---|---|
| UK: | 6 February 1984 |
| Personnel: | Backing vocals: Derek Forbes, Mel Gaynor |
| | Bass: Derek Forbes |
| | Drums: Mel Gaynor |
| | Female vocals: Kirsty MacColl (tracks 3, 6) |
| | Guitars: Charlie Burchill |
| | Keyboards: Michael MacNeil |
| | Vocals: Jim Kerr |
| Duration: | 45 minutes |
| Produced by: | Steve Lillywhite |
| Chart position: | UK: 1; US: 64 |

The chase for further commercial success was now on. Attaining that coveted UK No. 1 album was tantalisingly close. Jim Kerr was determined that the band would not simply offer up '*New Gold Dream—Part Two*'. Whatever they delivered to the record-buying public in 1984 had to be musically nothing like its predecessor.

The first jamming sessions for *Sparkle in the Rain* took place at The Chapel studios in Lincolnshire, a short distance from Skegness. A new year had just begun, and the band had only just completed the gruelling first leg of touring *New Gold Dream*, which had taken them down to Australia and New Zealand and across to Canada before winding up back home in Glasgow just a few days before Christmas in 1982 for two home gigs. The tour was set to continue during 1983 but before then, work started on the follow-up to *New Gold Dream*.

In February the band met with Alex Sadkin to discuss him producing the new album. Sadkin seemed as keen as the band to collaborate, but shortly afterwards he filled his schedule producing for Duran Duran, Classix Nouveaux and Thompson Twins, so Simple Minds found themselves seeking an alternative.

They chose Steve Lillywhite. Lillywhite had already established himself working with the likes of XTC, Joan Armatrading, U2 and, most recently, Big Country. In any case, the band would continue to tour through the spring and summer, so recording of the album wouldn't resume until after the final concert of the tour, the big U2 Homecoming concert held at Dublin's Phoenix Park on 14 August 1983. The band performed a new song—offering a taster of the new sound for the new album. The two-chord bass-pulsing 'Waterfront' was an immediate hit with the crowd. A review of the concert from *Number One* music magazine, dated 27 August 1983, declared that 'U2 are now crowd pleasers whereas Simple Minds are crowd transformers'.

Phoenix Park was a stand-alone concert that came a month after the band's run of summer festival slots in mainland Europe. They had turned down a support slot for the Police during the American leg of their *Synchronicity II* tour.

When interviewed in early 1984 in Australia, Kerr explained that this was done in favour of concentrating on recording:

> We'd have just been going through the motions [had they toured]. We still had the energy to get up on stage, but our heads were bursting with all these new ideas and we just had to get them out first. People thought 'this is your chance' and a lot of people thought we were crazy, but there you go. With all due respect to the Police, I think if our future were in the hands of ten or twelve dates with them, I don't think we'd have much of a future.

Writing and demo sessions recommenced at Rockfield Studio shortly after the Phoenix Park gig, with album recording sessions and mixing taking place at the Townhouse Studio, where the band were now joined by Lillywhite. The choice of Lillywhite came in for some criticism. Jim Kerr, when speaking to Billy Sloan just a couple of weeks after the album was released, shrugged this off: rightly so, given *Sparkle in the Rain*'s chart position when the interview took place:

> The thing about that [criticism over the choice of Lillywhite] is that these people; you get people, and they talk about production and this should'nae been this or this should'nae been that. No one knows what a production is until they've actually been in a studio and been there for six weeks. Other than that, they're only guessing and they're welcome to guess and speculate as much as they like. But we knew we were heading towards that [sound].

Kerr went on to talk about the new sound that was developing, through having worked on *Sparkle in the Rain*:

> Steve has a reputation for having a big drum sound—well we've got a drummer who's got the biggest drum sound in Britain, if not the world. And I just think it wasn't so much Steve giving us that. We were heading that way, and he just

> happened to bring it out. People say there's a distinctive Steve Lillywhite sound, that every band he works with sounds the same. Well, I'll be damned if Joan Armatrading sounds anything like Big Country to me.

Such criticisms seemingly had no bearing on how the album was received by the not-insubstantial Simple Minds fanbase and the broader music-loving public. As for Mel Gaynor's sound on the record, the drummer certainly was cementing his place in the Simple Minds line-up. It could be argued that as this is the first album on which he played the drums on all the songs, *Sparkle in the Rain* is Mel Gaynor's album, musically speaking. More broadly, the band appeared to have formed a more cohesive unit, with all band members contributing to the song-writing in a way that had not been apparent before. In an interview in 1984, shortly after the release of the album, Jim Kerr gave particular praise to Gaynor, saying:

> I feel at least six feet when he's behind me on stage. I can really feel him at the back, and he hits the kit so hard. Every night he just gets me up there and drives me on. I think Mel's got a really big future no matter what he does. He's got a great scope in music. Everything from reggae, to jazz, to funk and rock. I think since he's come in and really tightened the whole unit up. I think he and Derek Forbes are definitely a special rhythm unit.

In the week of its release in February 1984, *Sparkle in the Rain* entered the UK chart at No. 1 and spent a total of twenty-eight weeks on the chart during 1984. It went on to spend a further thirty weeks on the chart during 1986, enjoying chart rankings alongside the band's follow-up album, *Once Upon a Time*. The album also made the American Billboard 200 chart, peaking at No. 64 during the week ending 7 April 1984. It spent a total of twenty-four weeks on the Billboard 200 chart. Despite the album cultivating three top-forty singles for the band in the UK, curiously its Billboard album chart success did not result in any corresponding Billboard Hot 100 successes for its singles Stateside.

After the release, when interviewed about the album and comparing it to its predecessor, Jim Kerr said: 'When we were doing *New Gold Dream* there was a subconscious search for perfection. This time [with *Sparkle in the Rain*] it was more for performance'.

## The songs

### 'Up on the Catwalk'

Duration: 4.45

Right from the very beginning, Mel Gaynor makes his presence known on this album. His is the first voice you hear, and the crash of his snare and bass drum are also the first instruments heard. It's an immediate signal that this album is going to be different from its predecessor. The keyboards sound different too. The drums are very quickly accompanied by piano.

Jim Kerr's explanation of the song's lyrical narrative has been that part of the song was inspired by *The Master and Margarita*, a novel by Russian author Mikhail Bulgakov. However, while researching this book I came across an article in which Kerr stated the song was about 'the hypocrisy of Britain'.

In another interview, around the same time in early 1984, Kerr went into further detail:

> I'd like to think my resentment at the British malaise is not cynical, I just think it's better to be honest and to take it from there. What I'm bitter about is the way Britain presents itself media-wise, and I just can't stand the whole Thatcher regime. It hits you when you leave Britain—when you're here, you never think of it as an island, because the media still paint it as the centre of the universe or something, when we all know it's hardly that. That's what I'm saying in the songs, that things may be down, but I don't like to wallow in the muck.

Exactly which aspects of the novel inspired the song are unclear, but the disillusion that Kerr felt about mid-1980s Britain is more obvious.

The accompanying official video showcased a band as energetic as ever, with Kerr jumping, leaping and lunging around like a whirling dervish. A catwalk of sorts is on display behind the band, with a strange assortment of characters strutting their stuff as the single edit version of the song plays out.

The third single from the album, it entered the UK chart at No. 36 during the week ending 24 March 1984. It peaked at No. 27 two weeks later, spending a total of five weeks on the chart.

## 'Book of Brilliant Things'

Duration: 4.20

The song has a different musical arrangement on the album than it does when performed today. When interviewed in 1984 Jim Kerr described the song as 'a child's ode or a child's prayer'. He continued to elaborate: 'It's a song about learning and growing up. I think you're never too old to stop growing and learning, especially if you keep your eyes and ears open'.

During the *Once Upon a Time* tour of 1985–86, the song was reworked. Mick MacNeil added more synthesiser and piano elements to the track, including a longer intro. The tempo was slowed and it became more of a soul and gospel tune rather than one that was styled on the metre and sound of a locomotive engine, hence the lyric 'Our hearts beat like the wheels of a fast train all around the world'. There is also an example of Kerr's penchant for reusing lyrics, with the opening line 'Thank you for the voice, the eyes and the memories shine' having been used similarly in a previous song, the title track to *Sons and Fascination,* which contains the lines 'Thank you for the voice/Thank you for the eyes/Thank you for the good times'.

The song has been a regular feature in the band's live set, particularly in more recent years. It is now sung exclusively by additional vocalist Sarah Brown. It is a live favourite among the fanbase.

## 'Speed Your Love to Me'

Duration: 4.25

The second single from the album. An expression of burgeoning young love from the point of view of a young man, which brings to it an urgency that means it's adored equally by male and female Simple Minds fans. It's not your typical love song. Due to the new, rockier sound that the band had embraced, it has that loud, crashing drum style. It's no ballad. It's heady, visceral and quite manic. It expresses emotions in a way that teenage boys wish they could. 'You go to my head/With the flames that go higher'. It's no coincidence that at this point Simple Minds won themselves a new legion of fans that were in their early teens. As a 13-year-old at the time of the release of *Sparkle in the Rain*, I was increasingly exposed to the band's sound through watching music video programmes and seeing their videos for 'Waterfront', 'Speed Your Love to Me' and 'Up on the Catwalk'. Most Simple Minds fans I know today are of my generation: in their early-to-mid teens in 1984.

The video for 'Speed Your Love to Me' felt particularly exotic to a teenage Australian girl, with its imagery of the Firth of Clyde and Loch Lomond adding Caledonian romanticism. The videos for 'Waterfront' and 'Speed Your Love to Me' were the first to offer up any kind of Scottish identity to the band, at least visually.

The single was released in January 1984 and entered the UK chart at No. 20, its peak position during a four-week run.

## 'Waterfront'

Duration: 4.49

The musical manifestation of the song was instigated by bass player Derek Forbes. That opening pulse, swiftly followed by the crash of Mel Gaynor drums, cemented the two men as the enviable rhythmic backbone of the Simple Minds line-up. The guitar riff added by Charlie Burchill is probably his most recognisable, while Mick MacNeil's synths embrace and feed a subtle countermelody to Forbes' throbbing bass. It couldn't fail but become an immediate anthem.

The lead single from the album made its debut at Phoenix Park in Dublin on 14 August 1983. The reaction from the crowd must have helped in the decision-making process to choose it as the album's first cut. 'Waterfront' had been an instant hit with the Irish crowd. Jim Kerr felt the song's strength also lay in other areas:

> It's almost an anti-single. Everything else on the radio was verse/chorus, whereas 'Waterfront' just burst through, even on the tinniest, tinny speakers. The first time I heard it I jumped up and down. It's a real 'Come on, let's go!' song.

The song took initial lyrical shape sometime during the late spring and into early summer. Kerr was back in Glasgow and during several interviews he spoke about how the lyrics came about during the time he was there:

> This particular time I walked right along the front, and Glasgow was packed with empty ships, like ghost ships. Even from the factories you could hear from the echoes and the acoustics that they were all empty, just shells. And it was kinda special for me because all my people—my grandfather and that—worked on the front. So, I was looking about and there was this real sadness. I hope it doesn't sound too romantic, but I had a fantastic view which I didn't know you could get from there and I couldn't help but feel... you can sit around and say it's all finished; industry's finished, Glasgow's a ghost town. But the river was still going through, and there's a force there that you can't hold back. It was just moving on and moving on...

In another interview, Kerr expanded on his feelings about the city and his optimistic and (with hindsight) prescient outlook:

> There's a new sky above Glasgow. They've been through the darkness and come out. 'Waterfront' begins bleakly, walking around Glasgow's docks, thinking of the time when that front must have been Glasgow's crowning glory. People still talk about those docks as the lifeblood of the city but they're not, people are the city's lifeblood. Industry can come and go but the people remain, and they'll adapt. For me right now, it's impossible not to see light at the end of the tunnel.

Virgin had decided there would be two singles released prior to the album. 'Waterfront' was one, and 'Speed Your Love to Me' was chosen as the second. The video for 'Waterfront' was recorded around Glasgow, showing the band taking the Renfrew Ferry as well as performing live inside the Barrowland Ballroom to a crowd of ecstatic young concertgoers. Footage of the band was shot for the 'Speed Your Love to Me' video at the same time. The video shoot took place during the week that 'Waterfront' was released as a single.

The song entered the UK chart at No. 25, peaking at No. 13 the following week. The song has been a mainstay in the live set since its debut in Dublin in 1983. The only tour it has not featured in was the *5x5 Live* tour in 2012.

## 'East at Easter'

Duration: 3.30

Several Simple Minds songs from this period have been misinterpreted as having religious connotations, but I view these songs as having a theological aspect—making observations and questioning things rather than offering firm statements. When it comes to 'East at Easter', it is very easy to fall into the trap of believing it is a religious statement, given its title. The song is much more of a plea for peace and a call for an end to conflict and war. When interviewed around the release of *Sparkle in the Rain*, Jim Kerr said that he had initially written the lyrics to 'East at Easter' during the recording of *New Gold Dream*, so it could be argued that a little of *New Gold Dream—Part Two* had made it on to *Sparkle in the Rain*. In 1982 Britain had gone to war in the Falklands and, at the beginning of the summer, war had broken out in Lebanon. These events obviously weighed on Kerr's mind, like the assassination of Anwar Sadat in 1981, which was said to have inspired 'King is White and in the Crowd'. 'East at Easter' has had sporadic outings in the live set over the years.

## 'Street Hassle' (L. Reed)

Duration: 5.15

The song was first performed live at the Roskilde festival in Denmark on 1 July 1983. The band was awed by the crowd reaction. In an interview in early 1984, Jim Kerr described the effect the crowd had on him that night in Roskilde: 'It was amazing to see a hush go over 60,000 people and there was just this beautiful, serene feeling, and so we just carried it on into the studio'. When it came to the recording sessions for the album, Simple Minds offered a condensed version of the Lou Reed original, which had been segmented into three parts subtitled: 'Waltzing Matilda', 'Street Hassle' and 'Slipaway'. Simple Minds' version borrowed mostly from the 'Waltzing Matilda' and 'Slipaway' parts of the song. It was a bone of contention as to whether a five-minute condensed version could express the same depth of meaning and intensity of subject matter as Reed's 11-minute original. The main part of the Reed original (the 'Street Hassle' section) deals with a heroin overdose and one observer's notion about what to do with the dead body. It could be said that Simple Minds turned it into a sentimental love song, or a break-up song. There is more complexity in the Reed original. In explaining the decision to record the song, Kerr offered this:

> It was just a good balance to some of the more optimistic things that we were writing about. There was just something in the song that we really identified with. I never particularly felt that it was a cover version or anything like that. It's obviously a sensitive song. A few Lou Reed fans, a few 'inverted snobs', have criticised us for doing it, but I'm pretty proud that Lou Reed's got a song on what is a No. 1 album.

The song was performed during the *Once Upon a Time* tour during 1985–86 and a live version was captured at Ahoy in Rotterdam and was a track on the double 7-inch release of 'Sanctify Yourself'.

## 'White Hot Day'

Duration: 4.33

A song that has a tricky time signature, which may be the reason it was only performed live a handful of times, during warm-up shows in Glasgow and London in December 1983. It was also scrutinised by Jim Kerr as a second-side album track that could have benefited from more rehearsal time, thus producing 'better arrangements' and 'better songs'.

The lyrics weave into the repetitive nature of the song. Kerr was never one to shy away from lyrical repetition, and it seems he uses lyrical loops as his own way of providing a form of instrumentation. He has often remarked, when asked about his lyrics and the lack of lyric sheets in Simple Minds albums, that 'my lyrics aren't poetry. They go with the music'. When interviewed in 1982, Kerr also said, 'I don't attach too much importance to words. If they sound attractive and make a coherent picture, then great'.

'White Hot Day' is the track that serves as a hint as to where Simple Minds are headed next musically. An instrumental version of the song titled 'Bass Line' was chosen as the B-side for 'Speed Your Love to Me'.

## '"C" Moon Cry Like a Baby'

Duration: 4.21

A falling out between lovers? A breakdown in communication? Who exactly is this song about? It's the first use of another trope that Jim Kerr has used throughout his song-writing career: the one in which love conquers all. Except it doesn't seem to be helping poor '"C" Moon'. The middle eight of the song has one of the most fantastic crashing drum displays by Mel Gaynor to be captured on record. This album really heralded the arrival of Gaynor as a key element of the new Simple Minds sound. Jim Kerr would say in several interviews during that time that having Gaynor playing behind him made him feel '10 feet tall'. As for lachrymose '"C" Moon?' She's rarely been heard of since. The song was given limited live exposure during the *Tour du Monde* of 1984 and then had no further airings until the *Alive and Kicking* tour of 2003. The song then once again vanished from the live set.

## 'The Kick Inside of Me'

Duration: 4.45

In 1983, Jim Kerr suggested that this song 'could be a Sex Pistols backing track'. It has another of Derek Forbes' incredible bass rhythms. Discussing this track, Forbes has often said that he attacked his bass playing in such a frantic way that it made his fingers bleed. There is a rushed urgency to this tune which is encapsulated by Forbes' playing style, along with Kerr's raw and somewhat vitriolic vocal performance. If 'Waterfront' offered a 'Come on, let's go!' anthem, then this track sounded more punk than Johnny & the Self Abusers had ever been, with a fist-pumping 'Get it up ya!' to boot. The song was given initial exposure when the band recorded a live radio session for the David 'Kid' Jensen show on BBC Radio 1, which was broadcast in October 1983. Much like the previous track on the album, the song had limited live exposure, identical to '"C" Moon' in frequency.

### 'Shake Off the Ghosts'

Duration: 3.48

Continuing what has become a regular feature on Simple Minds albums, this slow tempo instrumental feels as if it provides a simmering down from all the frenetic energy and aural crash of what's gone before. It's preceded by Jim Kerr singing the words 'shake off the...' at the end of 'The Kick Inside of Me'. It's a very effective segue. Rather than something that sounds like it could be morose or ghoulish due to its title, to me it's like the smell of petrichor and the sight of a rainbow after a torrential downpour.

## Additional tracks

### 'A Brass Band in Africa'/'A Brass Band in African Chimes'

Duration: 5.10/9.22

An instrumental that was used as the B-side for 'Up on the Catwalk'. In the same way Jim Kerr had felt that 'Theme for Great Cities' was a complete song and did not require lyrics or a vocal performance to complete it, it was true for 'Brass Band'. The track was initially an idea from Mick MacNeil, as was 'Theme for Great Cities'. A longer, extended mix was used for the 12-inch single for 'Up on the Catwalk'. The extended version appears to have the chorus coda of 'Speed Your Love to Me' attached to it, or at least something that sounds similar. At over nine minutes in length, it is one of the longest Simple Minds instrumental mixes. Broken up into three distinct sections, the final section has a reprise of the guitar riff from 'Shake Off the Ghosts' within it.

9

# *Once Upon a Time*

| | |
|---|---|
| UK: | 21 October 1985 |
| Personnel: | Additional lead vocals: Robin Clark<br>Backing vocals: Carlos Alomar, Michael Been, The Simms Brothers<br>Bass: John Giblin<br>Drums: Mel Gaynor<br>Guitars: Charlie Burchill<br>Lead vocals: Jim Kerr<br>Percussion: Sue Hadjopoulos<br>Piano, synthesisers: Michael MacNeil |
| Duration: | 40 minutes |
| Produced by: | Bob Clearmountain and Jimmy Iovine |
| Chart position: | UK: 1; US: 10 |

Writing for the album began towards the end of 1984. The band reconvened in the autumn, a few weeks after they had returned to the UK from an extensive touring schedule throughout 1984 promoting *Sparkle in the Rain*, released in February. Now their sights were firmly set on cracking the United States.

The UK and much of mainland Europe had been won: *Sparkle in the Rain* entered the UK chart at No. 1 in its first week of release. It had also made the top twenty in several other countries around the world, predominantly in Europe but also in Australia, New Zealand and Canada. The album also made the Billboard 200 in the US, though there are no corresponding Billboard Hot 100 entries for any of its singles. After February 1985, there was a steady change in Simple Minds' fortunes Stateside. It was a slow climb. It took three months to build up but, eventually, the band began to trouble the Billboard chart with 'that song from the movie'. By the middle of May it took the No. 1 spot.

Propelled by the success of 'Don't You (Forget About Me)', the drive to break the American market had taken off. No one wants to be a one-hit wonder! And Simple Minds certainly didn't want to end up with that badge, especially not for a song that they hadn't penned themselves. A full-on assault began in earnest. Jamming sessions resulted in material gradually coming together.

By this point relations in the band were strained, and Derek Forbes was asked to leave. He was replaced by John Giblin, whose studio the band just happened to be conducting their writing sessions in.

Around the time of the release of 'Don't You' Jim Kerr secured a meeting with Jimmy Iovine for talks about him producing the next Simple Minds album (alongside Bob Clearmountain). Iovine required some convincing. He wanted reassurance from Kerr that the band already had material to record. Kerr laid on the charm and was adamant the band would be ready and have all the material required by the time of recording. Incredibly, Iovine was put at ease, most likely impressed by Kerr's overt cockiness. It was while Kerr was holed up in France during the spring, frantically penning lyrics for the tracks that would feature on *Once Upon a Time*, that news reached him that 'Don't You' had topped the Billboard chart.

By the end of June, the band were ready to shift Stateside to continue recording the album, having started at Virgin's Townhouse Studios in London a few weeks earlier. It was a busy time. The final production of the album took place alongside photo sessions with Anton Corbjin for the album cover photography, as well as video shoots for 'Alive and Kicking' and 'All the Things She Said'.

Another high point in the history of Simple Minds was just a few weeks away: their appearance at the JFK Stadium in Philadelphia for Live Aid. The concert took place on 13 July 1985, just four days after Jim Kerr's twenty-sixth birthday. After Live Aid, final recording sessions and mixing took place at Bearsville Studios near Woodstock in New York State, with the final mixes taking place in Right Track Studios in New York City.

The album produced three songs that took top-forty positions on the Billboard Hot 100 in the United States. From 'Alive and Kicking's first week in the Billboard chart on 12 October 1985, until the final week of 'All the Things She Said' appearing on the chart on 28 June 1986, Simple Minds spent a total of thirty-seven weeks in the Billboard Hot 100.

The album entered the UK chart at No. 1 during its first week and spent seventy-eight consecutive weeks on the chart from 2 November 1985 until 25 April 1987. It spent a further four weeks in the top 100 during May 1987, only toppled out of the chart by the release of *Live in the City of Light*. Of all the weeks the album spent on the chart, its only time at No. 1 was during the debut week.

The album entered the Billboard 200 chart at No. 69 in its first week and peaked at No. 10 in its seventeenth week on the chart. It spent a total of forty-two weeks on the Billboard chart from 9 November 1985 until 23 August 1986, with twenty-seven weeks of that forty-two-week run spent within the top forty. On 27 June 2025 the band played a concert at Glasgow's Bellahouston Park, at which they performed the whole album in celebration of its fortieth anniversary, along with other greatest hits.

## The songs

### 'Once Upon a Time'

Duration: 5.44

A fairy-tale title that could have easily seen the song fall victim to being deemed a throw-away gimmick, but musically it has serious clout! There is no let-up in Mel Gaynor's rhythmic dominance in the mid-1980s Simple Minds sound. The crash and bang are less brash than they were on *Sparkle in the Rain.* There is a more wholesome delivery to his playing on this album, revealing more funk and a style that harks back to his earlier drumming days when he was involved with the British funk scene. Nonetheless, Gaynor was pulling out all the stops to sonically steal the show. Not so fast, Mel! Within the opening chords of the song, every band member is clearly and audibly defined. John Giblin's bass playing is distinct from what fans had grown accustomed to with Derek Forbes, but the difference defined him. Charlie Burchill's guitar riffs are now identifiably his. Mick MacNeil's keyboards take on a new layered warmth, removed from the colder, edgier electronic hooks and loops of the past. Finally, Jim Kerr's vocals have now taken on a more soulful feel and delivery. And there is the added weapon of Robin Clark on additional vocal duties—a stellar move.

The song is uplifting, but what do the lyrics mean? Time is obviously a big marker here. Is this another way of saying time is a healer? An observation that we live in crazy times and being with someone that you can draw strength from will see you through? It was one of the last tracks to be written for the album, so it made sense for it to be the opener and titular tune, as it encapsulated the musical motif of the album perfectly.

### 'All the Things She Said'

Duration: 4.16

One of the earliest songs penned for the album. This had started life at jamming sessions during the recording of *Sparkle in the Rain,* but it was put aside and not worked on for the final cut of the album. It was picked up again during the early writing sessions for *Once Upon a Time* in late 1984 and progressed from there.

Lyrically, it was partly inspired by a magazine interview Jim Kerr had read featuring Danuta Wałęsa, the wife of Polish Solidarity chairman, Lech Wałęsa. In a magazine interview in 1993, Kerr said: '[She] was just saying this amazingly courageous stuff, and I think some of the lines came from that. It isn't what the song's about, but that was a sort of spark'. More broadly speaking, the song acknowledges the role women assume in family dynamics, particularly women left behind: keeping a family together while their husbands are either being held as political prisoners or in some other way kept far from home against their will.

On a more personal level for Kerr, it seems to reflect the significance women had in his own life. He'd been married just over a year at the time of writing the song and had become the father of a daughter.

The song was chosen as the third single from the album. A Virgin Records press release from the time states that the single was released on 1 April 1986, but it appears to have been released slightly earlier in the US, as it had already entered the Billboard chart for the week ending 5 April 1986. It was the least successful of the three singles released in America, although it still achieved a top-forty placement. It spent a total of 13 weeks on the chart, peaking at No. 28 during its ninth week. In the UK, it entered the chart at No. 15 on 12 April 1986. It spent a total of twelve weeks on the chart, peaking at No. 9.

The director of the video for 'Alive and Kicking', Zbigniew Rybczynski, also directed the video for 'All the Things She Said'. The video appears to have been recorded several weeks after the 'Alive and Kicking' video and features Kerr, Burchill and Robin Clark.

## 'Ghost Dancing'

Duration: 4.46

One of the earliest songs to be penned for the album and one of the earliest to have a debut live performance. In fact, 'Ghost Dancing' didn't have its live debut at Live Aid. It had been played several months earlier when the band played a string of gigs at the Barrowland Ballroom in Glasgow at the beginning of 1985. The music was already in place, but Jim Kerr had yet to write the lyrics for the new song, so he sang the words to 'I Travel' instead. Both songs begin with the same line: 'Cities, buildings falling down'. Although the musical structure has been changed somewhat, the keen listener can hear the strong similarities in the songs, not just in their shared opening lyrics. Kerr's political observations had understandably altered between writing 'I Travel' and working on 'Ghost Dancing'.

In an interview in 1989, Kerr reflected on his song-writing and performances from earlier in his career and singled out 'I Travel' for scrutiny:

> But now we've come through the voyeuristic phase, when I hear a song like 'I Travel', what pisses me off or embarrasses me is it's our *On the Road*. Our version of Kerouac in Europe; there were bombs going off in Bologna train station and in synagogues, and Baader-Meinhof. This was the year before Brixton and Toxteth and you could feel the weirdness. When I listen to the song, I sing it in the most affectedly unaffected way, whereas now, eight years on, if something happens, it appals me: how do I reject this, how do I show my protest, how do I take a kick at this? In the past there was all this artfulness—as distinct from art—that is awful.

Personally, I find his self-reflection harsh. Observing what was happening in 1980 and singing about it was important, and I don't feel he made it sound voyeuristic or trivialised it. There is certainly a noticeable change in the way Kerr was responding to and articulating the things happening in the world around him. One could argue that 'Ghost Dancing' had evolved from the observational stance of 'I Travel' into something more revolutionary.

In the booklet that accompanied the 2015 super-deluxe edition box set of *Once Upon a Time*, Jim Kerr is quoted as saying of 'Ghost Dancing', 'It's an echo of "I Travel" five years later. I describe world violence, destruction and the rule of evil.'

Released as the fourth and final single from the album in November 1986, it entered the UK chart at No. 22 and peaked the following week at No. 13, spending a total of ten weeks on the chart. All profits from the single were donated to Amnesty International.

The official music video was a composite of live footage recorded at Le Zenith in Paris and archival news and documentary footage. The audio used on the video is a live version of the song.

## 'Alive and Kicking'

Duration: 5.24

In the recent past, Jim Kerr has spoken during interviews about a dilemma he had regarding the opening line of this song. He said that at the time of recording the vocal for the song he became self-conscious about the words 'you turn me on' and wanted to change them. This resulted in playful consternation on the part of Jimmy Iovine who felt the line was perfect and needed to stay, telling Kerr his girlfriend called it 'the "You Turn Me On" song.' As the disagreement continued, at one point Kerr said that Iovine took out a collection of keys he had in his pockets and placed them on the table in front of him. 'Here; take my car, have my house. You're going to make me a poor man if you don't keep that line in. You might as well take it all now.' Kerr's explanation for wanting to make the change was that not only did he feel the line was a little too cheesy, but he also felt it would have sounded 'creepy' being sung by a 'little white nerdy guy from Glasgow with freckles'. However, Iovine won, and the line stayed in.

The song was a slow burner in construction, arising from the early days of the writing sessions at Barwell Court at the end of 1984. Even after the writing retreat Kerr had taken in Nice in spring 1985 only a rough draft of lyrics existed, hence his desire to change the opening line. The final construction of the song came under the directorship of Iovine. Once moulded into shape, it was the strongest contender for lead single.

Both musically and lyrically it is a life-affirming and uplifting song. Despite Kerr's reservations about the opening line, it cannot help but instil a feeling of positivity in the listener, and even the youngest ears can grasp its positive connotations with no sexually suggestive sentiment attached to it. There is an element of the love song about it. It suggests a view along the lines of 'Hey, we've built a foundation here but if it crumbles what's going to keep it together? A faith in love? The belief in the human spirit to conquer all? Love itself? Dreams? You can't just call it quits. You've got to fight for what you believe is worthwhile, fight for something worth saving.'

This is a universal desire and the song's lyrical drive is backed up by its musical grandeur. It has been used as a wedding song as much as it has been used during sporting events. It is both inspirational and aspirational in equal measure. Its trajectory in the UK and American charts mirrors its musicality.

The single entered the UK chart during the week ending 12 October 1985 at No. 12. The following week it climbed to No. 8 and peaked at No. 7 during its third week on the chart. It spent a total of sixteen weeks on the UK chart. It entered the Billboard Hot 100 during the week ending 19 October 1985 at No. 52. It peaked during its eleventh week on the chart (the week ending 28 December 1985) at No. 3. It spent a total of twenty weeks on the chart and shared time on the Billboard Hot 100 with the follow-up single, 'Sanctify Yourself'. The video also reflects the grand and cinematic feel of the song, having been shot near the Kaaterskill Waterfall as well as other areas of natural beauty within the Catskill Mountains in New York State. These landscapes could have very easily been mistaken for Scotland. The band were in the final stages of recording the album nearby in Woodstock, so the location of the Catskills was ideal.

After 'Don't You (Forget About Me)', 'Alive and Kicking' is Simple Minds' most-watched official music video on YouTube. At the time of writing, from the time it was uploaded on the band's YouTube account on 3 June 2009, the video has had over 131 million views. From the time of the tour that followed the release of *Once Upon a Time*, 'Alive and Kicking' has been a mainstay on the setlist of every Simple Minds tour with only one exception: *5x5 Live* in 2012. It has been predominantly performed as the final song of the night or during the encore.

## 'Oh Jungleland'

Duration: 5.12

The song is an ode to the band's home city of Glasgow. It was not the first time they had paid homage to their city of birth. Less than two years earlier, 'Waterfront' had been released as the lead single of their previous album, *Sparkle in the Rain*. 'Waterfront' portrayed Glasgow's shipbuilding foundations and industrial working-class heritage built on the banks of the Clyde, with the view that although the city was in some ways in decline, the river was constant. Conversely, 'Oh Jungleland' characterised the city as a concrete jungle full of tower blocks, housing schemes and close-knit communities. Kerr had envisaged a rejuvenated Glasgow and personally I am quite astounded by his optimistic view and prescience in imagining a future for Glasgow that few could have foreseen in 1985 (or even 1983 for that matter). Musically, the wonderfully woven bassline that John Giblin uses provides the kind of backbone that underpins the optimism that Kerr is reaching for in the lyrics. The 'kid called Hope' searching for the bright future, looking towards the Northern Lights 'above this high-rise land'.

In discussing the song with *Classic Pop* magazine in 2015 at the time of the release of the super-deluxe box set of *Once Upon a Time*, Jim Kerr described 'Oh Jungleland' as 'a really breathless driving rock track'. He went on to say, 'It reminded me of my adolescence, being teenage, with your heart in your mouth, running for the sake of running'. Within the middle eight there is a sort of short-breathed pant, which leads into the repetitive chant of 'Don't look back/Never look back'. Interestingly, these lines are not printed on the lyric sheets enclosed in copies of the album distributed overseas.

As much as the city itself can be a contradiction in that it can be both bleak and uplifting, Kerr's lyrics offer similar contradictions: Glasgow is 'home sweet home' but he says 'you make me feel so sad to leave here all alone'—he wants to run from the place but feels the eternal pull of it. The song is vivid in imagery, of children playing in the streets, grandfathers shuffling down grey pavements, smiles on work-weary faces, community, togetherness, but there is also always being on your guard and an undercurrent of nervous energy and tension. It's a love song for a city, but more for the people that make the city what it is.

An instrumental version of the song is used for the B-side of the 'Ghost Dancing' 7-inch single, and a special extended mix appears on the 12-inch single of 'Ghost Dancing' as well as on the CD single—the first Simple Minds single to be released on CD format. The song was a regular feature on the setlist until the early 1990s, but it was then placed on hiatus until 2002 and the *Floating World* tour. Since then it had not been played live, until Bellahouston Park on 27 June 2025.

## 'I Wish You Were Here'

Duration: 4.42

For such a young band, and for a band with such young members, this was not the first time that the death of someone close had been the subject of a Simple Minds song. Back in 1982 'Big Sleep' had produced a similar lament—not in musical terms, but in subject matter. Whereas 'Big Sleep' has something of the gothic and ethereal about it—a bleakness—'I Wish You Were Here' has more of an optimistic longing, a nostalgic warmth, a reminiscence. This is most likely a reflection of Jim Kerr's own view of death around the time of writing the song. He is quoted as saying of 'I Wish You Were Here', and on death, '"Footsteps" [its then working title] is a kind of lament for a lost friend. But death doesn't worry me ... I think acceptance is the only sensible attitude'. The backing vocals evoke a kind of gospel feel. A song that had never been performed live, until Bellahouston Park on 27 June 2025.

## 'Sanctify Yourself'

Duration: 5.00

One of the final songs to be written for the album. Apparently it was as much a dare as anything else and was instigated by Jimmy Iovine, aimed directly at the band members. He wanted them to exercise their soulful tendencies and lo, through MacNeil and Burchill jamming during the mixing stages at Right Track studios, and Kerr locked away to come up with lyrics, 'Sanctify Yourself' was born. And boy, has this tune got funk! Something within the lyrics harks back to all those early soul tunes, a kind of 'Simple Minds does Motown', with words about having the 'ground move round your feet' and 'love is all you need'—as much a nod to the 'soul love' as it is to The Beatles' *Our World* contribution of 1967, which desired peace in a time of East/West chill and the Vietnam War.

There is still enough Kerr ambiguity to keep the listener pondering, especially when it comes to the closing lines, 'Well I hope and I pray that maybe someday/ You'll come back down here and show me the way'. A prayer to Jesus? A hope for the Second Coming? It is easy to see why much of Kerr's writing has been perceived as having religious connotations, and this song is called 'Sanctify Yourself' after all. Perhaps it isn't so ambiguous? If only Jim Kerr didn't constantly refute people's theories about the meaning of his lyrics! Kerr talked about this in an interview in 1982, around the time of the release of *New Gold Dream (81-82-83-84)*:

> I purposefully don't put lyric sheets in just so as I don't get nuts writing in taking ambiguous meanings. Apart from that I get quite embarrassed by a lot of the words because when I'm saying them there's absolutely no way I could be saying anything else, it just fits, but sometimes they seem a lot more important sounding than was intended [...] It freaks me out sometimes, some of the words I write. I can never remember what would cause them to be there. There's just something about the sound of certain words that really makes you feel good or inspired or catches your attention.

The song was released as the second single for the album on 20 January 1986. It entered the UK chart at No. 17 and peaked at No. 10 in its second week of an eight-week run. It entered the Billboard Hot 100 at No. 64 and peaked at No. 14 in its eighth week on the chart. The official video for the song was filmed during the band's time in Brussels, with live colour footage recorded during the concert at Forest National near Brussels. The live footage has various composite images of the band members at landmarks around the city including the Atomium.

## 'Come a Long Way'

Duration: 5.08

It's a curious, ambiguous end track and it fades out, leaving the listener with more questions than answers. Not that Simple Minds are a band for giving their fans answers to questions. Is the chorus merely a statement on the whirlwind the band had been through since their formation in late 1977? It has a very haunting beginning, with a fade-up of Kerr's voice sounding like it's being played in reverse. Then straight into 'oohs' and 'yeahs' with the opening fill of drums, and the short shrieks of guitar. Once the ambiguous lyrics are dispensed with, what is left is a stunning outro of Mel Gaynor-style drumming prowess at its absolute finest. That outro could have gone on for easily another thirty seconds in my book. It's not just Gaynor's—Burchill, MacNeil and Giblin all play their part in those final flourishes of the song. It's the most satisfying end to what Jim Kerr described as 'one of our most complete albums'. On the band's most recent 2024 *Global* tour, the song made a welcome return to the setlist, and was performed occasionally during the latter stages of the tour.

# 10

# *Street Fighting Years*

| | |
|---|---|
| UK: | 2 May 1989 |
| Personnel: | Accordion: Michael MacNeil<br>Backing vocals: Lorna Bannon<br>Bagpipes: Roger Sharp<br>Bass: John Giblin, Stephen Lipson<br>Bodhran: Maureen Kerr<br>Cello: William Lithgow, Sheena McKenzie<br>Drums: Mel Gaynor, Manu Katche<br>Guest vocals: Lou Reed (track 4)<br>Guitars: Charlie Burchill<br>Keyboards: Michael MacNeil<br>Orchestral arrangements: John Altman<br>Pennywhistle: Maureen Kerr<br>Percussion: Abdul M'boup, Sidney Thiam, Leroy Williams<br>Piano: Michael MacNeil<br>Vocals: Jim Kerr |
| Duration: | 59 minutes (LP) 61 minutes (CD)<br>Produced by Trever Horn and Stephen Lipson |
| Chart position: | UK: 1; US: 70 |

It might not have seemed like it at the time, but the success of *Once Upon a Time* would hinder the creation of fresh music for several years. Firstly, an extensive world tour took Simple Minds out on the road for over twelve months, criss-crossing the globe—beginning in the US at the end of October 1985 and moving through Canada, the majority of north-west Europe, Japan, Australia, New Zealand and of course, the UK. The final concert was in Auckland, New Zealand on 9 November 1986. Six months later, the band's live recording *Live in the City of Light* was released.

After that it must have seemed like the band were resting. There were limited public appearances until the release of 'Belfast Child' in February 1989. There were three shows at the Barrowland Ballroom in December 1987 called *Cash for Kids*—the trio of shows raised funds for charity. Two shows in Brazil took place in January 1988, followed by the Nelson Mandela 70th Birthday concert on 11 June 1988—which had also included recording 'Mandela Day' some two weeks earlier—and that was followed by an appearance at the Nelson Mandela Free Rally at Hyde Park on 17 July.

Between these fleeting appearances, the band were writing and recording. They purchased a building by the banks of Loch Earn in Scotland and had a studio built there. The studio would come to be known as Bonny Wee Studios. Four years was a long time for Simple Minds to be away from the game. For one thing, they missed the opportunity to capitalise on their breakthrough in the US. Although the release of *Live in the City of Light* was an overwhelming success, particularly in the UK and across Europe, it crawled to a lowly No. 96 on the Billboard 200 chart in 1987. By the time of the album's release, another two years had elapsed.

*Street Fighting Years* entered the Billboard 200 chart at No. 138 and climbed to a peak of No. 70 three weeks later. The album spent a total of twelve weeks on the Billboard chart. By comparison to the American chart, it entered the UK chart at No. 1 and spent a total of 28 weeks in the top 100, of which twenty-two weeks were within the top forty. When discussing the overall political intent of the album and how those intentions chimed with ones of faith, Jim Kerr said in an STV interview in 1989:

> For me at this point, I've lost faith in the corporations of the churches, and I've lost faith in the politicians as well. I haven't lost faith, as such. I think the faith I have is much more of a human nature. The album's title track is dedicated to Victor Jara, who was a Chilean songwriter. But he was more of a songwriter/pop star/social commentator, and he was killed for his beliefs. When they asked him what he believed in, he said 'Well I believe in your hand in mine. I believe in friendship and community'. And where I stand just now, that's where my faith begins.

Further to this, when discussing the overall political issues and themes tackled on the album, Kerr said:

> I'm not saying rock music has to always be social, heavy-duty, weight of the world on your shoulders. I think it should be first and foremost entertainment. But as I keep saying, it can be more than just entertainment. And that's when it's at its best. When it's most potent. When it communicates, or transmits, or illuminates.

At the time of the release of 'Let It All Come Down'—part of the *Amsterdam* EP, the final single from the album—a press release issued with the single stated that sales of the album had exceeded three million copies and it had achieved a top album chart position in nine countries. It may not have made a dent in the American music market, but there was no denying it was an incredibly successful album.

## The songs

### 'Street Fighting Years'

Duration: 6.26

Right from the opening notes of the song—although admittedly, the bass does sound a little too like '(Sittin' On) The Dock of the Bay' to my ears—Simple Minds revealed a sharp turn in musical direction. After the first two verses the musical structure of the song takes on a grand cinematic scope. Orchestral strings and a haunting piano from Mick MacNeil produce the stirring feeling of emotional fragility, complementary to the lyrics. A third verse then evokes the longing for the return of something human and close. Then comes a bluesy, sliding guitar solo from Charlie Burchill, as drums build to a crescendo. By two-thirds of the way through the song it has been a musical drama with few but intense words.

In writing about the challenge of creating the lyrics for the song in a diary post in 2010, Jim Kerr stated:

> Recalling now the instrumental music to 'Street Fighting Years' as originally presented, the crux of the problem was that I could not tell if what I was listening to was a happy song, a sad song, a song of victory or a lament? The mood of the tune seemed to contain various experiences, like the same photographic landscape shot in all four seasons and then superimposed on each other.

Kerr then goes on to describe the lyrics as being a narrative that is:

> Mirroring someone's inner emotions during a massive end-of-summer storm. Occurring outside the window and from a position of relative safety, the character of the song in turn is using the display on show as a metaphor for the turbulence often so real within his and all our lives.

Then the song changes musically, and the tempo increases. There's a rush of lyrics from Kerr as the song builds and rises again. It's a voice that is becoming much more soulful. A few words become unintelligible in the flow, tangled up in a meld of emotion. In 2009, Kerr described the lyrics as his way of offering his condolences for the loss of the younger brother of a close friend who had been the victim of an unprovoked knife attack by a gang of youths. 'Therapy for me, the song despite being a requiem at heart, does however blossom with a final note of optimism'.

## 'Soul Crying Out'

Duration: 6.07

The song is said to be partly inspired by the Thatcher government's trial of the so-called poll tax in Scotland during the late 1980s. Driven by a more folk-rock sensibility with organs, piano, acoustic guitar and bongos underpinning the song's musical structure, deep tolling drums provide the theatrical thrust and forward momentum. Lyrically, Kerr's highlighting of the poll tax issue is stressed by the lines 'and the government says you're gonna pay, pay, pay/And you pay/Still you pay'. Of course, the song has a broader scope than just the poll tax situation, as it deals with the oppressed in various circumstances. The desire to escape and find a better means of existence is the overriding message of the song. In fact, Jim Kerr stated in a Facebook post in 2018 that the decline of industrialisation during the Conservative government's time in office from 1979 meant that 'job losses and unemployment caused never-ending heartbreak in equal measure', for families in Glasgow, through all of Scotland and beyond.

## 'Wall of Love'

Duration: 5.20

Lyrically, this tells a tale of the haves and have-nots. Lines are delivered about the elite and their ivory towers and those stuck starving in the ghettos and ramshackle quarters, living cheek by jowl. The proximity of their lives geographically is juxtaposed with the chasm of the financial and economic divide between them. The chorus declares that peace isn't enough—it needs to be backed up with love. Musically, it's a wall of sound with a wailing Burchill guitar as its backdrop and sweet melody underneath. Mel Gaynor's powerhouse drums are also a musical highlight. There's a more traditional rock sound on this track compared to other tracks on the album. The song was performed live during the *Street Fighting Years* tour in 1989 and on a selection of dates in Germany in the summer of 1990. It wasn't performed again until 2004 when it formed a medley with 'Great Leap Forward', a track from 1995's *Good News from the Next World* album.

## 'This is Your Land'

Duration: 6.22

A song that has a kind of patriotic symbolism, but from the way Jim Kerr talked about it at the time, there was something grander intended than a mere shot of jingoism. In an interview with STV in 1989, Kerr said:

> I'm not totally nationalist. I much prefer the notion of internationalism. And that's always been something that has given me a great feel with the band. The fact that we've been accepted in many places. We're a Scots band without making a hoo-ha kind of thing.

The song's broader theme is to make the most of what your life's circumstances have given you. Make it something worth fighting for—in a passive and peaceful way. Ballad-like in musical structure, with a mix of slide and acoustic guitars, the song's riff is reminiscent of the one Burchill used on 'Don't You (Forget About Me).'

The track was released as the album's lead single in the US, possibly due to its star guest vocal appearance by none other than Lou Reed. The much-documented influence The Velvet Underground and Lou Reed had on the band, and Kerr in particular, made this guest appearance a high point for him. In a post on the band's social media in 2013, which served as an obituary to Reed, Kerr told the story of the recording of Reed's vocal part in Paris. Kerr was waiting inside the studio:

> It was right then that the enormity of the situation enveloped me. You see, to me, Lou Reed was more than Sinatra ever could be. More than James Dean, Marlon Brando or even Pablo Picasso. And as for me? Well, I might have had some success with Simple Minds, who were after all a stadium act in those years, but for some reason all my confidence suddenly deserted me. Right then in fact, I once again felt like I was the 13-year-old butcher's boy, coming back from the town centre, with my copy of *Transformer* under my arm.

Released as the second single from the album in the UK on 10 April 1989, it spent three weeks in the top forty, peaking at No. 13. As for the success of the US lead single release? Sadly, the song failed to make any impact on the Billboard chart.

## 'Take a Step Back'

Duration: 4.23

The shortest song with lyrics on the album and one of few songs with rock acoustic drums. Its opening bars are strikingly similar to Kate Bush's 'Running Up That Hill'. By the band's own admission, it is probably the weakest track on the album. It was a hard song to build up, coming from the coda of another song that was worked on in the earlier writing sessions for the album in 1987. It was performed during the early dates of the *Street Fighting Years* tour in 1989, only to be dropped after a few shows. It has not been performed live since then.

## 'Kick It In'

Duration: 6.11

Another epic on the album, but this time it is more in the prog rock/trad rock/folk blues vein, led by a blend of organ-style keyboards and guitar. An 'Unauthorised Mix' produced a sound like an attempt to make 'Kick It In' like some kind of Frankie Goes to Hollywood throwback. At just over seven minutes in length, it's a rather wasted amount of time spent on an extended version of the song. 'Kick It In' was released as the album's third (UK) single on 17 July 1989. It spent a total of five weeks in the UK chart, four in the top forty, and two of those weeks within the top twenty, peaking at No. 15. The single-edit version retains all the punch of the track without too much compromise. The standard 12-inch version contains the full album version. A limited edition 12-inch was also released which featured the 'Unauthorised Mix' as well as a full-size poster in the sleeve.

## 'Let It All Come Down'

Duration: 4.56

The music was composed by John Giblin. The song was written during the early stages of the recording of the album. In an interview in 2024 regarding the recording of *Street Fighting Years*, Mick MacNeil stated that he worked on the drum programming for the song:

> There's a couple of really crappy things that pee me off that I put on the demo that I assumed Trevor [Horn] was going to come and make them sound internationally amazing, but they're still there! I remember having a bit of a battle with Trevor, particularly about the snare drum thing that was on 'Let It All Come Down'. I went 'surely you can't be serious? We'll get Mel in and get him to do a proper roll on that. That's me trying to program a snare roll with fifty thousand bloody midi notes running tight together. It sounds like a fart!'

The album track featured as part of the *Amsterdam* EP—the final single for the album—released on 27 November 1989. An edited version of the song was used for the 7-inch single of the EP. The full-length album version is on the 12-inch and CD single copies of the EP. It spent four weeks in the top forty of the UK chart, peaking at No. 18. The EP also featured the band's cover of Prince's 'Sign O' The Times' and the traditional English hymn 'Jerusalem'. The song has been included in the live set sporadically, most recently during the *Global* tour 2024.

## 'Mandela Day'

Duration: 5.45

This song came together speedily. Simple Minds were asked to take part in the Nelson Mandela 70th Birthday Tribute concert that was held at Wembley Stadium on 11 June 1988. Organisers of the concert, Tony Hollingsworth and Jerry Dammers, had given Simple Minds the impression that all acts involved would contribute newly written songs performed specifically for the concert. The band dutifully embarked on creating a song. While in London at Stephen Lipson's home studio working on the songs they were developing for *Street Fighting Years*, they wrote and recorded 'Mandela Day' in May 1988. In speaking about the concert in 1989, Jim Kerr said, 'The very fact that the concert took place is the kind of oxygen that the likes of Mandela and the people down there [in South Africa] need to breathe'. Kerr's lyrics, particularly in the chorus, proved to be marvellously prescient. Mandela was released from prison in February 1990, less than two years after the song was composed. The song was released commercially as part of the *Ballad of the Streets* EP in February 1989, as the B-side to 'Belfast Child'. The song remains a regular feature in the band's live set, particularly at concerts held in mainland Europe, where the song gained greater prominence and radio play compared to 'Belfast Child' in the UK.

### 'Belfast Child'

Duration: 6.39

The composition of the song began just a few days after the IRA bombing in Enniskillen. The first single from the album, released in February 1989 as an EP package titled the *Ballad of the Streets*, the song had started life many years earlier as a traditional folk song known as 'She Moved Through the Fair'. As it is claimed to have both Irish and Scottish roots, let's call it Celtic.

At the time of writing, 'Belfast Child' remains Simple Minds' only UK No. 1 single. On release it entered the UK chart at No. 2 before going on to spend the next two weeks in the top spot. It stayed in the top forty for a further four weeks. It also reached the No. 1 spot in the Netherlands and Ireland and reached the top twenty in several other countries. The song gained itself some trivial notoriety as being one of longest songs to reach the No. 1 spot, with a duration of 6 minutes and 39 seconds.

When discussing what motivated the writing of the song in 1989, Jim Kerr said:

> I wanted to write a song that offered some sort of hope or solidarity, or something. I don't know where the hope comes from, but I did want to write a song taking the point of view of somebody in the middle who perhaps doesn't think the army should be there but also sees no future in or vision in the barrel of a gun.

### 'Biko'

Duration: 7.34

To complete the political theme of the album, the band decided to close *Street Fighting Years* with a cover of Peter Gabriel's song detailing the atrocity which had befallen the anti-Apartheid activist, Stephen Biko, who died while in custody in Port Elizabeth, South Africa on 6 September 1977. It was the second cover song to be recorded and commercially released by the band. The first was their version of Lou Reed's 'Street Hassle', which appeared on *Sparkle in the Rain*. The band performed the song at the Nelson Mandela 70th Birthday Tribute concert at Wembley Stadium on 11 June 1988, alongside Gabriel.

## Additional tracks

### 'When Spirits Rise'

Duration: 2.01

A final curtain for Mick MacNeil's involvement with Simple Minds. The instrumental was composed by MacNeil, who had used a synth to emulate the sound of bagpipes. In the final stages of the recording of the album, a piper was hired to record bagpipes in the studio. The track was a bonus at the end of the cassette and CD formats of the album. It was used as the intro music for the band's stage arrival during the *Street Fighting Years* tour of 1989.

## 'Saturday Girl'

Duration: 6.08

The B-side to the single 'This is Your Land'. Lyrically, it's an ambiguous and abstract piece of writing. There's no specific narrative and it feels more like a Kerr lyric of old in that sense. Words are fragmented, offering snapshots rather than a complete short story or a cohesive narrative. It is nonetheless overtly romantic and mysteriously sensual. The song is a firm favourite among the hidden gems appreciated by the fanbase.

## 'Year of the Dragon'

Duration: 3.05

A solely Burchill-composed piece of music with a keyboard flourish reminiscent of the falling petals of a cherry blossom on a windswept spring afternoon in Kyoto. The title of the piece comes from the year of its continued composition, 1988: the year of the dragon in the Chinese zodiac. Its title was coined by Jim Kerr. Burchill had previously titled the song 'The Beautiful Circle' and had initially started working on the piece as a side project in 1987.

## 'Sign o' the Times'

Duration: 5.35

This was an idea that came from the recording sessions that happened in a studio in Amsterdam in the autumn of 1989. The US leg of the tour had been cancelled and to make use of the free time that resulted, the band decided to start writing the next album. They went into the studio in the Netherlands with Stephen Lipson. To get the creative juices flowing, the band hit upon recording a cover of Prince's 'Sign O' The Times'. This saw MacNeil and Lipson working closely together on the project. The song then featured as part of the *Amsterdam* EP, released on 27 November 1989, which coincidentally was Charlie Burchill's 30th birthday.

## 'Jerusalem'

Duration: 2.57

The trio of song-writing members of the band at that time, Jim Kerr, Charlie Burchill and Mick MacNeil, all loved the piece and decided that they would like to record a version of it. The start of this song gives off the air of an old 78 rpm recording of 'Jerusalem' playing away in the corner, only to be replaced by the current version with all the electronic bells and whistles, finished off with some electric guitar for good measure. The track features on the *Amsterdam* EP.

11

# *Real Life*

| | |
|---|---|
| UK: | 8 April 1991 |
| Personnel: | Backing vocals: Carol Kenyon, Sonia Morgan-Jones<br>Bass: Malcolm Foster, Stephen Lipson<br>Drums: Mel Gaynor<br>Guitars: Charlie Burchill<br>Keyboards: Charlie Burchill, Stephen Lipson, Peter John Vettese<br>Orchestral arrangements: Will Malone<br>Percussion: Andy Duncan<br>Shaft guitar: Alfred Bos (track 7)<br>String leader: Gavin Wright<br>Violin: Lisa Germano<br>Vocals: Jim Kerr |
| Duration: | 52 minutes |
| Produced by: | Stephen Lipson |
| Chart position: | UK: 2; US: 74 |

The album was released just two years after *Street Fighting Years*. Much had changed in the interim for Simple Minds. The beginning of a new decade seemed a symbolic harbinger of doom. Not only did original keyboard player Mick MacNeil leave the band, but manager Bruce Findlay had also decided to part company with the band.

One could argue that Jim Kerr and Charlie Burchill should have seen this as an opportunity to down tools for a period to recharge and regroup, but Simple Minds was a creative juggernaut for both Kerr and Burchill, and neither was particularly keen to try and slam the brakes on.

In sharing his observations about the recording of *Street Fighting Years* and what happened after in 2019 Jim Kerr said:

> When I think of those things now, we were exhausted—it sounds wimpy. What we needed was a couple of months break and then coming back to the table fresh could have sorted it all out. But then before you know it, someone's left and the train moves on, or it doesn't move on, or it goes somewhere else and that seems to be the story with bands.

The band had been working solidly: writing, recording and touring in a constant loop since 1978, with the ten-year period from 1979–89 being particularly prolific and prodigious. But there was to be no let up. Their persistence resulted in sustained commercial success as the album reached the higher echelons of the UK chart.

Released on 8 April 1991, it peaked on the chart at No. 2 and kept a place in the top ten for a total of five weeks and remained within the top forty for a further 12 weeks after that. The album also reached the top twenty album chart in several European countries as well as Down Under. Along with successes in the UK, Europe, Australia and New Zealand, the album spent eleven weeks on the Billboard 200, peaking at No. 74 in its second week on the chart.

The album cover art for *Street Fighting Years* pictured the band as a three-piece, with Kerr, Burchill and MacNeil featuring in photographs together. For *Real Life* the three-piece consisted of Kerr, Burchill and Mel Gaynor for promotional purposes.

Creatively, the song-writing was now once again a tight Kerr/Burchill partnership, except for three songs that appeared on the album (two of which Kerr/Burchill co-wrote with producer Stephen Lipson).

The album produced four singles, all of which made the top forty on the UK singles chart.

## The songs

### 'Real Life'

Duration: 4.54

In discussing the song on Facebook in 2017, Jim Kerr said: 'I think it's an incredible piece of music. Charlie [Burchill] is a genius. The "Gothic operatic" intro chords and atmosphere alone get me every time'. Kerr went on to explain that the lyrics came from a short story he had been writing during the period called 'Real Life', 'based on a group of young characters setting out to discover themselves'. He felt that the words in the story fitted in with a piece of music Burchill had written. Paula and Shane's lives play out like a flash fiction soap opera. In fact, the lyrical structure of the song could be likened to a three-act play. Two lovers meet in the big city having escaped provincial lives in pursuit of the 'American Dream', violence occurs in the form of gangland murders and, finally, there is human loss among the stars. The latter part is perhaps inspired by what had happened some five years previously in the Space Shuttle *Challenger* disaster in January 1986. The tragedy included the loss of Christa McAuliffe, the first teacher to go through NASA training and journey into space as part of the shuttle crew. It was the fourth single to be released from the album and spent three weeks in UK chart during October and November 1991, peaking at No. 34.

## 'See the Lights'

Duration: 4.28

The second single from the album, released on 13 May 1991. Two promotional videos were recorded for the song. One is a colour action-animation that leans heavily on A-ha's 'Take on Me' for its concept, while the other (and the one that was put forward for broader play), is a black and white film recorded at Bonny Wee Studios, as well as on location at St Fillans and Tyndrum in Scotland. The *Glittering Prize* VHS, released in 1992, contains a promotional video that is a composite of both videos. The single spent three weeks in the top forty of the UK chart, peaking at No. 20. It was Simple Minds' sixteenth top-twenty single in the UK charts within a decade. The single also made the American Billboard Hot 100, peaking at No. 40 and spending a total of ten weeks on the chart.

Musically, the song is driven by a bluesy bassline. Lyrically, the song's protagonist appears to be reeling from a break-up. It's a call for forgiveness—'I'm too proud to cry'—but 'If you can see the lights'—i.e. see your way to forgiveness—then we might be able to salvage this thing. Or perhaps the protagonist is resigned to the notion that the relationship has ended? The song has been a regular feature in the live set since its release.

A curious altering of a line in the song started in around 2009. Jim Kerr now sometimes changes the line from, 'Oh forgive me love, I'm too proud to cry' to 'I look right through your disguise,' much to the dismay of some fans. The reason for the change is unclear but is most likely down to simple artistic licence.

## 'Let There Be Love'

Duration: 4.56

The song was the lead single from the album and was released on 11 March 1991. When introducing the song to the audience during the band's soundcheck at the First Direct Arena in Leeds in 2024, Jim Kerr stated that the song was a favourite of both his and Charlie Burchill's, but this had not always been the case. He spoke about a cover of the song that was recorded by Australian band Icehouse and how the Icehouse version was not only superior, but also made both himself and Burchill conscious of and appreciative of the fact that it was a better song than they had previously thought. The track makes no apologies for what it is: a soft ballad. A love song. Beyond that, the broader message is for love to reign over everyone. This gave the song universal appeal and it became their sixth UK top-ten single. It also reached the top ten in several other countries throughout Europe and climbed to the No. 1 spot in Italy.

### 'Woman'

Duration: 4.42

A strong yet underrated song. It's a very sensual tune. There's some ambiguity within the lyrics. The narrator tells us about a woman with a 'Strange tattooed bird on her thigh'. There's a frisson going on. There's also a strong sense that this woman is becoming intangible and there's no clear sense of its cause. It's all a bit of a mystery. Is the woman an apparition? Is she a ghost? Is she real? Or is she just a figment of the narrator's imagination? Musically, the guitar and orchestral strings work sweetly together. Kerr's voice is soulful and scintillating. As much as the song is a ballad, it keeps a soft rock edge, with elements of funk and jazz mixed in. Burchill's guitar riff is bluesy with a blend of notes played legato then staccato. Stephen Lipson's involvement in the writing of this song perhaps added to its musical strength, making it arguably one of best tracks on *Real Life*.

### 'Stand by Love'

Duration: 4.08

The song was the album's third single, released on 12 August 1991. It spent a total of four weeks in the UK chart, peaking at No. 13 during its second week in the top forty. The song is a foot-tapping, hand-clapping bit of fun. The narrator is a restless wanderer looking for a great night out in the big city. If any song symbolises where Simple Minds are headed next musically, 'Stand by Love' is a solid indicator. The video for the song is a montage of live footage, most likely shot specifically for the music video.

### 'African Skies'

Duration: 4.51

The track tries to epitomise all things Africa in its sound and lyrics. The lyrics are quite sparse, perhaps in line with the vastness and scope of the continent itself. The band's then biographer, Alfred Bos, gets a personnel credit on this song for playing 'shaft guitar', which suggests that he plays a wah-wah blend of notes that add an underpinning of funk to the song. It's a bit 'bongos in the Congo'.

### 'Let the Children Speak'

Duration: 4.14

This starts very noticeably with the synth melody from 'Theme for Great Cities'. As we've seen, it is a recurring theme for Simple Minds to 'remake and remodel' their own songs. Sometimes that can be a very good thing, and the 'reimagining' works by making a statement beyond the musical structure. An example is the music for 'I Travel' adapted for 'Ghost Dancing'.

Occasionally, it doesn't work so well. Such is the case with 'Let the Children Speak'. It feels a little sacrilegious to use a tune that is a Simple Minds instrumental masterpiece and then put lyrics over it. Kerr himself said something similar in a Facebook post on 12 August 2017, in which he told the story of how 'Theme for Great Cities' came about. He said that in deciding that 'Theme' should remain an instrumental, his reasoning was 'I could find no need for me to go breathing all over the top of it—only so we could call it a "proper song."' He'd obviously changed his mind about this notion he'd had in 1981, because a decade later he does just that on 'Let the Children Speak'.

I'm also not quite sure how they managed to attribute the writing credits to this song as simply 'Kerr/Burchill', given that 'Theme for Great Cities' was originally credited as either 'Music: Simple Minds', or to the individual members of the band at the time of its composition: Kerr, Burchill, MacNeil, Forbes and McGee. An oversight, perhaps?

### 'Ghostrider'

Duration: 3.24

There's a worrying element to the lyrics of this song. There is a line that seems to suggest that if you fear the song's narrator, they may well produce excrement on your loved one. This seems an unlikely lyric to me, but it has been printed this way on the lyric sheet provided with the album. Personally, I believe the line is, '*Shooting* on the one you love if you're afraid of me.' This is much more sensible and feasible—if somewhat harsh. Surely the lyrics on the album's sleeve are a misprint? I enjoy the clever mondegreen used for the title of the song. Obviously, it's meant to be heard as a word association with 'ghost writer', reaffirmed by the use of 'paperback rider' in the lyrics as well. There's a blues feel to the song with its thumping drum beat and Hammond organ-style keyboards. It was performed as part of the live set on the *Real Life* tour in 1991, but has not been performed live since.

### 'Banging on the Door'

Duration: 5.40

A song of lament. The breakdown of a relationship. Possibly autobiographical? Jim Kerr and Chrissie Hynde had divorced the previous year, although they had been romantically estranged for some time prior to that. There's certainly no denying that the song contains one of the most downcast lines in any Simple Minds song, 'Some dreams grow old and then they just die'. Musically, the lyrics are accompanied by a mid-tempo soft-rock structure. The song has a long intro which Kerr described as a, 'beautiful intro. It sounds like a cloudscape and out of that comes this whole world of music from Charlie'. There is an acknowledgement that Burchill composed the song single-handedly.

### 'Travelling Man'

Duration: 3.34

A rocking number. Sensual in lyrical content at times. The protagonist is holed up in a seedy motel in a generically identifiable mid-west American town. Our traveller moves around from place to place, searching for a means of escape from an endless cycle they've got themselves caught up in. Musically, it's a sign

*Above*: Fan artwork of the lyrical interpretation of 'Real to Real'. (*Priptona Art*)

*Below*: Fan artwork of the lyrical interpretation of 'Sad Affair'. (*Priptona Art*)

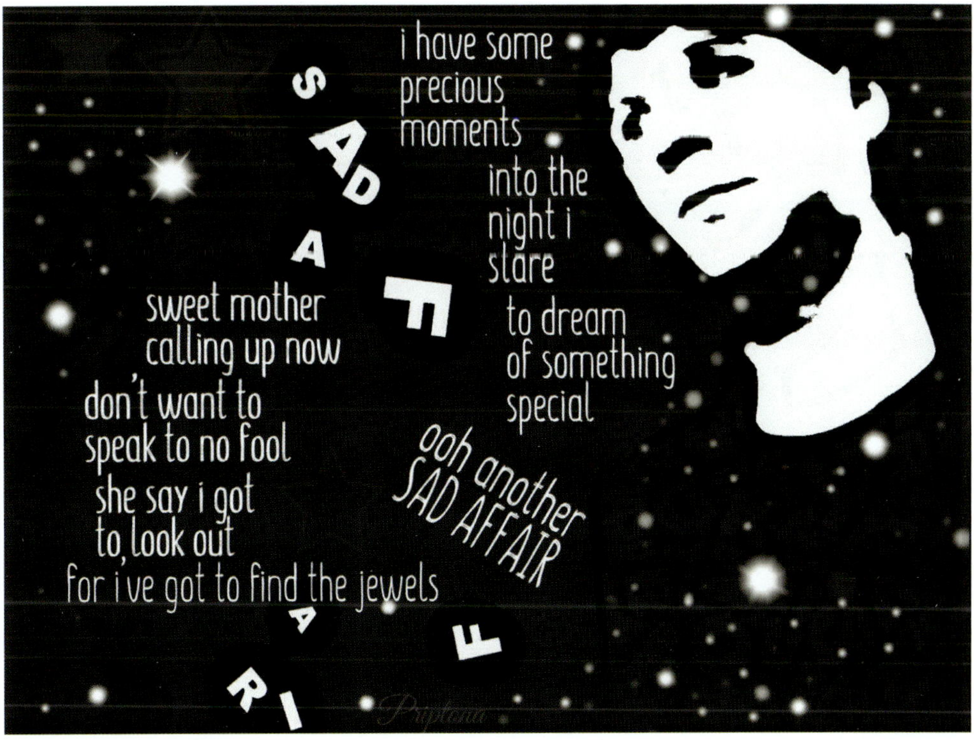

*Above*: Simple Minds concert poster for the Paradiso in Amsterdam, 29 March 1980. (*Author's collection*)

*Left*: Simple Minds at Tavistock Square, London, 26 October 1980. (*Virginia Turbett*)

*Right*: Jim Kerr on stage at Tiffany's in Glasgow in 1982. (*Simon Clegg*)

*Below*: Music paper advert for Simple Minds' first tour of Australia in 1981. (*Author's collection*)

*Above*: Music paper advert for the Lyceum concert in London during the New Gold Dream tour, 1982. (*Author's collection*)

*Below*: Fan artwork of the lyrical interpretation of 'Hunter and the Hunted'. (*Priptona Art*)

*Above*: Jim Kerr performing at Cambridge Corn Exchange, 21 April 2015. It was my first Simple Minds concert. (*Larelle Read*)

*Below*: Jim Kerr performing at Phoenix Park, Dublin, 14 August 1983. (*Richard Jones*)

*Above*: Jim Kerr performing at Phoenix Park, Dublin, 14 August 1983. (*Richard Jones*)

*Below*: Fan artwork of the lyrics of 'Waterfront'. (*Created by the author*)

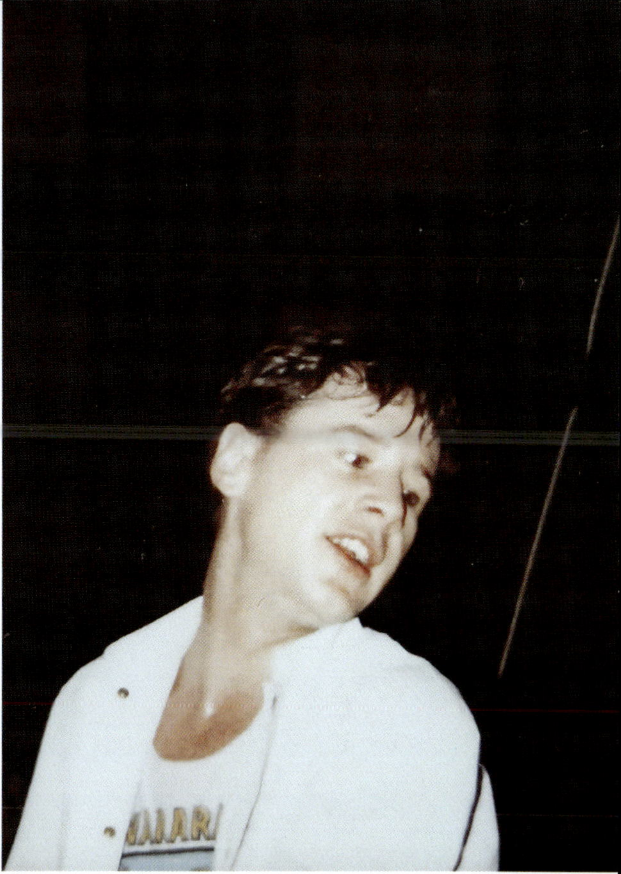

*Right* and *Below*: Jim Kerr on stage at the Barrowland Ballroom, 28 February 1984. (*Irene Kane*)

*Above*: Simple Minds performing at the Barrowland Ballroom, 28 February 1984. (*Virginia Turbett*)

*Left*: Charlie Burchill at the Barrowland Ballroom in early 1984. (*Jim Kerr*)

Derek Forbes at the Barrowland Ballroom in early 1984. (*Jim Kerr*)

'Let me see your hands'. Jim Kerr performing at the Barrowland Ballroom in 1984. (*Jim Kerr*)

The 'Barrowland Star'. Jim Kerr on the Barras stage in 1984. (*Jim Kerr*)

Jim Kerr strikes a signature move while performing on stage at the Barras in 1984. (*Jim Kerr*)

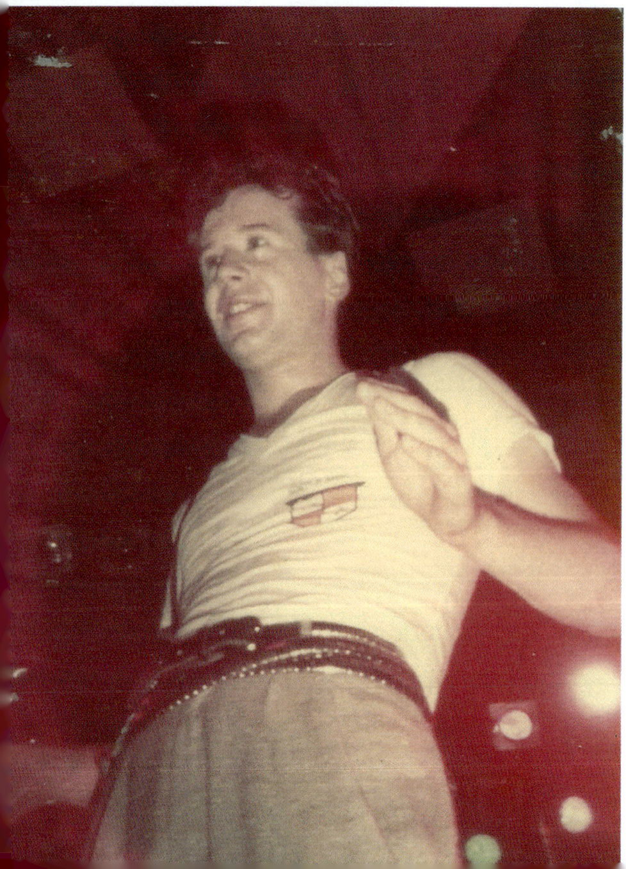

Jim Kerr acknowledging the crowd at the Barras in 1984. (*Jim Kerr*)

*Above*: Jim Kerr with Bono of U2 during soundcheck at the Barrowland Ballroom in January 1985. (*Jo Donnelly*)

*Below*: *Street Fighting Years* tour 1989 ticket stub. (*Gaz Williams, from private collection*)

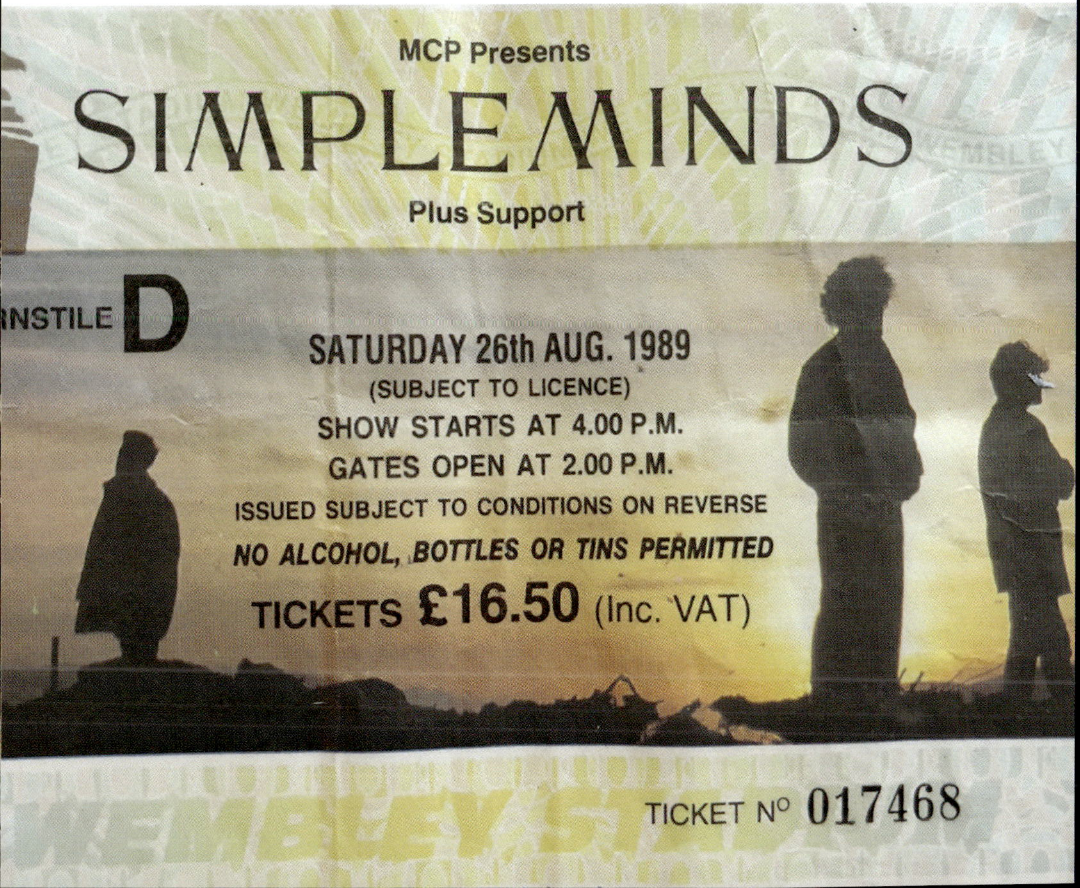

*Left*: *Real Life* Paris concert poster 1991. (*Gaz Williams, from private collection*)

*Below*: Jim Kerr and Sarah Brown on stage at the Olympia Theatre, Dublin, 26 March 2013. (*Martin Potappel*)

Musilac Festival bill poster at Aix-les-Bains, France, 11 July 2018. (*Larelle Read*)

Jim Kerr on stage at The Filimore, Detroit, 14 October 2018. (*Vidhya*)

*Left*: Jim Kerr on stage at Store Vega, Copenhagen, 10 March 2020. (*Larelle Read*)

*Below*: Fan artwork of Charlie Burchill. (*Priptona Art*)

*Above*: Charlie Burchill on stage at Store Vega, Copenhagen, 10 March 2020. The final show before touring ceased due to the Covid-19 pandemic. (*Larelle Read*)

*Below*: Me with Jim Kerr and Charlie Burchill taken at P&J Live, Aberdeen, 5 April 2022. (*Author's collection*)

*Left*: Jim Kerr on stage at Princes Street Gardens, Edinburgh, 13 August 2022. During a special one-off concert, Simple Minds performed New Gold Dream in its entirety. (*Yvonne Bird*)

*Below*: Simple Minds performing at the Ziggo Dome, Amsterdam, on 6 April 2024. (*Martin Potappel*)

of what's to come with Simple Minds. Possibly an even stronger indicator than 'Stand by Love', as 'Travelling Man' could easily slot into the track listing on the next album.

### 'Rivers of Ice'

Duration: 3.33

A romantic ballad. The melody of the song is based around a composition by Iain MacLachlan titled 'Dr Mackay's Farewell to Creagorry'. This is a traditional Scottish folk song usually played on bagpipes, but has also been played on accordion and violin. Simple Minds' version of the main melody is played on keyboards and bass. Lyrically, Jim Kerr provides a loving tale. Rivers have provided inspiration for several lyrics throughout Kerr's career as a song-writer. 'Waterfront', as well as songs such as 'She's a River' and 'Underneath the Ice' (though not mentioning a river directly, the lyrics allude to a river) all use a body of water as their source of inspiration.

The song was performed in the live set during the *Real Life* tour in 1991 and then had a long hiatus before returning to the set in 2015 and 2016, when it was performed by Catherine Anne Davies (aka The Anchoress) as a touring member of the band. It made another brief return to the set in 2020 as an instrumental prelude to 'Dolphins', but was subsequently replaced by 'Banging on the Door' when the remainder of the *40 Years of Hits* tour resumed in 2022.

### 'When Two Worlds Collide'

Duration: 3.57

Another dark and seedy affair but with a slower tempo that arrives on a fade-up. It has a stronger feeling of sophistication behind it than the track on the album two songs prior. Malcolm Foster's bass is bluesy and growling, while Burchill's guitar is sparse and mysterious. Kerr's words are initially delivered almost in a whisper, with a chorus delivered in a falsetto. It is a song about the underworld and how its elements can devastatingly invade the 'real' world of ordinary people. In writing about film director David Lynch in 2018 and focusing his attention on *Twin Peaks*, Kerr described his feelings about the song thus: 'When I hear our song, "[When] Two Worlds Collide", I feel certain that the kind of creeping sexuality that song exudes would have made it fit right in with what Lynch was then delivering to our screens'.

## Additional tracks

### 'Good Night'

Duration: 3.09

A soft ballad and a song that was initially touted by Kerr and Burchill for inclusion on the album, but it was chosen as a B-side to 'Let There Be Love' instead. The title of the song is an extract from the line, 'Go gentle in the good night when you go'. This is an almost direct lift from the first line of Dylan Thomas's poem known as 'Do Not Go Gentle into That Good Night'. Is the song a lament for a love lost? Or is it a requiem for a loved one? I would err on the side of the latter, given the presence of angels in one line of the song as well as the description of walking down a street alone. The song is a fan favourite as one of the more obscure numbers in the Simple Minds catalogue.

# 12

# *Good News from the Next World*

UK: 30 January 1995
Personnel: Backing vocals: Pat Hodges, Maxann Lewis, Stefani Spruill, Julia Waters
Bass: Mark Browne, Malcolm Foster, Marcus Miller, Lance Morrison
Drums: Tal Bergman, Vinnie Calaiuta, Mark Schulman
Guitars, keyboards: Charlie Burchill
Vocals: Jim Kerr
Duration: 48 minutes
Produced by: Keith Forsey
Chart position: UK: 2; US: 87

The nearly four-year break between the original material releases of *Once Upon a Time* and *Street Fighting Years* was repeated with the gap between *Real Life* and *Good News from the Next World*. It appeared the creative fecundity of the band was naturally slowing.

For some fans, the hard rock vibe that Kerr and Burchill decided to run with for the new album was too much of a change. Mel Gaynor was also absent from the recording (and subsequent tour). He'd cut his musical chops playing for heavy-metal band Samson shortly prior to joining Simple Minds, so his absence was strange considering it was his style of drumming that gave the band their bombastic appeal and sonic boom. Instead, three drummers were used on this album: Mark Schulman, Vinnie Calaiuta, and Tal Bergman. Bass duties were also shared by several players.

Despite the album dividing opinion with the fans, it was commercially successful, making it into the top five of the UK chart and spending several weeks in the top forty while also producing two top-twenty singles. It also made the Billboard 200 chart, peaking at No. 87 in its first week and spending another six weeks on the chart.

Although Gaynor's drumming style was an integral part of Simple Minds' music and their stadium-filling success, so also—from the earliest days—was the use of keyboards, particularly all that Mick MacNeil brought through synthesisers, sequencers, organs and acoustic piano. Alas for *Good News from the Next World*, hardly a single keyboard note was audible.

Simple Minds had gone full rock.

In speaking about the reason for the change in musical direction in 1995, Jim Kerr said:

> I think we let the technology go too far. I mean, it was great to get your own studio, and it was great to get all the equipment and all that kind of stuff. But you tend to start thinking that that's what it's about and it's not. Again, that comes to the forefront on this record [the focus on guitar and vocals]. There's not a lot going on, but it's still a very powerful sound. This whole idea of trying to make the songs work in a simpler form has rekindled my enthusiasm for the older songs. You must remember the first reason we got into the band was because it was fun. We got into it to avoid work. But the irony is that every day there is so much work to be done.

To some extent the decision to change musical direction helped to win back some of the American market that had been lost due to the 'too overtly Eurocentric' politically charged sentiment of *Street Fighting Years*. What also helped was the hiring of Keith Forsey as producer. Forsey was, of course, responsible for co-writing the band's most successful single in the United States, 'Don't You (Forget About Me)'. He had a solid history of producing albums, working with the likes of Billy Idol, among others. In discussing the writing process for the album in 1995, Kerr said:

> The real hard work is in the writing of the songs—the melodies and the text. We tried to make the songs stand the test on a guitar or a piano, and if it worked like that harmonically and the arrangement worked and the atmosphere was rich, then we knew we were onto a good thing.

## The songs

### 'She's a River'

Duration: 5.31

The first single off the album, released in the UK on 16 January 1995. It entered the UK chart at No. 9 and spent three weeks in the top forty and a total of ten weeks in the top 100. It also made the Billboard Hot 100, entering the chart on the week ending 18 February 1995 at No. 67, peaking at No. 52 and spent a total of nine weeks on the chart.

The song was inspired by the Hermann Hesse novel *Siddhartha*, in which the titular protagonist gains enlightenment by the banks of a river that 'speaks' to him. Of course, you don't need to be familiar with the Hesse novel to be able to appreciate the song's broader theme of finding a spiritual connection with a body of water—sacred or otherwise. Nor is it the first time Kerr had found inspiration in writing lyrics about a river. This time the river could be any river anywhere in the world that the listener finds a connection with. This Buddhist transcendental element to Simple Minds' music continued into the next album, with a more laid-back texture, rather than the strong rock tone of 'She's a River' that's led by the soaring riff from Burchill and Mark Schulman's cracking drums.

When interviewed in 1995, Jim Kerr said that the song was the last to be completed for the album. Furthermore, he said:

> We wanted it to be the song to bring us back. After being away for such a long time, you want something explosive, something that has a great sense of climax, and something that heralds this new phase. And in some ways, we also wanted something we thought would be—if I can say it—classic Simple Minds.

## 'Night Music'

Duration: 5.23

If any song Simple Minds has produced epitomises the magic that song-writing and creating music embodies for Jim Kerr, it is this track. Often Kerr has described the song-writing process as 'solving a puzzle', saying that it is mysterious how some songs evolve quickly and relatively effortlessly, while others are akin to drawing blood from a stone. This song contains a line that gives the album its title.

At the time of release, Kerr said:

> It refers to a period in the creation of the music where, I think for the first time ever, I had a block. I don't know what was happening, but my muse had gone. Initially that was fine, and we were working on the music, and Charlie was coming up with a lot of things but … it's funny, this whole place where you get inspired from—you call it the muse, or you call it the gift of vision or inspiration or whatever. No one really knows what it is but where does it come from and where does it go? We still don't know but when it goes, a certain panic sets in. And without trying to get purposefully mystical about it, it does seem *some place*. It does seem like another world, because it's not got a lot to do with logic. This world that offers us the raw material—my own antennae didn't seem tuned in. As I say, I don't know why and I don't know how it came back but I'm glad to say that a few months later it was as flowing as ever, which for me and for Charlie was a great thing. It was almost a small statement on that. I'd come in and say to Charlie 'you know we've got good news from the next world'.

## 'Hypnotised'

Duration: 5.53

The second single off the album. Although, like 'She's a River', it spent three weeks on the UK top forty singles chart, its place on the chart was lower overall. Released on 27 March 1995, it entered the UK chart at No. 18. Unlike the moderate success 'She's a River' had on the Billboard Hot 100, 'Hypnotised' failed to chart. A soft-rock ballad that features wonderfully sensual slide guitar work from Charlie Burchill, the lyrics of the song exude lust and desire, possibly referring to an illicit affair. 'Maybe it's a sin, I know, but it's not a crime', says the protagonist, but in contrast is the line 'All I've got now in my defence is my innocence'. The promotional video for the song has some surreal elements to it. It feels like one that may have been storyboarded because it plays out like a mini-film with a script in which the song's lyrics are the dialogue.

## 'Great Leap Forward'

Duration: 5.35

This arrives in your face with a guitar intro. The 'great leap forward' seems to be a metaphor for the propulsion of moving yourself forward in life—taking the next step—getting to the next level. Or perhaps it is more akin to taking a leap of faith? The protagonist seems to be recounting a near-death experience that spurs them on to make something more of their life. A 'poverty of expectation'—is that the definition of apathy? A simile that says don't let apathy drain your mental prosperity? Musically, it's heavily guitar based, with a strong rhythm and with a single keyboard note that strikes on the fifteenth bar of every sixteen bars of the verse.

## '7 Deadly Sins'

Duration: 5.10

Although you'd be forgiven for thinking that the song is about each of the deadly sins: lust, gluttony, sloth, greed, anger, envy and pride, Jim Kerr concentrates on just a few of the seven, namely lust, anger, envy and pride. Upon closer inspection, perhaps some things are just harder to find. Gluttony is possibly addressed in the line, 'Ever find when trouble calls/You're first in line and stick your finger in', or perhaps that's another sign of lust? Other than this I see no signs of gluttony or sloth being addressed. I guess they would be deemed the lesser of the sins—all of us are gluttons to some degree. Sloth is a different subject and is not as easy to define, but I see it as apathy and indifference which produces the 'laziness' attached to the modern-day interpretation of sloth—as in the laboured manoeuvrings of the animal. Lust provides the song's overriding sensual feel.

## 'And the Band Played On'

Duration: 5.32

One of the first songs to be completed for the album. It started out from sessions for *Street Fighting Years*. It is a song about the power of destiny and taking it firmly within your grasp. It feels like an autobiographical piece of lyrical writing by Jim Kerr, reflecting his feelings of where the band had been and where they were now. It's now a crusade of two—just himself and Charlie Burchill—and that declaration and intent is summed up in the lines of the song and its title.

### 'My Life'

Duration: 5.15

A force for positivity, this song encapsulates the sense of moving forward to what you feel may be your destiny, or the thing that gives you the ultimate purpose in life. If viewed in an autobiographical sense—and I do feel that much of the album has been written in a more obvious autobiographical way than other Simple Minds albums—one could view the first verse as an ode to music itself, as well as the forward momentum that Jim Kerr uses as a mantra for life: 'One step forward/Never look backward'. The second verse solidifies the notion of a continuing forward momentum being salvation. Musically, it is in keeping with the theme of the rest of the album. It has a traditional rock structure, heavy with guitar riffs and hooks.

### 'Criminal World'

Duration: 5.02

A track on the album that has a stronger melody to it. Much of the album features straight out rock chords and relies on a more traditional rock guitar-based sound. I find the melody that starts this track really engaging and it counters the guitar-rock form of the song very well. In a way it gives the vibe of a modern-day song about a past 'Wild West' cowboy showdown. I see and feel those sorts of images emanating from the song in both lyrical context and musical structure.

### 'This Time'

Duration: 4.58

One of the first batch of songs to be completed for the album. Love? Is that what this song's theme is? Or is it lust? 'Never go to bed without it'. Hmm. Or is it more a generalised 'good vibes' theme? Whatever it is, it is obviously something that feels intangible to Kerr. Something elusive that all too readily slips through your fingers. The key is once you find it to hold onto it ... this time.

## Additional tracks

### 'E55'

Duration: 5.10

An instrumental that was the B-side to 'She's a River' and a Charlie Burchill solo composition. In a post on the Simple Minds Facebook page in 2012, Jim Kerr explained that the piece had been inspired by a road route (encompassing two ferry crossings) from Helsingborg, Sweden, to Kalamata, Greece. The title of the track is the name of the highway that forms the final part of the road journey. Kerr said the track was 'based on some experience of travelling' the route.

## 'Celtic Strings'

Duration: 5.13

Another instrumental that was featured on a limited-edition CD single for 'She's a River'. It was an instrumental at the time as perhaps Kerr was stuck composing lyrics for it. Some things take time—and so lo and behold the music of this instrumental would return more than twenty years later as the track 'Barrowland Star' on the 2018 album *Walk Between Worlds*.

## '#4'

Duration: 4.30

Said to be an instrumental version of 'Hypnotised' and featured as a B-side to the single. I also hear—especially in the piano intro—the sound of a previous B-side titled 'Saturday Girl'. I think perhaps it might be a blend of the two tunes.

## 'Women and Ghosts'

Duration: 6.06

An instrumental that sounds very reminiscent of, or has elements of, 'Banging on the Door' from previous album *Real Life*. It also shares musical notes with the *Real Life* title track. Perhaps this is why the tune has the title that it does? 'Woman' is a track from the *Real Life* album, and this composition uses the 'ghosts' of songs from the previous album. I am merely theorising here. Saying that, it does strongly play out as a composite blend of elements of both the title track and 'Banging on the Door'. It's a long piece for an instrumental, running at just over six minutes, making it one of the longest instrumentals the band have recorded.

13

# *Neapolis*

| | |
|---|---|
| UK: | 16 March 1998 |
| Personnel: | Additional drums: Jim McDermott, Michael Niggs<br>Additional programming: Hamilton Lee<br>Bass: Derek Forbes<br>Drums: Mel Gaynor<br>Guitars, keyboards, programming: Charlie Burchill<br>Strings: The Dukes<br>Vocals: Jim Kerr |
| Duration: | 46 minutes |
| Produced by: | Charlie Burchill and Peter Walsh |
| Chart position: | Italy: 6; UK: 19; US: - |

The partnership between Simple Minds and Virgin came to an end at the beginning of 1996. Both sides seem to have been ready to part ways, and it initially appeared to be amicable. Simple Minds signed to the Chrysalis label. Composition of the album began in 1996 at Loch Earn. During those early writing sessions, 'Lightning' was one composition that formed, and several other ideas germinated for what would become 'Killing Andy Warhol', 'Glitterball' and 'Androgyny'. Production work continued through 1997, and the band road-tested songs planned for the album in their live sets through the summer, namely 'Glitterball' and 'War Babies'.

Familiar faces returned to the touring line-up in the form of Derek Forbes and Mel Gaynor. News of the album's release brought another surprise, with the return of Peter Walsh as the album's co-producer. Walsh had previously been at the production desk for *New Gold Dream (81-82-83-84)*. Forbes and Gaynor were also confirmed as being involved with the album. Gaynor had not been involved with the previous album, and Forbes had had no official involvement in any recordings with Simple Minds since early 1985.

The new record label led to a new drive in promotional content in relation to the album's release with extensive press, radio and television exposure at the beginning of 1998. During an interview promoting the album during that year Jim Kerr said, 'Things move at such a pace these days that it's hard to really grasp when and where we are. In fact, throughout the recording we were constantly on the move.' A look at the album's credits confirms this with a list of recording locations in Glasgow, London, Dublin, Paris and Italy.

The album was released on 16 March 1998. It crept into the top twenty of the UK chart at No. 19, and spent a further two weeks on the chart, relegated outside of the top forty. *Neapolis* was the band's first commercial flop in more than fifteen years. The album was released only on CD and cassette formats. It was not until Record Store Day 2023 and the twenty-fifth anniversary of the album that a special edition pressing of *Neapolis* was released on green vinyl.

## The songs

### 'Song for the Tribes'

Duration: 5.37

A song that evolved over several years. Its conception began during the *Street Fighting Years* sessions in 1987. The track is led by an acoustic guitar and stringed instruments, as well as a wonderfully repetitive bassline that features more prominently in the latter part of the song. In a post on the band website in 2008, Jim Kerr mentioned that the lyrics came together around the time of the UK general election in May 1997, which saw the return of a Labour government to office for the first time in eighteen years. The line 'feel real power in the darkness' is a theme that Kerr seems to return to at regular intervals. He uses similar lines in both 'And the Band Played On' and 'My Life', both tracks on the previous album.

In a diary post for the band website in 2006, Kerr said, 'Music is at its best when it brings things to light, illuminates us, sheds light on our lingering darkness. Even more so when it casts light into the heart of our darkness and in doing so invites us to "see".' The title of this post was 'Power in the Darkness'.

In the same 2008 post, Kerr mentioned the Goths he saw congregating around the Gallery of Modern Art (GoMA) on Royal Exchange Square in Glasgow, and stated that the song was inspired by them:

> [...] and all others who felt like I did when I was eighteen; self-obsessed, felt victimised, and hung about the very same Royal Exchange Square, dressed entirely in death-mass black, and feeling that I belonged to a lost generation that was entirely misunderstood by all who came before.

## 'Glitterball'

Duration: 4.55

The lead single from the album. It was released on 23 February 1998. The song received broad exposure, with the band making several television and radio appearances in the UK to promote both the single and *Neapolis*. These included guest spots on *Top of the Pops*, music channel VH1 and *The National Lottery Draw*, as well as Virgin Radio sessions where the song was performed.

In terms of musicality, the thumping guitar-based rock sound was pushed aside for a return to the Simple Minds of old, with an emphasis on melody and synth-driven hooks and loops with electric guitar working in partnership with keyboards rather than taking centre focus.

Conceptually, the song has a great premise behind it that perhaps doesn't quite come across in execution. At the time of release, Jim Kerr said: 'In "Glitterball" the imagery behind the song is "empty glamour". It's a small song about the emptiness in believing in bright and shiny things'. In a separate interview, Kerr said the song was about 'fashion victims and glamour junkies'. That makes it sound as though the song should have a harder edge to it, less in terms of musical styling perhaps, but in lyrical intent. It should be the younger sister to 'Love Song', but it's more like an elderly aunt. The intent is there but the execution doesn't quite hit the mark. As a result, it falls short commercially. It entered the UK chart at No. 18 and then spent a second and final week on the chart at No. 45.

## 'War Babies'

Duration: 5.03

In discussing the meaning of the song in an interview in 1998, Jim Kerr said:

> You could say it had a lovely melody in it. There was something uplifting about it as well, but there's something naive in the melody to me, something classical. It's not a war in the sense of Bosnia or wherever, it's more sort of emotional warfare. I could see it as a relationship song. There was something also intimate about it and it was my job to come up with a dialogue between whatever characters would be in this particular scenario.

He then talks about the lyrics playing out like an abstract scene from a film in which the viewer arrives *in medias res*. In Kerr's words: 'You don't know what led the characters to be this way but you're maybe grabbing just one scene and it [the song] just seemed to emerge this way'.

The song has provoked some bewilderment in the fanbase about why it was not the lead single for the album, as the consensus was that 'War Babies' was the stand-out track. However, the honour of lead single was bestowed upon 'Glitterball' to the dismay of many.

The second and final single from the album, 'War Babies' was released on 18 May 1998 and failed to make the top forty in the UK, troubling the chart for just a solitary week at No. 43. It appears a repeat of what happened to Simple Minds during the release of their first and second singles in 1979. Chrysalis decided to repeat the same tactic that Arista had used, keeping the stronger single back in favour of the weaker lead single, with a similar result. In 1979, 'Life in a Day' charted for two weeks peaking at No. 62, while 'Chelsea Girl' failed to make the chart. This time, 'Glitterball' charted at No. 18 when released. And although 'War Babies' also charted, it floundered in comparison. Despite this, fans see the song as one of the best Simple Minds compositions of the period.

## 'Tears of a Guy'

Duration: 4.48

A song that started its long evolution during the *Real Life* writing sessions in late 1989. It continued to be developed during the sessions for *Good News from the Next World*, seemingly being cast aside as it did not evolve in the way the band had hoped. Finally, in 1996, the track was picked up again. The lyrics seem to have an autobiographical touch as the protagonist tells of their personal struggles: 'But if I can't get to it/I can't get through it'—which could also be a reference to the creative block Jim Kerr said he was experiencing when he and Burchill started recording *Good News from the Next World*. There are other lines that suggest this might have been part of the song's meaning: 'Time goes/And the fountain still flows,' and 'But if I can't get cured/I must endure'. Again, the theme of a river as a significant natural feature and spiritual force personally for Kerr echoes in the line, 'So many rivers run to me'. Maybe his lyrical ideas are now flowing once again?

## 'Superman v Supersoul'

Duration: 4.47

The track has a very spiritual sound, underpinned by Bhangra-style percussion. Lyrically, Jim Kerr described the song as being about a man who finds himself staring into a painting depicting a scene from the *Bhagavad Gita* and then gets kind of sucked into the painting. According to Wikipedia, 'Kali Yuga' is a measure of time in Hinduism. Epochs are measured in Yugas. 'Kali Yuga' is the fourth and shortest of the Yugas. It is said to have started its most recent cycle in 3102 BCE and is meant to last 432,000 years in total, broken up into three cycles. Yuga is the time measurement itself, so 'Kali Yuga' is translated as meaning 'the age of Kali'—interpreted as 'the age of darkness', or 'the age of vice and misery', or 'the age of quarrel and hypocrisy'. The *Bhagavad Gita* seems to have been written during the age of Kali Yuga, so the line in the song 'Kali Yuga's miles away' is possibly meant to be taken in an emotional sense rather than in any actual metaphysical sense. I believe, from what I hear on this track as well as on 'Killing Andy Warhol', that these songs might have been those where Hamilton Lee was involved in the drum programming. Perhaps he was involved with other tracks on the album, but I would wager that he was certainly instrumental with these two, which is why I single them out.

## 'Lightning'

Duration: 5.35

This song has always been a personal favourite of mine. Without initially knowing what the song's theme was, I felt it was very sensual lyrically. It seemed to express a need or desire to embody someone else. Lines like, 'I want to touch/ Let me play' and 'I want to lie where you lay' seemed the most erotic notions, but my interpretations couldn't have been more wrong! The song is about wanting to embody another person, but not in an erotic way. Well, at least not outwardly. The narrator is an arms dealer who revels in the thought of the weapons he sells being used on perceived enemies; he wishes to live vicariously through the actions of the users of the weapons. It's akin to a pyromaniac deriving pleasure from watching as fire crews work to extinguish a blaze that they have deliberately started.

Musically, the song is up-tempo with a flash of synths and a great bassline. It begins with the fade-in tolling of some kind of klaxon—perhaps it's meant to represent the ticking of a bomb? It slowly builds, adding layers of instrumentation as it forms. After the middle eight and the bridge, the line 'I long to be where you are' is accompanied by a melodic flurry that is the high point of the song for me. It always sparks a frisson. Despite now knowing what the song's subject is, I still find it incredibly sexy.

## 'If I Had Wings'

Duration: 4.43

A slow-paced number that tells the story of wanting to have the means to perform the ultimate escape—the ability to fly. Or perhaps it is just the notion of being able to 'take flight' from one's own inner demons and escape the thoughts that keep us shackled and grounded? Of the songs on *Neapolis*, this track is probably the least discussed among the fanbase. It has never been performed live and has fallen into relative obscurity. It's another track that could have been formed musically with the help of Hamilton Lee, as the sound feels as though it has been influenced by the Transglobal Underground project that Lee was synonymous with at the time.

## 'Killing Andy Warhol'

Duration: 5.16

The title of the song is a comment that Jim Kerr overheard during a heated conversation between a pair of lovers, who were apparently Warhol fans. The details he has given about where he overheard this exchange have varied, with him mentioning a coffee shop inside a cinema when seeing the film *Basquait*, and a coffee shop at MoMA in New York City.

The concept of the song is a metaphorical 'killing'. Of course, there had been an assassination attempt on Warhol in 1968 in which he was seriously injured having been shot twice at close range, once in the chest and once in the torso.

He spent eight weeks in hospital. The song's title is a comment that Kerr heard within the coffee shop conversation as an outcry about how Warhol's perceived artistic legacy was being desecrated. A wider commentary on the superficiality of the world at large can be gleaned from the lyrics.

Musically, the song has a wonderful little guitar riff. It starts with that same kind of Asian subcontinent vibe with the percussion. Filled with hooks and loops, it feels most reminiscent of the synth-based early-eighties electronic dance era of Simple Minds.

### 'Androgyny'

Duration: 5.07

The last Kerr/Burchill attributed instrumental that appears on a Simple Minds album. I'm curious about why this track was attributed to both Jim Kerr and Charlie Burchill, considering Kerr has never played any musical instrument in Simple Minds other than the occasional rattle of a tambourine. (Although he did once try to convince me he could play the glockenspiel and triangle.) I am at a loss to understand exactly what Kerr brought to the writing of this piece of music, other than perhaps a directional guide about how the song should flow. A late-nineties electro-dance underrated gem, it conjures up a piercing sunset over an azure Ionian Sea.

14

# *Neon Lights*

| | |
|---|---|
| UK: | 8 October 2001 |
| Personnel: | Additional vocals: Kevin Burleigh, Gordy Goudie, Dee Miller<br>Arrangements: Charlie Burchill, Gordy Goudie<br>Bass: Charlie Burchill, Gordy Goudie<br>Drums: Gordy Goudie<br>Guitars, keyboards,programming: Charlie Burchill, Gordy Goudie<br>Vocals: Jim Kerr |
| Duration: | 42 minutes |
| Produced by: | Simple Minds, Gordy Goudie and Phunk Investigation with D. Tignino and E. Pat Legato |
| Chart position: | Germany: 58; UK: 141; US: - |

This is a curious beast in the Simple Minds catalogue: an album full of cover songs. Personally, I had second thoughts about including this album in the book. However, the album came at such a pivotal time in the band's existence, as well as falling under the discography definition of a studio album, that it felt important to include it.

The track list of the album reasserts all the influences the band tried so doggedly to shake off to achieve their own musical identity during their early days. From Roxy Music, David Bowie, The Velvet Underground, and Kraftwerk, to more surprising influences such as Van Morrison and Neil Young, as well as acknowledgements of contemporaries such as Echo and the Bunnymen and Pete Shelley, the album features an array of rock music sub-genres. The album was released under a new record label, Eagle Records—a subsidiary of UMG—on 8 October 2001.

Reflecting on the album's importance to the Simple Minds story on Facebook in 2018, Jim Kerr said that Simple Minds had 'come to a point where discussions had taken place regarding calling time on the band'. He recalled being 'convinced that it might be the right path to take', saying that the band were 'flatlining'. In describing the subsequent turnaround in fortunes, Kerr explained:

> So how did we get back on our feet? ... How to open up and let the faith in ourselves take over once again? There is no one single answer to all of that. Except to say, that we had to go back to the very beginning. Back to falling in love with writing and recording music. [...] It was nevertheless the act of recording *Neon Lights* that saved our ongoing creative lives. Without it, there would be no present Simple Minds. Sick men back then, working on that album became our first step to recovery. And nothing is possible without the first step.

In an interview conducted for a *Neon Lights* EPK, which remained unreleased until 2019 when it was added to a DVD that featured in the *Rejuvenation* box set, Kerr went into detail about the development of the album and the decisions made on the track selections, as well as explaining the choice of the album's title:

> When it came to covering the actual songs, it did take a kind of analytical approach; 'why was that, what is it, what was the overriding atmosphere?' And I enjoyed sifting through the sands of time to find 'it was that!' As with any great art you can never really put your finger on what exactly it was or is. And in fact, it's always, when it comes to music, sort of subjective. But certainly, you can try and articulate what it was or what it is for you. There is a kind of stigma attached to doing covers. We all know that because there have been so many poor ones done. Part of you is trying to emulate. Another part is trying to find, perhaps, something that wasn't emphasised on the original. And I suppose overall in the case of our band, trying to show off the genetics of where our sound came from. [...] Obviously, to go back when you're covering songs, there is a sense of romance involved. There's a sense of sentimentality. And for me, not only was it the music that instilled all these great dreams and possibilities but, indeed so did the cityscape. Being up on the eleventh floor, the panorama of the city was the accompanying pictures. *Neon Lights* does sum up the environment in which we listened to the music. I thought it was an appropriate title.

## The songs

### 'Gloria' by Them

Duration: 3.45

Written by Van Morrison and performed by Them. Released on Decca Records on 6 November 1964. Simple Minds had played the track live on and off through the years as a medley during other songs.

## 'The Man Who Sold the World' by David Bowie

Duration: 4.07

Written by David Bowie and the title track for his album, first released in the US in November 1970. Certain lines to the song are paraphrased from the poem 'Antigonish' by William Hughes Mearns. In discussing the cover version by Simple Minds, Kerr said:

> There is something in the melody for us with this song. There was something in the atmosphere of it that, again, it was fun to do. It was fun to try and recreate. And I think our version of 'The Man Who Sold the World' is the only and the most 'karaoke' type of situation on the album, where we were trying to '*Stars in your Eyes*' our way through David Bowie's great song.

## 'Homosapien' by Pete Shelley

Duration: 4.20

Written by Shelley and released as a single in September 1981. When talking about the choice to cover it, Kerr said, 'In the case of "Homosapien", it's just one of these songs that when it appeared I had always had in the back of my mind to try and write a song in that vein. "Homosapien", to me, is more like Pete Shelley doing Bowie. And now we're doing Pete Shelley doing Bowie.'

## 'Dancing Barefoot' by Patti Smith Group

Duration: 3.48

Written by Patti Smith and Ivan Kral and released as a single by the Patti Smith Group in May 1979. In discussing the choice to cover the song, Kerr stated:

> I remember seeing Patti Smith when she first came to Scotland, and she played during the Edinburgh Festival. I think it was 1977, and the sheer force—I can still recall wanting to create a band, or create a sound that could live up to that. We didn't go down Patti's earnest route. We probably took a more Pet Shop Boys approach to it. You see with these covers, not only can we cover the original, but we cover others who may have covered the originals this way.

In fact, the date of the Patti Smith Group concert was 30 August 1978 at the Odeon Theatre, Edinburgh. Which would have meant Simple Minds as a band were already in existence. The date would have fallen between their weekly residency at the Mars Bar. The Simple Minds version would be released as the lead track for an EP issued to promote *Neon Lights*. Other tracks on the EP included 'Gloria', as well as two tracks that were recorded during the album sessions but were not selected for inclusion on *Neon Lights*: 'Being Boiled' by The Human League and 'Love Will Tear Us Apart' by Joy Division. The EP was released on 10 September 2001.

## 'Neon Lights' by Kraftwerk

Duration: 4.16

Written by Ralf Hutter, Florian Schneider and Karl Bartos and released by Kraftwerk as a single in December 1978. Kerr said of the Simple Minds cover, 'The challenge that was staring us in the face was to take on a Kraftwerk song and try and give it a human heart. And in the case of "Neon Lights" it, unlike most Kraftwerk songs, we found it ... it's a little song that if you play it on an acoustic guitar, it's just a beautiful little folk song'.

## 'Hello, I Love You' by The Doors

Duration: 3.32

Written by The Doors and released as a single in June 1968. Kerr said of the Simple Minds cover, 'Through the years, Simple Minds have played endless covers of Doors songs. And I suppose, again, Charlie's version here is a more electronic, more industrial, sort of *Eraserhead* version of The Doors song'.

## 'Bring On the Dancing Horses' by Echo and the Bunnymen

Duration: 5.15

Written by Echo and the Bunnymen and released as a single in October 1985. Simple Minds decided that of their contemporaries it would be the song they chose to cover.

## 'The Needle and the Damage Done' by Neil Young

Duration: 4.15

Written by Neil Young and released as the B-side to the single 'Old Man' in April 1972. In discussing the choice to cover the song, Kerr said, 'We've chosen to expand on the song. Initially the original version of this is quite a small ballad. We've given it, I think, much more drama. And I think we've tried to highlight the lyrical content of the song'.

## 'For Your Pleasure' by Roxy Music

Duration: 4.08

Written by Bryan Ferry and performed by Roxy Music. The song is the title track of their second studio album, released in March 1973. Kerr said of their cover, 'Roxy Music [was] probably the predominant influence on Simple Minds in terms of the sound of the guitars and the synthesisers, melodies, etc. We've chosen, I think, a more obscure Roxy song, albeit the title of one their albums. We had great pleasure in recording this song. We hope we do it justice'.

## 'All Tomorrow's Parties' by The Velvet Underground and Nico

Duration: 3.35

Written by Lou Reed and performed by The Velvet Underground and Nico. It was released as a single in July 1966. Kerr's words on the choice were, 'true Velvet Underground fans will recognise it as being one of the dark horses of their incredible catalogue. The song itself, I think, is about the end of an era. We've chosen to close the album with this song. It's not the end of an era for us, but it's certainly a stopgap'.

# 15

# *Cry*

| | |
|---|---|
| UK: | 1 April 2002 |
| Personnel: | Acoustic guitar: Mark Kerr (track 5)<br>Additional vocals: Gordy Goudie, Mark Kerr, Daniele Tignino<br>Bass, guitars: Charlie Burchill, Gordy Goudie<br>Keyboards, drums,effects, programming: Charlie Burchill, Gordy Goudie, E. Pat Lego, Dono Maggiorana<br>Vocals: Jim Kerr |
| Duration: | 48 minutes |
| Produced by: | Jim Kerr, Gordy Goudie, Charlie Burchill and Planet Funk |
| Chart position: | Italy: 14; UK: 80; US: - |

The formation of the album started in late 2000. It was a tentative step. Jim Kerr was at a creative crossroads at this point in Simple Minds' history. On a personal level, he felt that he was at a creative impasse, and this would have an obvious effect on the future of Simple Minds. More focused writing sessions commenced in January 2001.

Current touring member of the band Gordy Goudie first became involved in working with Simple Minds during the early stages of 2001. Goudie also became heavily involved with the project coinciding with the production of *Cry*, *Neon Lights*, which also involved Jim Kerr's younger brother, Mark.

Aspects of *Cry*'s musicality and structure derived from Kerr's involvement in writing with Italian musicians and producers while he resided in Italy. There were several collaborative crossovers during the writing and production of the album. Some tracks involved writing between Jim Kerr and the Italian group of producers and musicians collectively known as Planet Funk, while others evolved from what remained of *Our Secrets Are the Same* and some were the result of writing collaborations between Charlie Burchill and Mark Kerr. Jim Kerr suggested that the theme of the album was 'rejuvenation or rebirth', particularly in terms of his own experience in 'getting involved in music once again'.

Upon release the album stalled at No. 80 on the UK chart. An observation by one reviewer was that it was more a Jim Kerr solo album than a Simple Minds album. Given the fractured development of the album and the minimal involvement of Charlie Burchill, you can see why the reviewer came to that conclusion. Burchill has only two song-writing credits on the album, and there is just one J. Kerr/Burchill composition.

## The songs

### 'Cry'

Duration: 3.55

Released as the lead single on 18 March 2002. It made the UK chart peaking at No. 47 in its first week of a two-week run. The single was released as two distinctly coloured digipak CDs: one bronze and one blue. The CDs had different track lists. The bronze-coloured cover contained the tracks 'Lead the Blind' and 'Homosapien [Vince Clarke Remix]', while the blue contained 'For What It's Worth' and 'The Garden'. Lyrically, 'Cry' is about a fraught relationship—an emotionally manipulative and damaging one—seemingly narrated by the victim. Musically, it's a rather slow-tempo number with a repetitive synth hook. Several remixes of the song were also released on CD and 12-inch vinyl, including: Clubinvest Mix, Phunk Investigation Radio Edit, Dubinvest, Tazz Glasgoal Remix, Tazz Dub, and Charly Fath 80's Remix.

### 'Spaceface'

Duration: 3.53

Released as the second single from the album on 17 June 2002, it conjures up a 'trip' to space both musically and lyrically. The female protagonist is described by the narrator as being 'big on aviation' and 'loves a levitation'. A metaphoric experience of a drug 'high'? Be it substance-induced or naturally occurring, this trip is one taken in the mind or perhaps through an 'astral travel' experience rather than any genuine journey into space. A dreamy and positive song. The song was performed live on the tours that followed from 2002–04. It also made the setlist on Jim Kerr's solo *Lostboy! AKA Jim Kerr* tour in 2010. Much like the 'Cry' single, 'Spaceface' also had several remixes produced: Stonebridge Club Mix, Stonebridge Radio Mix, Farfa Spacemix, Farfa Edit Mix, Tomcraft Remix, and Hardakt Remix.

## 'New Sunshine Morning'

Duration: 3.36

When discussing the album in 2002, Jim Kerr stated that he didn't realise the song was as good as it was until the band had recorded an acoustic version—alternatively titled 'New Sunrise'—in session for Radio Clyde:

> Some songs grow. Some songs ... once they're sort of committed—that's it, it's done. And then when you go back to it, you do it with a freer spirit or you do it with a more wide-open attack. I didn't realise it was such a good song. When we play it with an acoustic guitar and a voice, you go, 'Jeez, this thing's really, really powerful'. Inherently, it's a better song than I initially gave it credit for.

## 'One Step Closer'

Duration: 6.06

Arguably the album's strongest and most commercially mainstream song. As such, it was a highlight of the tour that coincided with the release of the album in 2002, with 'Spaceface' and 'New Sunshine Morning' the other songs from the album to feature in the set on the tour. The song was released as a single towards the end of 2002. On reflecting on the song in a post on the band's social media in 2018, Jim Kerr said:

> Heraldic, symphonic, dreamy, and loaded with emotion. Written at the turn of the century, it came across as a musical footnote to time passing, historically shifting from one era into another. A world moving both distant and closer ... to who knows what?

## 'Face in the Sun'

Duration: 3.57

The song was penned by Kerr's younger brother, Mark. In an interview in 2002 Jim Kerr likened 'Face in the Sun' to an early David Bowie pre-Ziggy Stardust song. Kerr also suggested that the track was 'a great song that works in antithesis to the more "charged-up electronic" tracks on the album'. That 'it's a good switch' from the strong electronic dance vibes to softer acoustic sounds.

## 'Disconnected'

Duration: 3.37

When interviewed in 2002 Jim Kerr said:

> Some songs just land in your lap and this was one of those songs. From the point of when I knew the title of the song, the lyrics just poured out. It's almost like a nursery rhyme, but it deceived me. When I then took full note of it, it was saying some pretty poignant things. On the surface it seems like a little bouncy

superficial song, but it hits on home truths. So, when I say it landed in my lap I mean on a subconscious level. I didn't intentionally sit down to write a song like it, but in the case of 'Disconnected', it's a little loaded song.

### 'Lazy Lately'

Duration: 4.02

A composition by Charlie Burchill and Mark Kerr. It exudes a summer feel with its acoustic guitars. This may be a controversial statement, but I feel this song gives credence to the tired old accusation that Simple Minds are a 'lesser' U2. It's U2 circa *Zooropa*, which means the tune is a pastiche of something that was already nearly a decade old. Listen to 'Lazy Lately' and then compare it with 'Lemon' or 'Numb' from the *Zooropa* album and hopefully you'll understand what I mean. Jim Kerr's falsetto voice sits uncomfortably and sounds a little too much like he's trying to emulate Bono to my ears.

### 'Sugar'

Duration: 3.13

A metaphor for sex? Or perhaps it is more the chase of a 'hit', with Jim Kerr of being back in love with music and creating songs? The song is image rich, with scenes of Mediterranean sunshine and heat-haze. It is the only J. Kerr/Burchill composition on the album.

### 'Sleeping Girl'

Duration: 4.11

A collaborative track involving Jim Kerr working with the Phunk Investigation team. Other tracks on the album had additional Italian DJs and producers involved, like Planet Funk. Much like its title, it has a dreamy quality to it. One of several tracks that creates a sense of bright and glaring Ionian Sea sun flares, the imagery of 'Sleeping Girl' reflects a setting sun, with a cooling breeze wafting in through muslin curtains draped over patio doors. Musically, it has elements in it that remind me of Garbage's 'Stupid Girl'.

### 'Cry Again'

Duration: 3.35

Ostensibly the same song as the opening title track, but given an acoustic musical arrangement and slowed in tempo. It is much more of a melancholic lament about a fractured relationship, rather than the melodically pop tale of a broken relationship that the album opener offers. As a result, it is more emotionally raw. Kerr's vocal on this version is very effective in conveying the desperate state of the narrator of the song.

### 'Slave Nation'

Duration: 3.01

Another darker piece, the penultimate track on *Cry*. As the album's tracks lead us towards its end, they seem to become increasingly dark. Our narrator—Kerr himself this time?—seems to be suggesting that being caught inside a slave nation is 'alright'. I guess it all depends on what we're enslaved to? Ourselves? Other people? Governments? Dictatorial regimes? Modernity? Technology? Spiritual enlightenment? Vices such as drugs, alcohol and sex? A slow blues number that fades down into a stringed segue into the final track.

### 'The Floating World' (V. Clarke)

Duration: 4.23

To date, this is the last officially released original instrumental to feature on a Simple Minds album. Written by Vince Clarke, it is given a rather curious description by Jim Kerr in the liner notes. 'Coming from the heart of Boy Wonder, haunted by the smiling ghost of Billy MacKenzie ... goldfish swimming in cool pools ... and the world is moving on'. Cryptic, to say the least! The only association I can make with the reference to 'Boy Wonder' is that Kerr was referring to the 1988 novel by American writer James Robert Baker. The track made its way onto the decks of DJs in dance clubs across Europe in the early 2000s. The track's title gave the subsequent tour, coinciding with the release of *Cry*, its name.

## Additional tracks

### 'Lead the Blind'

Duration: 3.59

A track that featured on the brown-covered digipak single release of 'Cry', written by Charlie Burchill and Jim Kerr's brother, Mark. There's a catchy chorus that I believe has the line, 'If you're not sold on the way it's told' and a repetition of the phrase 'It's an easy show/Easy show'. There are allusions to the weather, dancing and zombies. Tellingly, there is a line that declares 'But I don't know what this means/To me'. Likewise! The musical structure sounds very similar to the other Burchill/Mark Kerr penned track, 'Lazy Lately'.

Bonus tracks usually are not quite in keeping with the rest of an album. I'm unsure what caused 'Lead the Blind' to be left off the main album, as to me it sounds quite in keeping with the rest of the recordings from the *Cry* sessions. There was also running time left on the CD.

### 'The Garden'

Duration: 3.12

A song that was a legacy from the recording sessions of *Our Secrets Are the Same*. It featured on the blue-covered digipak single release of 'Cry', along with 'For What It's Worth'. The song was written with Kevin Hunter. Some years later, in 2006, when writing a post about a band tour break in Bali, Jim Kerr wrote about the song in relation to the feelings he was experiencing while recharging his energies:

> It has always struck me as having an incredible sensual power. 'Bordering on the mystical, that song' is how Kevin Hunter our then producer would put it. I agree with him entirely. Amazingly it is my experience that on occasion some song lyrics just seem to appear from who knows where, announcing themselves as if almost in a dream. 'The Garden' is an example of when that occurred as it was almost as though some force demanded that song to be written and made real. I do love it when that happens, and I am happy to move over and let events unfold wherein the song seemingly writes itself.

## 'For What It's Worth' (S. Stills)

Duration: 3.43

This cover of the Buffalo Springfield song written by Stephen Stills featured on the blue-covered digipak release of the 'Cry' single. The song was most likely recorded during the recording sessions for *Neon Lights*, which at times happened in conjunction with the *Cry* sessions. In years to come the song would feature on the setlist for much of the *Acoustic* tour of 2017, and the song would be performed as a duet between Jim Kerr and fellow Scottish music artist KT Tunstall.

## 'New Sunrise'

Duration: 4.16

An acoustic version of the album track 'New Sunshine Morning'. The song featured on the single releases of 'Spaceface' and 'New Sunshine Morning'.

16

# *Our Secrets Are the Same*

| | |
|---|---|
| UK: | 18 October 2004 |
| Personnel: | Additional keyboards: Chris Fudurich<br>Backing vocals: Kevin Hunter, Mark Kerr<br>Bass: Eddy Duffy<br>Drums: Mark Kerr<br>Guitars: Charlie Burchill, Kevin Hunter<br>Keyboards: Charlie Burchill<br>Percussion: Eddy Duffy<br>Vocals: Jim Kerr |
| Duration: | 40 minutes |
| Produced by: | Charlie Burchill and Kevin Hunter |
| Chart position: | UK: -; US: - |

The album has had a marred history. Recording started in 1999, directly after the band had recorded and released *Neapolis*. Their record company at the time, Chrysalis, was initially very keen on the fresh music produced, but Chrysalis was experiencing its own upheaval, eventually merging with EMI. This led to delays to the album's projected release, with dates moving forward several times. Eventually, Simple Minds were dropped from EMI completely. In the interim, the album had been leaked with CD-R copies surreptitiously making their way into the hands of fans.

The album appeared to be the metaphorical last gasp of a band that seemed on the brink of collapse in 1999. Artistically, it was a strong record. It all seemed to be a matter of timing—and unfortunately, that timing was not in Simple Minds' favour. You could argue that had the album found its way to a commercial release in 1999, it would likely have fared better than its predecessor, *Neapolis*. Thus, the only conclusion to come to is that the band's crisis point was somehow needed.

In a post on the Simple Minds website in late December 2009, Jim Kerr stated that one executive at Chrysalis-EMI had 'confessed that had [the album] come from a brand-new artist they would be delighted with the prospects for it'. I place the album here in the chronology of the band's output because in 2004 *Our Secrets Are the Same* at last obtained a commercial release with inclusion on *Silver Box*, issued by Virgin Records. Interestingly, the idea was touted that the album would get its own stand-alone release in 2003, but this did not happen.

The other four CDs on *Silver Box* are presented as a chronological band anthology with a selection of demos, radio sessions, and live performances. It was released on 18 October 2004. All songs on *Our Secrets Are the Same* were composed by Jim Kerr, Charlie Burchill and Kevin Hunter unless otherwise stated.

## The songs

### 'Swimming Towards the Sun' (K. Hunter and K. Stevens)

Duration: 4.32

It's a dark number. One that relays a tale of drug abuse, suburban struggle, feminine attachment, gun-wielding death and a society fractured by oppression. A new version of 'Sign O' The Times', maybe? An update? There's a languid energy to it. Also, an element delivered in the line 'I'm swimming towards the sun' as if it's Icarus under water. Instead of flying, we're swimming. Destined to sink, perhaps? Icarus's wings melted. The song was subsequently rerecorded and included on the deluxe edition of 2014's *Big Music*. As far as live performances go, its only appearance was during Jim Kerr's solo *Lostboy! AKA Jim Kerr* tour in 2010.

### 'Jeweller to the Stars'

Duration: 3.27

The song's lyrics were inspired by Jim Kerr seeing an advert in a newspaper. Some years later, Kerr would describe his song-writing partner and band guitarist Charlie Burchill as 'the jeweller'. The lyrics can almost be read as moments of misgiving or thoughts of doubt, decline or destruction. But there is salvation at hand through this craftsman of wearable gems. There's a feeling of 'fight or be damned' in the words. It's almost an ode to Charlie Burchill himself, the 'Jeweller to the stars/That's who you are'. Simple Minds will keep on keeping on with Burchill there to help guide the way. The song was eventually rerecorded and commercially released as 'The Jeweller (Part 2)' on *Black & White 050505*.

### 'Space'

Duration: 4.15

A slow ballad that lyrically appears to be a break-up song. A miscommunication between lovers. Perhaps all is not lost? The answer to a prayer that conjures up the thought of 'think of me and I'll appear' is suggested through the narrator of the song. Jim Kerr described its theme as, 'Space being the metaphor for emotional alienation'. The band felt it was such a strong tune that it was performed during the *Floating World* tour in 2002, and the *Alive and Kicking* tour of 2003. Another song that had bold pop sensibilities, much like 'Jeweller to the Stars', it was rerecorded for commercial release, finally appearing on the compilation *Celebrate: The Greatest Hits +*, released in 2013. As a result, it was performed live during the subsequent tours of 2013 and 2014. Two remixed versions by Johnson Somerset were also produced.

## 'Death By Chocolate'

Duration: 3.35

A song that was inspired in part by the works of author Yukio Mishima, particularly his novel *The Sailor Who Fell from Grace with the Sea*. Jim Kerr goes so far as to directly cite the author, 'Mishima made the final act/Too sweet for us to bear', as well as giving a nod to the book with the line 'I will fall for you/ Like a sailor falls to the sea'. It was given one solitary live airing during a concert in Zermatt, Switzerland in 2016, possibly as a trial run for inclusion in the set for the *Acoustic* tour in 2017. As it was its only live performance the song obviously failed the litmus test.

## 'Waiting at the End of the World'

Duration: 3.25

A song that seems to be looking back to the narrator's halcyon days before the apocalypse. The tarot cards within the lyrics declare it so: the end of the world is nigh. Musically, the song also has a nostalgic glint, harking back to the earliest Simple Minds sounds that fuelled *Life in a Day*. There is even a nod within Kerr's lyrics to one of the band's big influences, with the line 'Said she looked like Nico/ From the Velvet Underground'. Is it not the desire of many a human being to have their life flash before them before they shuffle off this mortal coil in one last nostalgic look back? Maybe it will make the departure less painful?

## 'Neon Cowboys'

Duration: 3.51

The song was originally titled 'Christians'. In a description of the song in the liner notes for *Silver Box*, Jim Kerr wrote about 'silent philosophers, ghosts at the bar' and mentioned Edward Hopper. With that in mind, I feel the imagery of Hopper's *Nighthawks* present within Kerr's description of the song. But when reading the lyrics, I also see drifters and nomads making their way across a vast area of countryside. Bedouin tribes on desert treks. American pioneers making their way westward to the new promised land. For the barflies and the self-proclaimed philosophers, it's a journey of the mind. The narrator in the song pleads for company. They don't want to be making this journey alone. 'Stay with me tonight', is their request in this slow tempo tale. A song unlike any other Simple Minds song that exists.

## 'She Knows'

Duration: 4.07

Secrets and intimacy are the overriding themes of this song. A coupling of an illicit nature, perhaps? A man who's falling hard for someone unsuitable, maybe? Or perhaps he's been stung too many times, but he feels himself falling again nonetheless. There's an addiction to it that's inescapable. What is there left to do but have fate seal itself? The final sixty seconds of the song are reminiscent of U2's 'The Fly'. The track is languid and sensual in delivery.

## 'Hello'

Duration: 3.23

A sensual song that evokes the feelings of an enduring love, or a wonderful love affair that seems as if it will stand the test of time. Or perhaps not? Perhaps it is meant to be fantastic while it lasts, as fleeting as that may be? Like ships in the night that cross paths, create beautiful music and then ... depart without the merest hint of regret. The song was chosen by Michael Davis, the director of the film *The Match*, for inclusion on its soundtrack, but in the end the song didn't make it onto the film's score. It remains one of Simple Minds' more obscure tracks.

## 'Happy is the Man' (M. Kerr)

Duration: 4.23

The decision to record this song, written by Jim Kerr's brother Mark, was explained in the liner notes in *Silver Box* by the frontman:

> It was me who was 'bouncing off the walls' when this tune got under my skin. Written by Mark Kerr, I reckon he stole the song from me, while I was dreaming it up thinking about Zimmerman. Only fair to steal it back then. What are brothers for, if you cannot play with their toys?

## 'Sleeping'

Duration: 4.30

Sometimes you feel you need to run away from the responsibilities that pervade your life. Sometimes sleep feels like the ultimate escape. When you try too hard, work too hard, the body screams for rest and recuperation. We can all have too much of a good thing and there needs to be an equilibrium. Sleep can also be a metaphor for ignorance, or perhaps in this case despondency or weariness. At a slow tempo, it's as languid as an afternoon siesta and mildly hypnotic.

# 17

# *Black and White 050505*

| | |
|---|---|
| UK: | 12 September 2005 |
| Personnel: | Additional guitars: Jez Coad<br>Backing vocals: John Biancale, Daniele Tignino<br>Bass: Eddy Duffy<br>Drums: Mel Gaynor<br>Guitars: Charlie Burchill<br>Keyboards: Charlie Burchill, Jez Coad, Andy Gillespie<br>Percussion: Eddy Duffy, Mel Gaynor<br>Vocals: Jim Kerr |
| Duration: | 41 minutes |
| Produced by: | Jez Coad and Simple Minds |
| Chart position: | Germany: 6; UK: 37; US: - |

The process of writing the album started tentatively in 2002. Such had been the momentum of the band from their earliest days that once an album was completed, writing for the next would immediately commence. This *Black and White* period was little different. There was already material left over from the production of *Cry*.

One early contender for inclusion on the new album was a song called 'Freedom Angel'. The band recorded the song in session for Billy Sloan on Radio Clyde in April 2002. Several other songs had been penned by this point, including the album tracks 'Underneath the Ice' and 'Dolphins' as well as 'Light Travels', which didn't make an album appearance until the follow-up, *Graffiti Soul*. Then, during a two-month stint for Night of the Proms in the latter months of 2002, Burchill and Kerr were able to accumulate ideas and get some further early-stage writing done for the album during the days on tour.

In 2003, the band toured during the latter half of the year. In 2004, writing resumed with recording sessions for the album taking place between tour dates throughout the year.

Although the system of writing was little altered since 1979, the rate of album releases had changed. The band also switched record companies after the release of *Cry*, signing to Sanctuary Records in early 2005. Production of the album ended on 25 May 2005, hence the '050505' numbering in the title.

Gone were the Mediterranean chilled vibes of *Cry*. The band was back to its rock roots, as sonically *Real Life* and *Good News from the Next World* had more in common with *Black and White* than *Neapolis* or *Cry*.

In talking about the process of recording the album in 2005, Jim Kerr spoke about the influence his move to Sicily had on the forward momentum of his artistic endeavours. Kerr also spoke about the broader influence that Italy was having on the music he and Burchill were creating:

> One of the big things that happened in my life was about five or six years ago, just at the period when I was perhaps feeling a little lost in my artistic life, I finally decided to pursue one of my passions: to live in the south of Italy. And I think this decision to live in Sicily really reinvigorated me as a person [...] And in a sense, it seems a little over-romantic to say 'reborn', but I do say that, to a large extent, I have been reborn. The album was pretty much written in Italy, in Sicily. In the sense that [...] I live there and my partner, Charlie Burchill, lives in Rome. So, it's just along the road, as the Roman Empire will tell you. People say, 'Well, how does it influence the music?' It doesn't influence it in the sense of writing those famous Neapolitan melodies. But it influences it in the sense, I believe, that if you get up in the morning and you feel good then there's more of a chance that you'll do good work. You will want to be creative. You will be up for the challenge.

The album was released in the UK and Europe on 12 September 2005. Release was delayed by one day for other parts of the world, including the United States. September was proving to be an auspicious month for Simple Minds, with previous albums *Empires and Dance*, *Sons and Fascination*, *Sister Feelings Call* and *New Gold Dream (81-82-83-84)* all having been released in the same month.

*Black and White 050505* entered the UK charts at No. 37, only to fall to No. 74 in the following week of its two-week run on the chart.

## The songs

### 'Stay Visible'

Duration: 5.19

This track started out under the title of 'Immigrants'. The lyrics were inspired in part by the novel *The Blinding Absence of Light* by Tahar Ben Jelloun.

Its plot centres around a group of prisoners kept in small, darkened cells in a mountainous region of Morocco. They survive their incarceration by creating fantasy worlds as a means of escaping their mental (and physical) suffering. The song was performed live during the band's tour in the summer of 2005, chosen as a forerunner song prior to the album's release. It was then showcased during the 2006 *Black and White* tour. It has appeared on the setlist sporadically ever since.

## 'Home'

Duration: 4.23

The lead single from the album was released on 5 September 2005. It stalled just outside the top forty, peaking at No. 41 for a solitary week. A traditional sounding rock anthem with a catchy yet melodic guitar from Burchill and signature Mel Gaynor drums with fills and thrills, it is backed up by a great rhythmic bass from Eddy Duffy. Lyrically, the track seems semi-autobiographical, with Kerr expressing the wanderlust that has been evident throughout his life as frontman to a band that consistently tours the world, playing live in front of many thousands of fans night after night for several months a year. 'God gave me travelling shoes/God gave me the wanderer's eye'. In describing the song's meaning, Kerr said it is the 'idea of an imagined return journey' to the state of 'enlightened consciousness with regards to its environment' that a foetus developing in the womb seems to possess. He likened this latter foetal state as being as 'spiritually ... in a perfect paradise state' of existence.

## 'Stranger'

Duration: 4.08

A pure pop-rock song. Signature Mel Gaynor drums and rock guitar riffs from Charlie Burchill, with lyrics co-penned by Jim Kerr and Italian musician Daniele Tignino that are upbeat and uplifting. A song about a burgeoning love? The protagonist seems to suggest that they have fallen under the spell of love at first sight. The intrigue of the 'beautiful stranger' borders on the obsessive, expressed by the imploring words 'tell me who you are'. The overt pop sensibilities of the song continue right through to the 'sha-la-la-la' backing vocals. A version of the song subtitled 'London Mix' was released as a digital download on iTunes on 11 November 2005 and was later released on CD in Europe, including the album version of the track plus extra material. It was played live for a few years before being recorded for the album and was also performed during the tour prior to the release of the album in 2005. It was then showcased during the 2006 *Black and White* tour but has not been performed since.

## 'Different World [TAORMINA.ME]'

Duration: 4.37

Lyrically, it is a song that describes the feeling of rebirth and creative reinvigoration experienced by Kerr when he returns to his home of Taormina in Sicily. In a post on Facebook in 2015, Kerr elaborated: 'Felt both rejuvenated and inspired after my recent trip to Sicily. For more than twenty years I have been going to Taormina, each time I come back with new ideas for songs. Much as I did with "Different World".' The lyrics for this track were co-written with the album's co-producer, Jez Coad.

## 'Underneath the Ice'

Duration: 4.45

A song that seems to suggest that the narrator or protagonist is looking for meaning in their life. Trying to find its significance, while others are 'skating by' as if they know what it's all about and are doing just fine, thank you very much. A sort of plea for salvation. Musically, a slow tempo song, leaning into the Simple Minds signature blend of big drums, catchy keyboards, guitar hooks and playful melodies. It plays with that duality of 'uplifting melancholia' present in many of the band's songs. Another song that was performed during the 2006 *Black and White* tour but has not been performed since.

## 'The Jeweller (Part 2)'

Duration: 4.18

It's a strange quirk that the same song in both musical structure and lyrics would have two slightly differing titles. I'm still unsure why there is a distinction, other than to separate the different recorded versions. This is something that Simple Minds have done with several songs over the past twenty-five years, and they have never altered any of the previous song titles. If they did alter the title, it would be because they had altered or changed the lyrics (i.e. 'Cocteau Twins' retitled 'No Cure', 'Sweet Things' retitled 'Destiny' and so on). In any case, the song first appeared (as 'Jeweller to the Stars') on *Our Secrets Are the Same*. It was then rerecorded and appeared on *Black and White 050505*. Jim Kerr has said that the lyrics were initially inspired by a jewellery advertisement he saw in a newspaper. Kerr has also described Charlie Burchill as 'the jeweller'. No doubt he feels as if his song-writing partner offers musical gems to the world. Indeed, Burchill's sliding guitar riff gives the track its sonic sophistication. Lyrically, the song seems to convey the notion that, when the deepness of space is overwhelming, when you feel out of your depth and out on a limb all alone, your dearest friend gives you a grounding and brings you home. Much like the album opener, 'Stay Visible', the song was performed live during the summer tour of 2005 and went on to be showcased during the *Black and White* tour of 2006. However, unlike 'Stay Visible', 'The Jeweller' has not been performed since 2006.

## 'A Life Shot in Black and White'

Duration: 3.35

A song that tries to weave its narrative through portraying the feelings and emotions that images in black and white can leave upon the human psyche. An acknowledgement of the past with an eye on the future, taking great memories and carrying them forward. A slow tempo track with a quiet drama. Sonically, it presents itself with the atmosphere of a black and white photograph. An image that leaves an indelible mark. The song was showcased live in 2006 during the *Black and White* tour. It has not been performed live since.

### 'Kiss the Ground'

Duration: 4.06

Musically brought together by Charlie Burchill, with the band's former keyboard player Andy Gillespie. Burchill's guitar is at its most honorary 'The Edge' in sound on this track. Jim Kerr's lyrics conjure up Middle Eastern vibes with their description of temples, sandstorms and bombed-out streets. War zones and cultural buildings are juxtaposed. The title of the song brings to mind the image of Pope John Paul II kissing the ground whenever he set foot on the soil of a new country. Perhaps within that image lies what Kerr was trying to express lyrically: the earth itself is more sacred than any religious text. Yet another track that was showcased during the 2006 *Black and White* tour, then never performed again.

### 'Dolphins'

Duration: 5.57

An atmospheric piece that, at one time, Jim Kerr said was about a man contemplating ending his life. He finds himself by a shore and thinks about the dolphins he sees swimming in the water. Do the dolphins save him, or assist him? It's unclear, as the protagonist of the song proclaims that dolphins 'drag me down'. Does he mean that metaphorically or physically?

More recently, when asked about the inspiration for 'Dolphins', Kerr explained it was about drug addiction. The protagonist is caught in the grip of heroin addiction and the 'dolphins drag me down' line is the addict describing the sensation of a hit. Not in a glamorising of drug abuse sense, but in the sense that there is a feeling of freedom that comes at a cost. The addict wishes that it could be obtained by the act of swimming with dolphins.

Musically, it's a slow melodic piece. The guitar melody by Burchill is a melancholic siren's call, reverberating through the scenes that Kerr's lyrics conjure. First performed live during the *Black and White* tour of 2006, the song has been a regular feature in the band's live set ever since.

## Additional tracks

### 'Bird on a Wire'

Duration: 3.50

The song appeared as a track on both the 'Home' and 'Stranger' singles, and is another legacy from the recording sessions for *Our Secrets Are the Same* that was released as bonus material. Kevin Hunter gains a writing credit. Lyrically, the song seems to be inspired by Jim Kerr's dalliance with Eastern philosophy, the teachings of Buddha, and reading both *Siddhartha* and the *Bhagavad Gita*. There are mentions of Buddha and a parade within the lyrics which allude to the *Bhagavad Gita*. This spiritual quest of Kerr's seemed to spawn several songs in the mid to late 1990s, including 'She's a River', 'Superman v Supersoul', 'If I Had Wings' and 'The Garden'. Musically, it's more like a blend of the rockier aspects of 'She's a River' blended with the softer world music vibe of 'Superman v Supersoul'.

## 'Too Much Television' (S. Kelly)

Duration: 4.19

A commentary on the modern phenomenon of the 24-hour availability of television around the world, with channels dedicated to scrolling news, non-stop music videos, exclusive children's channels and an endless rotation of films, as well as the rise of the reality television star. Written by Sean Kelly, who also accompanied Jim Kerr for vocals on the song, it was released as a special standalone digital download single on iTunes on 14 August 2005.

## 'Mighty Joe Moon' (G.L. Phillips)

Duration: 3.43

This was a cover version of the song performed by Grant Lee Buffalo and is the title track of their 1994 album. It appeared on the maxi-single release of 'Home', which also featured a remix of 'Home' as well as its official music video.

# 18

# *Graffiti Soul*

| | |
|---|---|
| UK: | 25 May 2009 |
| Personnel: | Additional drums: Jez Coad<br>Additional keyboards: Jez Coad, Andy Gillespie<br>Backing vocals: Jez Coad, Gordy Goudie, Sonia Jones, Katie Kissoon<br>Bass: Eddy Duffy<br>Drums: Mel Gaynor<br>Guitars, keyboards: Charlie Burchill, Gordy Goudie (track 2)<br>Percussion: Tom Hooper<br>Timpani: Jez Coad<br>Vocals: Jim Kerr |
| Duration: | 43 minutes (standard edition), 87 minutes (deluxe edition) |
| Produced by: | Jez Coad and Simple Minds |
| Chart position: | Switzerland: 8; UK: 10; US: - |

Writing for the album began in the autumn of 2006, after the band had completed a summer tour with a finale at Princes Street Gardens as part of the T on the Fringe festival in Edinburgh. There had already been some potential album material generated during the *Black and White* recording sessions, as well as material in the vault from writing sessions for *Cry*. Two tracks in particular, 'Light Travels' and 'Fortune Teller' (the then title of what would be renamed 'Magic', appearing on 2018 release *Walk Between Worlds*) had not made the list for inclusion on *Black and White* and were now forerunners for inclusion on *Graffiti Soul*. Jim Kerr had written in a diary post in 2007, twelve months prior to the T on the Fringe finale concert, that the band were ready to continue with producing material for their next album, although writing sessions did not appear to commence until the spring of 2008. Kerr intimated that so much material had been written that there was potential for the release of a double album.

Recording sessions took place at Rockfield Studios during the summer, the first time the band had been back to these studios to record since *Sparkle in the Rain* in the autumn of 1983. Recording for *Graffiti Soul* was completed in autumn 2008. News of the album's release was announced on the Simple Minds website on 13 February 2009 with a release date of 25 May 2009.

The album entered the UK chart at No. 10. The first top-ten album released by Simple Minds since *Good News from the Next World* in 1995, the album spent a total of four weeks in the UK top 100. It was set to offer three singles in total: 'Rockets', 'Stars Will Lead the Way' and 'This Is It'. Information on the Simple Minds website for *Graffiti Soul* confirms this, but I can find no evidence that 'This Is It' was ever released as a single.

During an interview to promote the album for a German radio station, Jim Kerr expressed gratitude to the Simple Minds fans that had been offering feedback and were involved in the promotion of the album, referring to these fans as 'graffiti soldiers'.

## The songs

### 'Moscow Underground'

Duration: 5.01

The opening track on *Graffiti Soul* starts with real intent. There is an immediate delivery within the first few chords of how the whole album will play out sonically. It stamps a feeling of something very fresh, but also reaching back to Simple Minds' past. It's a track that would not have sounded out of place on *Empires and Dance* or *Sons and Fascination*. As far as bass-playing style is concerned, I feel that Eddy Duffy was as close to Derek Forbes stylistically as any other bass player that has worked with Simple Minds. Lyrically, 'Moscow Underground' has a dark tone. It also manages to do what a wealth of other earlier Simple Minds songs had done, which is to be paradoxically uplifting yet melancholic. Performed live during the *Graffiti Soul* tour of 2009, it was a firm favourite among the fans. It has had sporadic inclusion in the set since its debut.

### 'Rockets'

Duration: 4.35

The album's lead single was released on 18 May 2009 as a digital download one week before the release of the album. 'Rockets' has a more classic pop-rock feel to it, opening with a Burchill guitar riff and underpinned by a solid rhythm section provided by Mel Gaynor on drums and Eddy Duffy on bass. Lyrically, the song appears to be about lovers in adversarial conflict. The lovers seem to relish their conflict, and the protagonist expresses a regret or lament when the relationship feels too quiet and comfortable. They appear to revel in the conflict in a 'what's better than sex? Make-up sex!' kind of way. It's a cycle the lovers seem reluctant to break. Does this mean that the relationship is doomed to fail? When interviewed on Belgian radio station Nostalgie in 2009, Jim Kerr described the song's subject as 'love wars ... then making peace and making love, and then still clashing'.

## 'Stars Will Lead the Way'

Duration: 3.25

A crack of snare and bass drum leads straight into a high and gleaming guitar riff from Burchill. A riff that, when played to Kerr in its early development, sparked an instant drive to work on the song further and consider it for inclusion on the future *Graffiti Soul* album. Kerr also described it as the point at which he found the momentum to get back into the recording studio.

Lyrically, it's a song about finding your way forward and not losing hope. The protagonist delivers a monologue of lament on decisions made which have resulted in them losing their way. The middle eight section sees the protagonist at the height of their disillusionment. But with another crack of drums and the return of that guitar riff, there is a light-bulb moment. There are some wonderful backing vocal harmonies on the track, provided by Katie Kissoon and Sonja Jones.

When marking the passing of scientist Stephen Hawking on the Simple Minds Facebook page on 14 March 2018, Jim Kerr posted a link to YouTube for 'Stars Will Lead the Way', accompanied by words by Hawking: 'Remember to look up at the stars and not down at your feet ... however difficult life may seem, there is always something you can do and succeed at. It matters that you just don't give up'. The song was released as a digital download, the album's second single, on 20 July 2009.

## 'Light Travels'

Duration: 4.12

Initially written by Sean Kelly and demoed during the *Black and White 050505* sessions. A cyclical piece with a gorgeously evocative melody that is played as a tender guitar riff by Burchill. Continuing the theme established by the previous track, the song exudes the mantra of 'keeping the faith'. There is light at the end of the tunnel. After the storm, the sun shines through again. These words of resilience in the lyrics give the song a more universal appeal. Kerr and Burchill worked on expanding what was initially a demo loop from Kelly and brought to it the signature Simple Minds uplifting heart. A rarity occurs on this track—the use of a key change. It rarely happens in Simple Minds songs, but it is used with aplomb on this track.

## 'Kiss and Fly'

Duration: 5.01

Inspired lyrically by Jim Kerr wanting to make use of a term he had spotted on a sign at Nice airport, 'Kiss and Fly' has otherwise ambiguous lyrics which make it feel more like a Simple Minds track of old. Kerr is masterful at making words sound cohesive and creating imagery in the mind, but if you dig a little deeper his words can leave you perplexed. Musically, it's a ballsy affair with a signature Mel Gaynor drum all over it, especially during the solo fill before the middle eight and bridge. The fading jangly guitar towards the end of the track sounds like Burchill channelling The Edge or Johnny Marr. Interestingly, both men have gone on record to say that it was Burchill's guitar playing that inspired their styles.

## 'Graffiti Soul'

Duration: 4.48

The song was one that sat on the backburner for a while. It arose from ideas sparked by Burchill and keyboard player Andy Gillespie. There were some early lyrics by Kerr, but the track was shelved until around 2008 during writing sessions for the album. Whatever the stumbling blocks were, they were overcome to such an extent that the song became the title track for the album.

When discussing the inspiration for the lyrics, Kerr spoke about his commute to producer Jez Coad's residence in greater London and a particular train journey when he overheard a conversation between a group of young men talking about the graffiti on the London underground trains. One described a particular artist's tag work as having 'graffiti soul'. There is also reference in the album liner notes to Kerr being quoted in a very early interview describing the band's music as having 'graffiti of the heart and soul'.

During an interview with the Belgian radio station Nostalgie in 2009, Kerr stated that Burchill had written the music for the song several years earlier. He also said he thought the word graffiti was of Italian origin, but had subsequently learned it came from Greek. In fact, Kerr was partly correct. The word as it is known today is of Italian origin—from the word 'graffiato', meaning 'scratched'. The word 'graffiato' originates from the Greek 'graphein' meaning 'to write'.

## 'Blood Type O'

Duration: 3.48

A slower tempo track, full of mystical sounds and imagery—one of which is the use of a Stylophone, of all things. The song also ends with the tones of an incoming Skype call. Speaking during promotional interviews prior to release, Kerr pondered whether Simple Minds might have been the first band to sample a Skype call tone on a song.

Kerr also said that the inspiration for the song's lyrics came partly from an article he had read from a Japanese newspaper about the recruitment of a baseball player for one of the US Major League teams, which said that this player exuded 'blood type O' qualities. In Japanese culture, 'type O' people are perceived to be 'natural leaders, ambitious, outgoing, confident and strong'. With O+ being the most common blood type in the world, that makes for a lot of ambitious confident leaders out there.

In an interview with Belgian radio station Nostalgie in May 2009, Kerr stated that the idea for the Skype call tone at the end of the song was his idea, but he didn't really know why he thought of it. He just said to the band 'let's do it'.

### 'This Is It'

Duration: 4.52

A song that was touted by Kerr and Burchill to the early members of Simple Minds when there was a tentative suggestion that they record two cover songs in celebration of thirty years as a live performing band in 2008, involving former members Derek Forbes, Mick MacNeil and Brian McGee. All sides initially seemed keen, with MacNeil, Forbes and McGee eager to be involved in the project. However, once in the studio things didn't go to plan, and the reunion floundered. Both Burchill and Kerr felt the song was too strong to be put on the shelf and decided to record it for the new Simple Minds album.

In discussing the track in a Facebook post in 2016, Kerr said:

> I guess some songs are destined to get all the attention while others languish in the semi-obscure. Books, movies, music, whatever ... I was always attracted to the obscure. Anyway, this is a cool song I reckon, and Charlie's sci-fi guitar on the coda always gets me in an emotional sense. We really should have made it much louder.

## Additional tracks

### 'Shadows and Light'

Duration: 2.50

A track that was recorded during the sessions at Rockfield but stylistically wasn't really in keeping with the theme of the album and was therefore added as a bonus track. The track contains a wonderful keyboard melody which has a rocking guitar riff to accompany it. An ambiguous track, lyrically. One gets the sense it's tenuously trying to speak of the Yin and Yang of life. The ups and the downs, good and bad. The contrast between the shadows and the light.

### 'Rockin' In the Free World' (N. Young)

Duration: 4.17

This was placed as a bonus track and was recorded with several other songs covered by the band. On the band's 2001 album, *Neon Lights*, they had covered another Neil Young song, 'The Needle and the Damage Done'. It seemed an obvious choice to cover this song, as Simple Minds were feeling a renaissance, having dug their way out of a creative low at the turn of the millennium. Not only was the sentiment of the song partly a rallying cry to 'keep on rocking', but it was also twinned with the hope that there would be a free world for all. The deluxe version of *Graffiti Soul* contained a bonus CD with recorded cover songs listed in track order below.

### *Searching for the Lost Boys*

This bonus 37-minute CD came into being due to the band giving themselves time to play around in the recording studio, partly to keep the momentum going once the main album recording session was over for the day. Conversely, some recording days started this way—with an impromptu covers jam. A song would be hastily chosen and band members would give themselves a limited amount of time—usually around 30 minutes—then they'd record a cover version of a song. Much merriment and enthusiasm ensued during these sessions, to the extent that a deluxe version of the album featuring a second CD containing a number of these covers was released.

## Track list

'Rockin' in the Free World' by Neil Young
'A Song from Under the Floorboards' by Magazine
'Christine' by Siouxsie and the Banshees
'(Get A) Grip (On Yourself)' by The Stranglers
'Let the Day Begin' by The Call
'(What's So Funny 'Bout) Peace, Love and Understanding' by Brinsley Schwarz
'Teardrop' by Massive Attack
'Whisky in the Jar' by Thin Lizzy
'Sloop John B' by The Beach Boys

19

# *Big Music*

| | |
|---|---|
| UK: | 3 November 2014 |
| Personnel: | Acoustic guitar: Gavin Goldberg<br>Additional guitars: Owen Parker<br>Additional programming: Iain Cook, Andy Gillespie, Steve Osborne, Owen Parker, Paul Statham<br>Backing vocals: Sarah Brown, Andy Gillespie, Gavin Goldberg, Clinton Outten AKA Roachie, Owen Parker<br>Bass: Ged Grimes<br>Drums: Mel Gaynor<br>Guitars: Charlie Burchill<br>Keyboards, programming: Charlie Burchill, Gavin Goldberg, Andy Wright<br>Vocals: Jim Kerr |
| Duration: | 52 minutes (standard edition), 129 minutes (deluxe edition + DVD) |
| Produced by: | Gavin Goldberg, Andy Wright, Simple Minds, Steve Osborne and Owen Parker |
| Chart position: | UK: 12; US: - |

The release of *Graffiti Soul* in 2009 saw Simple Minds achieve their best UK albums chart position in more than a decade. Despite this continued forward momentum to reclaim the hearts and minds of the general music-loving public, it would be another five years before the band released their follow-up to *Graffiti Soul*. Several tracks for *Big Music* had already been demoed by the spring of 2009, and in early 2010 more songs were added to this list.

There were certain personal factors that forced the progression onto the backburner. Firstly, Charlie Burchill decided to take some time out from writing and recording. This came at a time when Jim Kerr admitted to feeling his most creatively potent for some time, and he was reluctant to lose the momentum gained from the band making *Graffiti Soul*.

So, as Burchill stepped away for a sabbatical, Kerr kept writing and decided to produce his first and only (to date) solo offering, *Lostboy! AKA Jim Kerr*. Released in May 2010, Kerr toured the album with a cluster of dates with an ensemble of musicians, including Simple Minds drummer Mel Gaynor, keyboard player Andy Gillespie, backing vocalist Sarah Brown and future band bassist Ged Grimes. The tour was broken up into two parts and alternated between Simple Minds concerts that took place in the summer.

A second tour that started in October 2010 was cut short due to Kerr's mother's ongoing treatment for cancer. Irene Kerr passed away on 8 December 2010.

Simple Minds' tour commitments resumed in 2011, as well as writing and recording. Recording of demos for *Big Music* continued intermittently through 2012, with album recording sessions commencing in 2013. Final album recording sessions took place in the late summer of 2014. Some songs recorded during these sessions did not make the final cut for the album and to date have not yet been released.

As with *Sons and Fascination* and *Sister Feelings Call*, little from the sessions was discarded. The deluxe edition of the album is filled with an 18-song track list spread over two CDs, similar to 1981's *Sons/Sister* with their 15-track total output. The deluxe edition also featured a DVD containing full music videos, video clips and behind-the-scenes footage and band interviews. The album spent a total of four weeks in the UK chart, peaking at No. 12 in the first week. Details of the album posted on the Simple Minds website on release day state that four singles for the album had been released, listed in alphabetical order: 'Blindfolded', 'Honest Town', 'Let the Day Begin' and 'Midnight Walking'.

## The songs

### 'Blindfolded'

Duration: 5.24

Continuing the band's recent run of strong opening album tracks, 'Blindfolded' showcased the album's concept of being both a nod to the past electronic pulse of Simple Minds' Euro-dance vibe of the early 1980s, while offering a fresh and current twist. The song begins with a programmed beat and high guitar riff that builds to a crescendo, which moves to a guitar accompanied by drum and bass. The guitar simmers, making way for Kerr's vocals that almost channel Bob Dylan in their dilatory delivery.

The lyrics drive a mysterious narrative that implies that the characters portrayed in the lyrics are 'blindfolded'—a state that suggests ignorance or a mode of survival, of self-preservation in the presence of adversity. The chorus adds to the notion that to be blindfolded is to be ignorant to compassion and understanding. Is the character of Sugar, for example, blinded by seeing the 'fortune' she has already amassed? Is the man in the cellar a prisoner-of-war? Is the young child in the desert also a victim of conflict? Is Sugar an arms dealer? And how did the saints end up blindfolded too?

The song was debuted with a video premiere and posted on the band's Facebook page on 5 September 2014. Lyrics for the song were posted with a link to the YouTube video. In a Facebook post in November 2015 regarding a *Guardian* newspaper interview with producer Tony Visconti discussing the imminent release of David Bowie's album *Blackstar*, Jim Kerr mentioned that the interview had stated that Bowie had written about ISIS on *Blackstar* and declared that 'Blindfolded' had been about the same subject matter.

## 'Midnight Walking'

Duration: 3.54

A melodic shimmer of keyboards opens the track and is then quickly joined by drums and bass that exude an appealing 4/4 signature funk tone.

The song began in March 2013 when Simple Minds were on tour and playing a music festival in Tromso, Norway. The band had been informed of a great opportunity to experience the *Aurora Borealis* (Northern Lights) if they ventured out into the forest that evening (the night before the gig). Jim Kerr had fallen asleep earlier in the evening listening to a piece of music given to him by keyboard player Andy Gillespie. Awoken by a call from Charlie Burchill some hours later, Kerr was then too tired to join the rest of the band on the trek to view the natural light spectacle.

However, the missed opportunity sparked the initial idea for the song. When Kerr awoke again in the early hours of the morning, he was instantly spurred to write down lyrics that had formed in his mind.

Some of the lyrics suggest the internal imagery of Godfrey Reggio's 1982 non-narrative documentary *Koyaanisqatsi*, and its depiction of modern-day human existence. 'Koyaanisqatsi' is a Native American Hopi word meaning 'life out of balance'. The accompanying video for 'Midnight Walking', directed by Roger Sargent, uses timelapse footage reminiscent of Reggio's film. One wonders whether Sargent was influenced by Reggio's work?

The song was the fourth and final single from *Big Music*. The video was premiered on the Guardian newspaper website on 24 March 2015, followed by a digital download release including several mixes on 20 April 2015.

## 'Honest Town'

Duration: 4.47

Subtle guitar with an accompanying slow and melodic synth intros the song. Its title comes from Kerr's mother Irene often referring to Glasgow as 'an honest town'. The song is a lament and a homage to the city, as well as a dedication to Kerr's mother. The city meant so much to Irene that when the Kerr family entertained the idea of emigrating to Australia when Jim was around eight years old, the pull of the city was so strong that it was her decision to stay that kept the family in Glasgow.

On a personal level I can appreciate this, experiencing it on its flip side. Having been born in Sydney, growing up and living there until my late twenties and then moving to England and living there for twenty years before finally relocating and settling in Glasgow, I can relate to the city's magical pull.

The song was the result of Kerr working with Chvrches member Iain Cook on what was to be Kerr's follow-up to solo project *Lostboy! AKA Jim Kerr*. The song was one of several collaboratively penned compositions that made it onto *Big Music*.

As lead single, 'Honest Town' made its premiere on BBC Radio 2 on 24 September 2014 and was released on streaming services shortly after. A video for the song was released on YouTube the following week.

## 'Big Music'

Duration: 4.12

The song had been around for some time and kept being put on the backburner by Jim Kerr as he felt he couldn't quite get a handle on the lyrics. Then, finally, the most unlikely of inspirations came. Kerr went to see Prince in concert and, in a story relayed by Kerr in explaining the concept of the song, Prince performed a style of music that meant he veered away from playing the bigger hits from his back catalogue. This had frustrated Kerr, as he had been expecting to hear all the recognisable signature tunes. Kerr found himself at the gig cursing what he was being exposed to and wishing to be swept away by the anthemic tracks that he knew well as a Prince fan.

In an interview for the EPK for the album Kerr said:

> I remember standing during the gig and just thinking, 'Give me the music. Give me the songs! Give me the songs that make me feel ecstatic. Give me the songs that change my world'. Because Prince is one of these artists that indeed could lay claim to that.

Musically, it comes in with the full Simple Minds atmospheric bombast. It starts quietly with some soft programmed percussion and synths then builds to a thumping arrival of drums, bass and riffing guitar. The joy of live music is the motto of this track. As such, the song was in the live set during Simple Minds tours from 2013 until 2018.

## 'Human'

Duration: 3.42

This track feels like the weakest link in the chain on *Big Music*. A standard modern pop song. It has a good musical motif, expressed in the guitar riff and keyboard melody. The chorus is catchy, but the song doesn't feel powerful enough. It could have been one that sat on the backburner, as its subject matter seems to allude to Kerr's creative crisis in the late 90s/early 00s. I feel that the 'la, la la' lines towards the end of the song are a bad parody of the ones that have so much power in 'Don't You (Forget About Me)'. They seem to weaken the intent of the song. 'Human' would have fared better without them. I can't help but feel that its place on the standard edition of the album should have been given to a stronger track, either 'Liaison' or 'Bittersweet', which were both relegated to bonuses on the deluxe edition of the album.

## 'Blood Diamonds'

Duration: 4.21

A soft layer of guitar chords slowly merges into a sweet melodic synth hook and a deft electronic drum accompaniment. The guitar hook is soft and rhythmic. The overall feel is that of a ballad. Another track that was composed between Kerr, Burchill and Iain Cook. It's a song of lament and lost love. A love that has ended, either by intent or by accident. There may have been a parting of the ways in a physical sense—a death, or the desire of a physical separation—but the bonding of souls and hearts remains unshakeable. The physical bond may die, but the spiritual bond endures.

Within the chorus, Kerr uses a technique similar to one known in poetry as an enjambment where two lines of poetry 'run over' without punctuation. Kerr plays with the effect for the lines 'Once we were blood/diamonds to the end', blood diamonds being a term used for diamonds mined in a war zone. Perhaps it was a conscious effort on Kerr's part to give the term a more emotionally uplifting meaning?

## 'Let the Day Begin' (M. Been)

Duration: 5.10

Jim Kerr has often mentioned the influence that the band The Call had on Simple Minds musically, and that of band member Michael Been on him personally. When Simple Minds toured the United States in the mid-1980s, The Call were their support. In fact, Been confessed to Kerr the influence the bass chords on 'Waterfront' had on the musicality of 'Let the Day Begin'. In this sense, Simple Minds choosing to cover The Call's song is Simple Minds covering The Call abstractly 'covering' Simple Minds. 'Let the Day Begin' had originally been recorded for the bonus CD *Searching for the Lost Boys*, which was included in the deluxe edition of *Graffiti Soul*. When recording tracks for *Big Music*, Simple Minds decided to rerecord the track for the album. An invitation was put out via the band's social media for fans to submit a short video of their daily routine and a selection of the entries were chosen to feature in a video for the track. The video for 'Let the Day Begin' premiered on 12 December 2014 on the Simple Minds website. A digital download release of the song followed.

## 'Concrete and Cherry Blossom'

Duration: 3.33

With a signature Mel Gaynor blast of drums opening the track, married with a programming crank and a bass that follows with a wonderful hook underpinning a fantastic guitar riff, it's a great rock song. Another song inspired by Glasgow, it had originally come to life during the recording of *Graffiti Soul*. Jim Kerr said in interviews that the inspiration for the lyrics came from a conversational exchange between himself and some young boys in Glasgow, in which one of the boys expressed a desire to live in Japan. This led to the idea of the fusion of the concrete of the Glasgow streets and the cherry blossoms that grow there melding with the symbolism of the trees in Japan and the cityscape of Tokyo.

## 'Imagination'

Duration: 3.42

The track started life as a Burchill instrumental titled 'Odyssey'. During a radio interview in 2015 Kerr said that when the music was given to him for writing lyrics, he initially felt it was so strong it didn't require his lyrical input. Then, having read the words of a professor stating that 'the greatest quality man has is imagination', Kerr was inspired to write lyrics with the concept of the human imagination as their theme.

## 'Kill or Cure'

Duration: 4.12

This track started out as a *Lostboy! AKA* song intended for inclusion on Jim Kerr's follow-up solo album. It germinated from writing sessions with Paul Statham for Kerr's solo album in 2009. It was performed during several Lostboy! AKA gigs in 2010. From there the track was added to musically by Charlie Burchill. During the latter stages of the recording sessions, *Big Music* co-producers Andy Wright and Gavin Goldberg decided to mix the track in such a way that it perplexed Kerr and he wasn't keen. He soon U-turned on his feeling and the song was added to the album. It is sensual, with a repetitive chorus that conveys the notion that the only person who can help you is you.

## 'Broken Glass Park'

Duration: 4.41

Originally written in 2010 and destined to be a track on Jim Kerr's solo work as Lostboy! AKA—in fact the song was performed as part of the Lostboy! AKA live set—it was eventually added to the Simple Minds repertoire. It was performed live during the Simple Minds tours of 2011 and recorded for the *Celebrate: Greatest Hits* compilation released in 2013. It was then rerecorded and added to *Big Music*. The music was initially written by Owen Parker, a writer Kerr had worked with for other Lostboy! AKA tracks. Kerr's lyrics are strongly autobiographical, with the 'broken glass park' in question a thinly veiled nod to Queen's Park in Glasgow's southside, the hangout of choice for Kerr, Burchill and their friends during the mid to late 1970s. This was the period when the band that would eventually become Simple Minds was forming.

### 'Spirited Away'

Duration: 4.09

Another musical composition written with Owen Parker around the same time as 'Broken Glass Park.' It is one of the most tender ballads in the band's more recent repertoire. Jim Kerr, when discussing the song during a radio interview around the time of the album's release, said that lyrically it's driven along via a first-person perspective. He also mentioned the fact that co-producer on *Big Music* Andy Wright had steered him towards opening the track *in medias res*. By Kerr's account it means the song begins with what was once the second verse. What happened to the first verse? Who knows? The song describes a separation, a chasm between two people, possibly relatives (taking note of the line 'together since birth')—and perhaps suggesting the death of one that seems to happen to unintendedly or accidentally. It is both soft and subtly heart-breaking.

## Deluxe Edition tracks

### 'Swimming Towards the Sun'

Duration: 5.16

A new recording of the Hunter/Stevens song that Simple Minds had originally recorded for *Our Secrets Are the Same* in 1999. The musical composition remained the same although it was rerecorded by the band. Jim Kerr also added some newly written lyrics to the song.

### 'Bittersweet'

Duration: 3.58

A dark and sensual song with Jim Kerr delivering the words in a Cohen-esque style –*Sprechgesang*—lowering his voice to a bass tone during the opening chords. The song initially came to life as a demo during the *Black and White 050505* recording sessions in 2005 under the title of 'Secret Love'. It was then worked on further during the *Graffiti Soul* sessions in 2009 but eventually dropped from the album, only to finally make it on to the deluxe edition of *Big Music*. It was also performed live by the band during the subsequent tour of the album in 2015. A quote (most likely from Kerr) when a link to the song was posted on the band's Facebook page in January 2015 said, 'The dark has its light side—the light side, its dark'.

### 'Liaison'

Duration: 4.37

One of the dark horses chosen for the deluxe edition of *Big Music* as it was deemed not 'in keeping' with the tone of the standard edition of the album. It includes a synth melody that is reminiscent of Mick MacNeil's earlier work. Obviously, the memories of MacNeil's work and his influence still seep into some of Burchill's own synth layering.

It was a song that Kerr and Burchill worked on with producer Steve Hillage, whom they had previously worked with on *Sons and Fascination/Sister Feelings Call*. A 30-year gap between collaborations had not diminished the influences each party brought with them into the studio with sessions taking place in Edinburgh.

Both this song and 'Bittersweet' quickly became fan favourites, which led to some perplexity as to why these two tracks were not chosen for the standard version of the album. In responding to this line of questioning from fans, Jim Kerr said it was a decision taken due to the feeling that these two songs were stylistically different to the rest of the album. With its strong reception from fans, 'Liaison' found itself in the live set on the *Big Music* tour of 2015.

## 'Riders On the Storm' (The Doors)

Duration: 3.47

A cover of the original classic track by The Doors. Both Burchill and Kerr had namechecked The Doors as an influence on the music of Simple Minds many times. In a 2023 look at the life of Jim Morrison that Jim Kerr recorded for the BBC Radio 4 series *Archive on 4*, Kerr recounted the story of the first time he'd heard the song, seated in the family car with his younger brother Paul, while waiting for their father who was having a pint in a pub (different times!) during an afternoon drive. The weather being constantly changeable in the west of Scotland, Kerr recalled a looming storm making itself present while the song played over the car radio. The lyrics about a killer at large sent a spine-tingling frisson through the 11-year-old Kerr as he and his brother waited for their father to return. The song had left an indelible mark. It was another piece of bonus material that found its way onto the live set for the *Big Music* tour of 2015.

## 'Dancing Barefoot' (P. Smith and I. Kral)

Duration: 4.02

A new recording of the Patti Smith Group song, this time sung by band member and backing vocalist Sarah Brown. The song had been previously recorded and released as a track by the band on *Neon Lights*, as well as being released as a single from the album in 2001. This track was also performed by Brown during the *Big Music* tour of 2015.

## 'Blindfolded [Reprise]'

Duration: 4.23

This was the original recording of the song from the early sessions that had taken place with Steve Hillage. This version is the Hillage-produced version. It has no drum track and the lyrics are subtly different to the main album version.

20

# *Acoustic*

| | |
|---|---|
| UK: | 11 November 2016 (CD), 25 November 2016 (LP) |
| Personnel: | Accordion: Charlie Burchill<br>Additional arrangements: Gordy Goudie<br>Arrangements: Charlie Burchill<br>Backing vocals: Sarah Brown, Ged Grimes, KT Tunstall (track 2)<br>Bass: Ged Grimes, KT Tunstall (track 2)<br>Guitars: Charlie Burchill, Gordy Goudie, KT Tunstall (track 2)<br>Harmonica: Gordy Goudie<br>Percussion: Cherisse Osei<br>Vocal arrangement: KT Tunstall (track 2)<br>Vocals: Jim Kerr, KT Tunstall (track 2) |
| Duration: | 58 minutes (CD), 111 minutes (LP) |
| Produced by: | Gavin Goldberg, Andy Wright and Simple Minds |
| Chart position: | UK: 16; US: - |

## Track list

'The American'
'Promised You a Miracle'
'Glittering Prize'
'See the Lights'
'New Gold Dream (81-82-83-84)'
'Someone Somewhere in Summertime'
'Waterfront'

'Sanctify Yourself'
'Chelsea Girl'
'Alive and Kicking'
'Don't You (Forget About Me)'
'Long Black Train'

## LP bonus tracks

'Stand by Love'
'Speed Your Love to Me'
'Light Travels'

This was a concept that had been bandied around on and off for several years but would quickly be dismissed, particularly by Jim Kerr who seemed worried that if the band went ahead with the idea, it would end up a 'bongos on the beach'-style endeavour. On a more serious note, Kerr felt their songs had such power and such sonic scope that to record acoustic versions would potentially dilute this.

In 2014, with the chance to try out a few songs on the *Chris Evans Breakfast Show* on BBC Radio 2, Kerr had a change of heart, spurred on by the fans who had listened to the show and lapped up the acoustically arranged songs. Thus, the real potential of the concept started to form. But promotion of *Big Music* was to dominate band activities for the immediate future, taking up the vast majority of 2015.

The following year was a naturally occurring 'rest year' for the band. There was a very limited amount of touring scheduled for 2016 and, as such, Simple Minds could road test the concept of the acoustic theme. If they were to produce an album, naturally a tour would follow. And if they were to do an acoustic album, the tour that would follow its release would have to have an acoustically arranged set. During the early months of 2016, it was all systems go on making the acoustic concept a reality.

The album was released in two physical formats, CD and LP. In a reverse to the norm, it was the double vinyl LP that featured bonus material, while the CD was a standard edition housed in a cardboard cover. With a double LP containing the same number of tracks on the CD spread over three sides of vinyl, it left one side spare for extra tracks. These tracks became highly sought after by fans who had only purchased the CD format of the album.

As is the consistent trend with Simple Minds, particularly in their more recent years, a cover song was chosen for the album. This time it was a track by Richard Hawley titled 'Long Black Train'.

The album was officially showcased live with a debut performance of the entire album plus extras for the BBC *In Concert* series produced by Radio 2. The band performed at the Hackney Empire on 10 November 2016, the eve of the release of *Acoustic*. Between April and June 2017, the band toured the *Acoustic* album with a 48-date tour of mainland Europe, the UK and Ireland.

The album entered the UK chart on release and stayed within the top 100 for a total of six weeks, spending the first two weeks within the top forty, peaking at No. 16 in the first week of release.

# 21

# *Walk Between Worlds*

| | |
|---|---|
| UK: | 2 February 2018 |
| Personnel: | Acoustic guitar: Gordy Goudie<br>Additional backing vocals: Catherine AD (AKA The Anchoress), Gavin Goldberg, Clinton Outten AKA Roachie, Emily Parker, Hatty Parker, Andy Wright<br>Bass: Ged Grimes<br>Drums and percussion: Mel Gaynor, Cherisse Osei<br>Guitars: Charlie Burchill<br>Keyboards: Charlie Burchill, Owen Parker<br>Piano: Peter John Vettese<br>Programming: Charlie Burchill, Gavin Goldberg, Owen Parker, Andy Wright<br>Vocals: Sarah Brown, Jim Kerr |
| Duration: | 41 minutes |
| Produced by: | Gavin Goldberg, Andy Wright and Simple Minds |
| Chart position: | UK: 4; US: - |

As with most Simple Minds albums, writing and recording for the new album started immediately after the completion of the previous one. In this case, recording for *Walk Between Worlds* began straight after *Big Music* was completed. In fact, after the *Big Music* tours of 2015, the band largely rested during 2016, with just a handful of concerts taking place throughout the year. The largest concert of 2016 saw them perform at the Hackney Empire as part of the BBC's *In Concert* series. Simple Minds performed an acoustic set, the majority of which would appear on the *Acoustic* album that was released the day after the concert.

In 2017, a short tour of Australia and New Zealand (not incorporating the *Acoustic* set), as well as an *Acoustic* tour in Europe and the UK, followed. Between the two tours, recording for *Walk Between Worlds* was completed.

Jim Kerr kept fans on social media updated with band activity between tours, discussing songs that were being worked on. During the earlier recording sessions for the album, Kerr posted about 'Silent Kiss'. He had also mentioned 'Planet Zero', but this track would not get an official release until the following album.

*Walk Between Worlds* was officially announced as the follow-up to *Big Music* (in terms of original material) on Simple Minds' social media platforms on 20 November 2017. On the day of release, Jim Kerr and Charlie Burchill appeared at HMV in Glasgow for an album signing. *Walk Between Worlds* entered the UK chart at No. 4, their first album to make the top five since *Good News from the Next World.*

## The songs

### 'Magic'

Duration: 4.35

Hope springs eternal in many of Jim Kerr's lyrics. A track like 'Magic', initially titled 'Fortune Teller' and evolving from the *Black and White 050505* recording sessions, is a prime example of the fountain of hope that springs forth in Kerr's song-writing. He credits this vision as being sparked by his partnership with Charlie Burchill. Of course, one excels in life through focus and drive, but luck also plays a part—as if by magic.

The song is fundamentally autobiographical, encapsulating the image of the young, directionless Kerr during his mid-teens. Focused on the period before leaving school, when he'd become disheartened about the fact that football stardom would forever elude him, he had not yet realised that an alternative path was going to offer itself.

Electronic drum fills with synth programming intro the track musically, swiftly accompanied by a sweet, short melodic guitar riff. The whole rhythm and tone of the song opens the theme of the ethereal underbelly of the album.

### 'Summer'

Duration: 4.57

Ged Grimes channels former Simple Minds bassist Derek Forbes with the opening chords to this bright, shining 21st-century party anthem. As the full set of instrumentation comes in, an anthemic vocalese chorus of 'a-a-a-o' drives the melody. The track conjures up an atmosphere of great times with a meteorological smorgasbord: of course, with the band's original members hailing from Glasgow, there is a sharp hint of reality in the opening lines of 'Here comes summer/Here comes rain' and 'Here comes lightning now/I like the way it shoots'. Released as a digital single for the album in May 2018, several mixes of the track were produced including versions by Gary Numan and Ade Fenton, released the same month.

## 'Utopia'

Duration: 4.15

Opening with a fade-in of an eerie and haunting guitar riff and then accompanied by a soft drum almost playing in reverse and a wonderful wash of synths, 'Utopia' feels immediately otherworldly. A soft, almost breathless vocal by Kerr includes words that provide abstract images of a record playing and dancing, the Northern Lights, snowflakes and kisses, a sense of euphoria and transcendental transportation. It is a song that ripples my skin with goosebumps. Its slow pace gives it trip-hop sensibilities. One could well imagine it being a long-lost track from Massive Attack.

The cleverness of Kerr's lyrics is most apparent in the enjambment over the lines ''Cause I can't tell if these memories belong to/Utopia'. That is an example of poetic art. When heard and not read, you can appreciate the sonic enjambment—I can't tell if the memories I have of Utopia are mine or yours. Or is it more a sense of questioning if the memories are real or surreal and not of this place?

## 'The Signal and the Noise'

Duration: 5.19

A fabulous catchy synth hook intros the track, which then merges with a catchy rhythm section centre foundation. Finally, the body of the song's melody is brought in by Burchill's guitar. There is something foreboding and epic in the musical structure, bringing a much heavier meaning to the lyrics, which drive home the idea of keeping a positive focus in a world of negativity. Be sure to see the wood for the trees, be true to yourself and those you love, do good and be virtuous. Negativity is the enemy and positivity is key. The song received a radio debut during Steve Lamacq's BBC Radio 6 Music show in early January 2018. The following week, the track was available as a digital single and made available on streaming services.

## 'In Dreams'

Duration: 4.16

A short, programmed flurry, then the angelic tones of Sarah Brown deliver the choral lines of 'In dreams nothing says we're unable/In dreams forever's never too long'. It's a rather mystical, abstract lyrical verse—both tangibly aspirational and sensual. Again, there is a subliminal meteorological thread weaving through the tracks on *Walk Between Worlds*. This track talks about a 'freeze' that 'hits from the east' which, given the timing of the album's release and subsequent tour, seemed prescient as the UK was about to be hit by 'the Beast from the East' (a strong Arctic blast leading to blizzard-like weather conditions in the late winter of 2018).

## 'Barrowland Star'

Duration: 6.25

The track begins with a pop sensibility, but ends with full sweeping rock glory with a guitar solo from Charlie Burchill, the likes of which had never been heard on a Simple Minds song before. The song feels autobiographical in nature, but Kerr downplayed the idea of it being directly about the band when I spoke to him about the lyrics around the time of its release. The song conjures up all the imagery of a night at the Barrowland Ballroom in Glasgow, from the viewpoint of a young band performing there. The venue had all but been abandoned during the 1970s, intermittently used as a roller disco hall. In 1983 Simple Minds decided to use the ballroom to record their 'Waterfront' video, and perform gigs to showcase the *Sparkle in the Rain* album a few months later. Then the venue re-emerged as the world-renowned concert hall it is today. Locally, the venue is synonymous with Simple Minds, explaining their choice to open the *Walk Between Worlds* tour there.

### 'Walk Between Worlds'

Duration: 5.13
One of the most musically cinematic and orchestrally epic openings to a Simple Minds song. What ends the previous track musically segues perfectly into the opening of this. The song speaks of a world in chaos that is only compounded by constant conflict. It's a call for understanding of different sides, thoughts and feelings. A need for centre ground, to 'walk between worlds' and see both sides of the argument, and thus perhaps attain a more peaceful and cohesive existence.

### 'Sense of Discovery'

Duration: 6.27
Initially written in partnership with Owen Parker in 2009, the song began life as a track for Jim Kerr's solo project, being performed live in the touring set when Kerr toured *Lostboy! AKA Jim Kerr* during 2010. The track was destined to be included on a follow-up to the album. But as the continuation of the project was placed on hiatus, so was the song. At the time Kerr felt the song was somehow incomplete—missing a certain element that he struggled to put a finger on. The song resurfaced during the recording of *Walk Between Worlds*. Charlie Burchill added to the musical structure of the song, which included the evocative wavering programmed intro to the song, and Kerr decided it should be recorded as a Simple Minds track. In the latter stages of the recording sessions for *Walk Between Worlds*, Kerr had a lyrical breakthrough and found the missing piece—a choral harmony akin to those used on 'Alive and Kicking', with added lyrics.

## Deluxe Edition tracks

### 'Silent Kiss'

Duration: 4.58
The melody reminds me of a pentatonic scale that is used primarily in East Asian music. Kerr sings in a slightly higher register than is normal for him. There's an urgency in his voice when he sings the opening lyrics 'Think of me/Will you

please think of me'. Then there's a nostalgia for what feels like was a more wondrous time: a dalliance with a lover before the reality leads to a 'move back home'. There is something beautifully ethereal about this track. It could have been on *New Gold Dream*; it has that kind of celestial quality to it. The song was deemed not to be in keeping with the theme of *Walk Between Worlds*, so it became a deluxe edition bonus track.

### 'Angel Underneath My Skin' (M. Kerr and E. Karst)

Duration: 3.34

A song written by Kerr's brother Mark, along with Erikah Karst. It had been on the backburner for some years before being recorded and appearing as a bonus track on *Walk Between Worlds*. It is one of several Mark Kerr-penned tracks that have been recorded and released on Simple Minds albums. The theme of the track feels in keeping with the recurring themes of Simple Minds songs: dark, otherworldly, but ultimately full of hope.

### 'Dirty Old Town' (E. MacColl)

Duration: 4.54

A track that was performed extensively during the *Acoustic t*our, this live version was recorded at the London Palladium on 27 May 2017, and subsequently became a deluxe edition bonus track.

22

# *Direction of the Heart*

| | |
|---|---|
| UK: | 21 October 2022 |
| Personnel: | Backing vocals: Sarah Brown, Gary Clark, Gavin Goldberg, Jim Kerr, Kathleen MacInnes, Andy Wright<br>Bass: Charlie Burchill, Ged Grimes<br>Drums: Cherisse Osei<br>Guest vocals: Russell Mael (track 3)<br>Guitars: Charlie Burchill, Ged Grimes<br>Gong: Ged Grimes<br>Keyboards, programming: Charlie Burchill, Ged Grimes<br>Synths: Andy Gillespie, Ged Grimes<br>Vocals: Jim Kerr |
| Duration: | 38 minutes, 48 minutes (deluxe edition), 57 minutes (super deluxe edition) |
| Produced by: | Gavin Goldberg, Andy Wright and Simple Minds |
| Chart position: | UK: 4; US: - |

Recording of the album began in Sicily in 2020. During the worldwide lockdown resulting from the Covid-19 pandemic, Kerr's hotel Villa Angela in Taormina was temporarily closed for the peak tourist seasons of 2020 and 2021. After initially being holed up in Scotland during the early stages of lockdown, Kerr managed to travel to France and then on to Italy in the summer of 2020.

Reunited with Burchill once he arrived in Sicily, and with an unused space in the form of the hotel, the duo decided to make use of the hotel for recording purposes. Reflecting on this period Kerr said: 'Within my experience it is in periods of crisis that opportunity often presents itself. In our case, cut off from the rest of the world at that moment, we took the opportunity to do the best work we could under those circumstances'.

It is highly probable that some recording of demo tracks for the album took place in 2019, particularly during the earlier months of the year and before Kerr's father's illness escalated in severity.

Further recording sessions happened in Germany and the UK in 2021. Details of the album's release were unveiled on the Simple Minds website and through their social media on 14 June 2022.

Upon release the album made it to No. 4 in the UK chart, repeating the result of *Walk Between Worlds* in 2018.

During an interview with music journalist Kyle Meredith in December 2022, Kerr was asked what the overriding story was that the band wanted to convey through the album. Kerr's response was:

> We wanted to conjure up the ghosts of the past because that's all you can do—try to conjure it up but ... that was then, this is now. We've changed. You've changed. The world has changed. Technology has changed, but there are certain things—certain sounds, and a certain attitude that we felt if we get right conjures up those early days of Simple Minds. And that's great, but we don't just want to be wallowing in nostalgia. We want it to feel 'in the moment', we want it to feel contemporary but, hang on ... that's a contradiction in terms? It may well be, but there is a sweet spot somewhere within where those two things can bridge and that's where we were hoping we could land.

## The songs

### 'Vision Thing'

Duration: 4.39

A song that Jim Kerr states was inspired by his father, Jimmy, as the person who fuelled the younger Kerr's aspirations for carving out a successful life for himself. In similar vein to 'Magic' as the opening track for *Walk Between Worlds*, 'Vision Thing' signals an intent and introduces the overall theme and tone for the album. The song started life as a yet-to-be-titled song in the summer of 2019. Kerr states on the band's Facebook page that he felt this new tune, even in its embryonic stage, was destined to be the opening track for the next Simple Minds album. It was the lead single from the album and was released on the same day as the announcement of the album's release, 14 June 2022.

### 'First You Jump'

Duration: 4.23

The track opens with a lovely keyboard melody, which is then followed with a rocking riff and crashing drums. Quite the signature Simple Minds intro. The guitar, drums and bass simmer to make way for Kerr's voice, which delivers lyrics that ponder a life in decline, a feeling of a world in flux and a personal crisis. A life spinning out of control, unable to see the wood for the trees. Yet you need to take the plunge—you must commit to the jump first, as only then will you get the wings to fly. Life is full of risks and sometimes we must take those risks to make our lives better. To create a better future for ourselves and become 'what you're meant to'. Such is the allegory that filters through this rocking tune. The song is powerful and uplifting. The track was written in partnership with current Simple Minds bassist, Ged Grimes. The song was released as the second single from *Direction of the Heart* on 5 September 2022, with a video featuring the entire band recorded at the Teatro Antico di Taormina in Sicily in July 2022.

### 'Human Traffic'

Duration: 4.17

Released as a single on 9 December 2022, the title of the track was truncated to 'Traffic'. The song was described in promotional information on the band's social media as being 'JG Ballard-inspired'. In reading the lyrics to the song 'There's a novel that's in my brain/About a drowning man and he's waving', I had theorised that the lyrics might have been inspired by a specific Ballard work, but I cannot find anything to substantiate this theory. Therefore, I can only assume that this description is somewhat erroneous and should read as being 'Ballard-esque'. The novelist's work is steeped in a dystopian science-fiction realm.

Further detailing the inspiration for the lyrics, Jim Kerr is quoted as saying 'I ended up writing about a game called "Human Traffic", where the people get so immersed they can no longer tell the difference between reality and the game.' This reminds me somewhat of the Pokémon Go craze in 2016.

The origins of the song go back to summer 2009. A demo recording was made during sessions in February 2010 when the band were gathering potential material for *Big Music*. The song was originally titled 'Human Trafficking' and perhaps the line 'Friday trucks them in from the sea' is a legacy of these lyrical beginnings.

The song's musicality is juxtaposed with the lyrics of the track. Kerr described the addition of Sparks' Russell Mael on vocals as an attempt to add 'some laughing gas to the song'. The single release contains an acoustic mix of the song with alternative lyrics to the chorus 'high on dreams and memories' as opposed to 'high on fumes and misery'.

### 'Who Killed Truth?'

Duration: 3.58

When discussing the song Kerr said:

> I've always liked artists that tackle the big themes, the themes of the day and, it's always good if you can be a little Zeitgeist-y. It's a phrase that I saw pop up quite a bit over the last few years, especially in America—'who killed truth?' It's a great song title. It could even be Shakespearean, could it not? I can imagine

one of the characters in Hamlet saying, 'But sire, who killed truth?' So, it's kind of timeless. It's just beautiful.

## 'Solstice Kiss'

Duration: 5.23

Another song written in partnership with bass player Ged Grimes, who is responsible for creating the musical structure of the tune. When discussing the song's development, Jim Kerr said:

> When Ged came up with the instrumental idea, I could feel the mists in it. You could feel a bright winter morning—or I could anyway. And my job as a lyric writer apart from coming up with complimentary melodies is to try and tell the listener what the picture is to this music. I could just feel a landscape in it and a romance as well. It was such a sweet, haunting melody. I would have been writing it about this time of year [late autumn], in Scotland, heading towards solstice—and it all just bled into the song.

The finishing touches to the song were recorded in Sicily during the Covid-19 pandemic in 2020. On the album's release, the track quickly became a fan favourite. Eventually the song was released as the fourth and final single from the album on 6 October 2023, as a special black and gold spattered 12-inch vinyl record. It entered the UK physical singles chart on 19 October at a peak position of No. 2.

The song was also used during a promotional advertising campaign for the Macallan whisky distillery titled 'The Spirit of 1926,' a dramatisation featuring actress Emily Mortimer. The short film recounts the story of the most expensive bottle of Macallan to be sold and how Janet Harbinson, known affectionately as Nettie, came to play a major part in its creation.

The Macallan website also featured a video interview with Jim Kerr and Charlie Burchill about Simple Minds' involvement with the promotional film, as well as an edited version of the song featuring concert footage recorded at the Teatro Antico di Taormina in July 2022, combined with footage of Kerr and Burchill walking around the grounds of the Macallan distillery. The song was a highlight of the opening leg of the *Global* tour 2024.

During an interview after the album's release, Kerr intimated that 'Solstice Kiss' might not have appeared on the album were it not for the interest the Macallan distillery took in it when looking for a piece of music from Simple Minds to use for 'The Spirit of 1926' campaign.

## 'Act of Love'

Duration: 4.02

A song whose earliest incarnation coincides with the formation of Simple Minds. The song was the then unsigned band's opening track at their inaugural gig at

Satellite City, Glasgow, on 17 January 1978. It remained in the set as they played various venues including a weekly residency at the Mars Bar, located just off St Enoch Square, during 1978. The song's riff and basic musical structure were written by Charlie Burchill just a few days before Simple Minds' first official gig. Jim Kerr quickly came up with lyrics for the piece and they had produced a thrilling and rocking opening number. The song evolved during the months that followed when Mick MacNeil and Derek Forbes joined the band. Eventually the song lost its prestige as new tunes were written on a regular basis. By the end of 1978, the song had faded into obscurity.

That was until 1998, when the very limited run of *The Early Years 1977-1978* CD was released but subsequently withdrawn. A demo version of 'Act of Love', recorded at Glasgow's CaVa Studios, featured on the CD.

Twenty years later Kerr came across a YouTube clip of a remix that incorporated the riff from 'Act of Love'. He thought it sounded great and felt that he and Burchill needed to go back to the song and complete it. From there, work started on preparing the song for commercial release. New lyrics were written, backing vocals put in and some new musical elements added.

Finally, on 17 January 2022, on the forty-fourth anniversary of the band's first gig, 'Act of Love' was released as a special stand-alone digital single, achieving minor UK singles chart success. Although added to the album, it is not considered its first/lead single.

During an interview Jim Kerr had with Kyle Meredith in December 2022, Kerr said of the track: 'And even the song title itself, "Act of Love". When people say "Oh, you've been making records, making music for forty years now. What keeps you doing it?" It's the love of it that keeps us doing it'.

### 'Natural'

Duration: 3.26

An upbeat song that has a modern disco feel to it. Lyrically, the song appears to be about trying to escape the worst that the world has to offer by experiencing the good things. A cleansing, the washing away of negativity with positive reinforcement—to 'feel natural'. A way of navigating losing direction and getting back on the right path. Perhaps through a shared experience? Musically, it's filled with synths and distorted guitar riffs. It's an energising tune but possibly not the strongest track on the album and most likely destined to remain an 'album-only' obscurity.

### 'Planet Zero'

Duration: 4.10

A song that had been through various stages of progression, with talk of it being a track on several Simple Minds albums including *Big Music* and *Walk Between Worlds*.

The first recording sessions involving the song saw Burchill and Kerr entering the recording studio with producer Steve Hillage during August 2011. The duo had previously worked with Hillage on 1981's twin offering *Sons and Fascination/Sister Feelings Call*. The recording sessions with Hillage in 2011 resulted in the production of several demo tracks, 'Planet Zero' among them.

Further development of the song continued in 2012 with a full musical production recorded during sessions for *Big Music* in 2014. This recording was a strong contender for inclusion on *Big Music*, but the consensus was that the song still required further work, and it was placed on the backburner once again.

In a Facebook post in 2014, Jim Kerr was adamant the song would eventually have a commercial release. It took another eight years, but Kerr was true to his word. Writing about it during its development, Kerr described the track as 'thundering space-rock' and suggested its sound was that of 'Prince set to the background of Hawkwind'. This description conjures 'Silver Machine' blended with 'When Doves Cry', which really does come close to the mark in describing the sound of 'Planet Zero'.

Lyrically, the song seems to imply the Earth is going to rack and ruin and we should pin our hopes on the mystical 'Planet Zero'. If any song were Ballard-inspired, it's surely this track, with its talk of a 'whole world on fire' and 'all those other mysteries'. It's a sci-fi fascination.

### 'The Walls Came Down' (M. Been)

Duration: 3.54

Simple Minds' tendency to include a cover song continues, this time with another track by The Call. It was the band's debut single, released in 1983 and featured on their album *Modern Romans*, released the same year. The decision to cover this track came from its political bite. Jim Kerr felt that the song had renewed relevance in the current social and political climate, especially in relation to the Russian invasion of Ukraine. The song was performed live during the recommencement of the *40 Years of Hits* tour in 2022, which, by way of timing, acted as a showcase for songs that would feature on *Direction of the Heart*.

## Deluxe Edition tracks

### 'Direction of the Heart'

Duration: 4.55

The song was originally released as a B-side on the special edition 'Magic' 7-inch single that came as part of the deluxe bundle releases for *Walk Between Worlds*. The track was rerecorded in Taormina in 2022 during the sessions for the album and added as a bonus track on the deluxe edition with the full title of 'Direction of the Heart (Taormina 2022)'. It seems a curious decision to make the title track of the album a deluxe edition bonus track only. Lyrically, it's a song that suggests you follow your heart, and that true passions should be explored and worked on. Musically, it has a heavy electronic vibe, which I feel gets a little 'overcooked' in the Taormina 2022 version. Sometimes rerecords add a new element or dimension to a song, but at other times something gets lost or overworked. I feel the latter happened in this case, but that is entirely a personal observation.

### 'Wondertimes'

Duration: 4.54

The song sounds more akin to a legacy track from *Graffiti Soul* to my ears. It has the same kind of musical motif as tracks on *Graffiti Soul*, minus the mystical intro synths and programming at the beginning of the track. The drum sounds more like Mel Gaynor's. There are acoustic drums on the song, yet Cherisse Osei is not credited as playing drums on this track, which I find strange as she gets credit for playing on other tracks on the album. My guess is that because no one has been credited for the drums on 'Wondertimes' Mel Gaynor is playing. Lyrically, it could be seen as a love song with lines such as, 'And I need you like no other'. It sounds as if Kerr is referring to a person? But he could be referring to a feeling. My feeling is that the song is about Kerr and Burchill and the band, and their past with the band and those past 'wondertimes'. However, they're still happening. There's a forward momentum. In continuing to tour the world and play live, they always 'go back to wondertimes'.

APPENDIX I

# Non-Album Singles and Solo Releases

## 'Don't You (Forget About Me)'

Written by Keith Forsey and Steve Schiff

| | |
|---|---|
| US: | February 1985 |
| UK: | 9 April 1985 |
| Personnel: | Bass: Derek Forbes<br>Drums, percussion: Mel Gaynor<br>Guitars: Charlie Burchill<br>Keyboards: Charlie Burchill, Michael MacNeil<br>Vocals: Jim Kerr |
| Duration: | 4:20 |
| Produced by: | Keith Forsey |
| Chart position: | UK: 7; US: 1 |

The story behind this song is a well-known to ardent Simple Minds fans. However, for the casual fan or the new fan that may have only recently discovered Simple Minds, the story might not be as familiar. It started in the later stages of 1984.

There are a few urban legends floating around that have been told over the years. Some include the offering of the song to Billy Idol—a plausible notion given that the producer of Idol's output at the time was the song's co-writer, Keith Forsey. It was reputedly also offered to Bryan Ferry. Yet another myth involved the supposed coercion to record the song from Kerr's then wife, Chrissie Hynde. When I asked Kerr about this several years ago he refuted it, declaring the claim was 'news to me'.

Another tale involved a recording of a demo made by Forsey and co-writer Steve Schiff, with a copy of it being given to Mick MacNeil who then pocketed the cassette, forgetting to let the other band members know about it until

Forsey contacted them later. One thing is clear from the stories that have been told about this song for the past forty years: both the director of *The Breakfast Club,* John Hughes, and Forsey, were adamant Simple Minds should record the song. Extra clout on the side of Hughes and Forsey came from Simple Minds' US record label A&M. They had a vested interest in getting Simple Minds to agree to record the song, as A&M's movie-production offshoot, A&M Films, was funding the production of the movie.

Of course, at that time the band weren't very keen on recording a song that wasn't their own composition, unless they decided to cover a song for their own reasons—usually in homage to a musical influence. Combine this with a relatively unknown director with just one film under his belt (although he had written the script of several others), involving a plot about high-school teens on detention—a rather alien concept to a group of Glaswegian men—and the band's reluctance to be involved can be justified.

Up to this point, the only cover Simple Minds had commercially released was a version of 'Street Hassle' for *Sparkle in the Rain.* Recording 'Don't You (Forget About Me)' was a different thing entirely. A new song, never previously commercially released, to be recorded as Simple Minds. Jim Kerr recalled when discussing the song that the band liked Keith Forsey more than they liked the song. With Forsey pestering the band to the point of irritation, they finally relented and decided to spend an afternoon recording the song for him. This was seen mostly as an exercise in getting him off their backs.

At the beginning of 1985, the single was on the production line at the pressing plant being prepared for release to coincide with the film's release in cinemas in the United States on 15 February 1985. The film's soundtrack and the 7-inch single of 'Don't You (Forget About Me)' were released the following week.

It was a slow ride up the charts. It took twelve weeks for the single to hit its peak No. 1 position on the Billboard Hot 100 and it would spend another ten weeks making its descent out, claiming a spot on the Billboard Hot 100 each week between 23 February and 20 July 1985.

In comparison to the song's success in America, the song peaked at No. 7 in the UK chart but spent an incredible sixty-five weeks in the top 100 through 1985 and 1986. It spent its first nine weeks in the UK chart within the top forty. Who could have foreseen that they would achieve a No. 1 single Stateside before they managed to reach the same chart position in the UK? The promotional video for the single became one of the most heavily played videos on MTV in 1985. The Simple Minds official YouTube account uploaded the video for 'Don't You (Forget About Me)' on 3 December 2010. As of March 2025, the video has been viewed more than 358 million times. On the Simple Minds Facebook page on 20 December 2024, it was announced that the song had exceeded one billion streams on music streaming service Spotify.

The box office success of *The Breakfast Club* and chart success of the song has led 'Don't You (Forget About Me)' to be the most successful single of Simple

Minds' career. Whatever doubts the band had about the track prior to its release quickly ebbed away as it climbed the charts.

In front of an estimated audience of 1.9 billion television viewers around the world, and in front of almost 90,000 people at the JFK Stadium in Philadelphia, Simple Minds performed the hit at Live Aid on 13 July 1985. In recent years, Jim Kerr has referred to 'Don't You (Forget About Me)' as the 'black hit from space'.

## 'Stagefright'

UK: 3 June 2011 (free digital download)
Personnel: backing vocals: Sarah Brown; bass: Ged Grimes; drums: Mel Gaynor; guitars: Charlie Burchill; keyboards: Andy Gillespie; vocals: Jim Kerr
Duration: 4:10
Produced by: Gavin Goldberg, Andy Wright and Simple Minds
Chart position: UK: -; US: -

'Stagefright' was a song that developed during the recording sessions for *Graffiti Soul*. The song was subsequently recorded in 2010 and eventually released as an exclusive download via Facebook in June 2011. The track was then included on the 3CD version of the *Celebrate: Greatest Hits* + compilation released in 2013. It appeared on the live set during the *Greatest Hits* forest tour of 2011. Lyrically, it details the story of a touring band playing to audiences and the positive connections generated between musical artists and their fans at concerts, bordering on the hyperbolic and cliched tales of 'sex, drugs and rock 'n' roll'. The recording required a slight change to one line of the lyrics to make it radio friendly.

## *Lostboy! AKA Jim Kerr*

UK: 17 May 2010
Personnel: additional arrangements, guitars, programming: Andy Gillespie, Owen Parker, Paul Statham; backing vocals: Jez Coad, Miss Jo Cocker, Martin Hanlin; bass: Charlie Jones; drums: Mel Gaynor; guitars, keyboards, programming: Jez Coad; vocals: Lostboy! (AKA Jim Kerr)
Duration: 48 minutes (standard CD) 60 minutes (deluxe limited-edition CD)
Produced by: Jez Coad
Chart position: UK: 94

The decade between 1999 and 2009 saw a 180 degree turn in the mindset of Jim Kerr. As the previous millennium was nearing its end, Kerr felt he was at a creative nadir, and that Simple Minds may have run their course. The album the band had produced that year, *Our Secrets are the Same*, was stifled by lukewarm interest from their record label and a leaked copy of the album spreading out through the fanbase. The following ten years would see Kerr rekindle his passion for making music and a sea change in the fortunes of Simple Minds.

By 2009, when the band released *Graffiti Soul*, they had returned to UK top-ten albums chart success. For Kerr, his writing had once again become prolific, and he was eager to continue to write and record as the hunger returned. Charlie Burchill had other commitments and, as a result, Kerr decided that this might be the time to go solo. He made it clear from the beginning that Simple Minds would continue, but despite Burchill's absence he didn't want to waste time and so Lostboy! AKA was born.

Kerr chose to work on the project with Jez Coad, having previously worked with him on the two most recent Simple Minds albums. As well as Coad, other musicians involved in the project included Paul Statham and Owen Parker, who teamed up with Kerr for writing compositions. Some of the writing began before Kerr had even whole-heartedly committed to the solo project. As a copious collection of compositions gathered, Kerr noticed some were not in keeping with what he felt were Simple Minds songs. A dilemma on what to do with this material was answered by the question of whether there was another creative side to Jim Kerr beyond being lyricist, vocalist and frontman for Simple Minds.

In a diary post at the beginning of January 2010, Kerr stated:

> Somehow, I had tuned into the boy that I used to be—the passionate kid that I had left behind. And mysterious as that all was, there was no denying how thrilled I was to be reconnecting with the energetic outlook and liberating values at the core of that distantly familiar character. Rapidly I then began considering what kind of songs could be created if I could now immerse myself in engaging fully with that young ghost. 'Lostboy! AKA' is the result of that curiosity, and I am exhilarated by it. No mere dance with the past, thanks to the vision of co-writer and producer Jez Coad, much of these songs feel to me that they could be signals from tomorrow. It's only a first step, but I can easily imagine taking this new relationship much further in parallel with the continuing great story of Simple Minds.

To the uninitiated it could have been seen as a self-indulgent vanity project, but this view would be doing Kerr's solo work a disservice. The album was recorded in the later months of 2009 after Simple Minds had been on the road touring *Graffiti Soul*. *Lostboy! AKA Jim Kerr* was released on 17 May 2010. A position in the UK albums chart was achieved for a solitary week, scraping in at No. 94. To me, this is not indicative of the calibre of the compositions on the album.

On a final note, in an interview at the time of the album's release, Kerr more than hinted that there would be a follow-up album for *Lostboy! AKA Jim Kerr*. Now, some fifteen years since the release of the album, it seems unlikely that a follow-up will happen.

## 'Refugee'

Duration: 4.11

The album begins with full intent, although it comes in with a slam after a mid-tempo electronic start. A slap of Mel Gaynor snare drum and off we go on the Lostboy! AKA journey. Salvation offered to the dispossessed and the oppressed. Further penance for the self-proclaimed 'affectedly unaffected' way Kerr said he delivered 'I Travel'? Who knows?

## 'She Fell in Love with Silence'

Duration: 4.32

A song for which Kerr, when discussing its inspiration, provided two slightly differing accounts.

The first was that a friend he knew had been in an abusive relationship and once she had found the courage to escape and leave, she found solace in nature and getting used to feeling comfort in silence. Silence no longer instilled a dooming sense of foreboding and a palpable rising fear; it had become freedom and liberation.

The second was a similar story of freedom and liberation from an abusive relationship, but the woman at the centre had altered in proximity to Kerr from a close friend to a woman interviewed in a newspaper article as a survivor of domestic abuse.

Either way, the song is an uplifting celebration of regaining freedom of expression and the escape from domestic violence.

## 'Shadowland'

Duration: 4.08

An ode to Lostboy! AKA himself? A feeling that Kerr is bringing an alternative version, or a truer version of his younger self out into the light? In an interview discussing Lostboy! AKA at the time of the album's release, Kerr said a rather curious thing: 'I started to imagine if that kid (Kerr himself, aged between 18 and 22) had access to the studio I had access to (in the present day); access to the musicians, access to the equipment—what kind of music would he make now, given what I could recall of his passions'. The strange thing is, he had it! The 18 to 22-year-old Jim Kerr had access to all that. Music production hadn't advanced so far as to be thoroughly alien in 2009. It almost sounds as if Kerr wished to start all over again, or approach things differently. The result could have been failure. It was such a curious statement. A notion of erasing the foundations of success.

## 'Return of the King'

Duration: 3.48

Inspired by an evening spent in the presence of Billy MacKenzie, in which Kerr related an anecdote. Apparently MacKenzie had grown disillusioned with David Bowie's (then) current musical direction, so decided the only thing for it was to write Bowie a song. Kerr dedicated the track to MacKenzie in the album's liner notes.

## 'Red Letter Day'

Duration: 4.20

A red-letter day is an auspicious or celebratory day. There is a woman at the centre of the song—'she knows why my heart moves towards it', one line ambiguously states. 'It' could be any number of things: love, marriage, ambition, music—assuming Kerr/Lostboy! AKA himself is the narrator of the track and it's autobiographical.

## 'Remember Asia'

Duration: 3.47

A song inspired by an incident that happened during a night in Japan when an earthquake warning klaxon disturbed patrons in a hotel, with two patrons caught in a rather tricky situation as the warning siren rang out. In an interview at the time of the album's release, Kerr hinted that the song's theme was autobiographical.

## 'Bulletproof Heart'

Duration: 4.32

Not so much a cover of the Fingerprintz original, but a reimagining of the track, as Kerr altered and added some lyrics. The song is said to be about the Irish Troubles, but could more broadly be about any city deemed to be dangerous. It could just as easily have been about Glasgow.

## 'Lostboy'

Duration: 3.50

Inspired by a night spent in New York with a close friend in 1979 when Simple Minds were on their first trip Stateside. Kerr remembered this friend reminiscing about their recent past together. When I first heard the track, I felt it sounded more like an ode to Lostboy! AKA himself, and that Kerr was expressing a nostalgia for the young man he'd once been. It seemed to be a recollection of the version of Jim Kerr who had an acute vision, lashings of self-belief and ambition to burn.

## 'Nail Thru My Heart'

Duration: 5.12

This could be seen as a sequel (or even perhaps a prequel) to 'New Warm Skin', the obscure B-side of 'I Travel'. The lines 'Is this a war/Is this a god' can be heard before the first verse begins and again at the end of the second verse—but with the lines reversed. Curiously the subject matter of the song seems to bear little relation to the alleged subject matter of 'New Warm Skin': plastic surgery. I have always felt that there was something much deeper under the surface (excuse the pun) of 'New Warm Skin'. 'Nail Thru My Heart' compounds that view.

### 'Soloman Solohead'

Duration: 3.26

It's quite heavy and dark. It's as near to true 'heavy rock' as Jim Kerr has ever got, as far as I am aware. Again, rather ambiguous subject matter. It could be interpreted as a sequel to 'Boys from Brazil' perhaps?

### 'The Wait: Parts 1+2'

Duration: 5.51

The track starts with a mid-tempo beat, the type that suggests a resting heartbeat. There's something that conjures an anticipation within the musical structure, expressed through electronic drums, synths and electric guitar. It puts you in the place of a sprinter at the running track, limbering up before placing yourself on the blocks awaiting the starter's pistol. The runners are off around the three-minute mark. Acoustic drums come in and lyrically Kerr offers the details of the runner coming to the finish line successful. The glory! But it's not enough. It's not the end goal. This race was just the start. But isn't 'the race the prize'? No matter about that now, there is something to celebrate all the same. Winning is transient, as are the celebrations it brings. But life itself is worth celebrating. Quite possibly the finest song Jim Kerr has ever written that isn't a Simple Minds song.

## Deluxe limited edition tracks

### 'Mr Silversmith'

Duration: 4.19

A heavy, dark, menacing piece. It has drums but they are buried down in the mix. Musically the song feels like a sibling to 'Soloman Solohead' without the prominent use of drums. Lyrically, it appears to be a song about deception. The main repetition of lyrics is 'You can walk away/But you can't hide'. A lyrical trope that has been used countless time by others in the past.

### 'Karma to This Rain'

Duration: 4.19

Musically a traditional classic rock feel with acoustic guitar and heavy, low bass lines. Kerr is channelling Dylan meeting Neil Young with his vocals on this track. Lyrically, the song suggests that actions have consequences, some karmic.

### 'Sad Stone Child'

Duration: 4.01

An emotionally intense song with lyrics such as, 'Feelings kill us when we can't explain them/There is only meaning without words/In this silence there's a hole inside us/That is only speaking when it hurts'. Musically, the song has a slow tempo and is very melancholic. A haunting other voice (possibly also Kerr) starts each verse with words delivered *Sprechgesang*-style.

## Additional tracks

### 'Jet Black the Night'

Duration: 4.14

The track sounds like a *Graffiti Soul* outtake and the guitar much like Burchill's, although it is most likely to be Jez Coad playing. It has a contemporary rock feel. The premise of the song appears to suggest that the darkness of night has a healing property. Darkness need not be full of fear and dread, but an opportunity for rest and repair, a reset. This was the A-side of a special 7-inch red vinyl bonus disc that was available with a limited edition signed release of the standard CD.

### 'What Goes On'

Duration: 4.07

A cover of The Velvet Underground song written by Lou Reed and released by The Velvet Underground in 1969. Kerr is a life-long Velvet Underground and Lou Reed fan. Released as the B-side of the special edition 7-inch red vinyl CD package.

APPENDIX II

# Select Discography

## Live albums

Of the live albums that have been officially released by Simple Minds during their career, I have chosen to highlight the most significant and/or commercially successful of those released. This section of the book would be far too lengthy to list them all.

*LIVE IN THE CITY OF LIGHT*
UK: 26 May 1987
Duration: 82 minutes
Produced by: Bruce Lampcov
Chart position: UK: 1; US: 96

**Track listing**
'Ghost Dancing'
'Big Sleep'
'Waterfront'
'Promised You a Miracle'
'Someone Somewhere in Summertime'
'Oh Jungleland'
'Alive and Kicking'
'Don't You (Forget About Me)'
'Once Upon a Time'
'Book of Brilliant Things'
'East at Easter'
'Sanctify Yourself'
'Love Song'
'Sun City, Dance to the Music (medley)'
'New Gold Dream'

The first official live album recorded during the most extensive world tour of Simple Minds' career to date. The album contains recordings—all bar one song—from their concerts at Le Zenith in Paris held on 12 and 13 August 1986.

In discussing the reason for choosing to record the shows in Paris for the album on Facebook in 2017, Jim Kerr said that it had been a prior show at Le Zenith in 1984 during the *Tour du Monde* that was partly responsible. The memory of the audience's reaction to the show that night in 1984 convinced the band that Paris would firstly be great for audience participation and give the band the atmosphere they desired, and, secondly; the shows in Paris in 1986 came midway through the tour, considered to be an optimal point when the band had honed and perfected the shows. Recording at this point would avoid any potential lacklustre performance that may have crept in during the final months of the tour.

Kerr's recall and calculations were slightly off with this explanation in terms of the show's placement on the tour. In fact, the tour had surpassed 120 dates prior to the Paris shows, meaning the tour was closer to its end than its middle.

Among Simple Minds fans, it is seen as the pinnacle of the band's live performances. However, a minority feel the double album did not capture the true essence of Simple Minds live, believing the recordings were overproduced and removed the authenticity of the genuine live music experience. This point is supported by the employment of various overdubs and other post-production techniques on the album.

As previously stated, the tour was and remains the biggest the band had embarked upon with over 150 dates over a 12-month period from October 1985 to November 1986. The touring line-up of the band extended to include vocalist Robin Clark and percussionist Sue Hadjopoulous on the road with Kerr, Burchill, MacNeil, Giblin and Gaynor.

On release the album entered the UK chart at No. 1 and spent a total of twenty-one weeks on the chart. The album would subsequently re-enter the chart in June 1988 and August 1989. Jim Kerr, Charlie Burchill and Mick MacNeil made in-store appearances at HMV stores in Edinburgh on 1 June 1987 and Newcastle on 2 June. Band members signed albums for fans during these appearances.

As well as the album's success in the UK, it broke into the top-twenty charts of several other European countries as well as in the Antipodes. The album went double platinum in sales in the UK, shifting over 600,000 units.

## *5x5 Live*

UK: 19 November 2012 (2CD), 23 April 2022 (3LP)
Duration: 139 minutes
Produced by: Olivier Gerard
Chart position: Italy: 80; UK: 129; US: -

**Track listing**

'Into'

'70 Cities as Love Brings the Fall'

'Thirty Frames a Second'
'Today I Died Again'
'Celebrate'
'Life in a Day'
'Calling Your Name'
'Scar'
'King Is White and in the Crowd'
'Hunter and the Hunted'
'Wasteland'
'Love Song'
'This Fear of Gods'
'Pleasantly Disturbed'
'Room'
'The American'
'In Trance as Mission'
'Sons and Fascination'
'Sweat in Bullet'
'Changeling'
'Factory'
'Big Sleep'
'Premonition'
'Promised You a Miracle'
'Someone Somewhere in Summertime'
'Theme for Great Cities'
'Glittering Prize'
'Someone'
'Chelsea Girl'
'New Gold Dream (81-82-83-84)'

The tour was announced on the Simple Minds website on 22 November 2011, and was one of the first major tours that new band management Quietus Management had organised. It is said that the head management consultant and founder of the company, Ian Grenfell, touted the idea of touring the *X5* compilation box set to Kerr and Burchill. The tour had a limited run of dates through Europe and the UK—just sixteen shows in all. It was one of the most highly anticipated tours in the band's more recent history.

The concept behind it was to perform songs exclusively from the first five (technically six) albums of the band's back catalogue. *Sons and Fascination* and *Sister Feelings Call* were melded into one for the purposes of the tour and to give the tour its alliterative and mathematically pleasing title. Considered a tour of 'non hits', this was something of a misnomer as several of the songs performed were indeed UK top-forty hits, chiefly 'Promised You a Miracle', 'Glittering Prize' and 'Someone Somewhere in Summertime'. Other songs had been minor hits in the UK at the time of their release: 'Life in a Day', 'The American', 'Love Song' and 'Sweat in Bullet' all made it into the top seventy-five of the UK singles charts.

The tour commenced on 14 February 2012, opening in Lisbon, and concluded on 4 March 2012 in Dublin. Four UK dates saw the band play the O2 Academy in Birmingham, Barrowland Ballroom in Glasgow, Roundhouse in London, and the Ritz in Manchester.

In April 2022, to mark the fifteenth anniversary of Record Store Day, a limited edition 3LP coloured vinyl version of *5x5 Live* was released in an exclusive limited run of 2,000 copies. Considering its limited run and release primarily for RSD in 2022, the 3LP album made it onto the UK Official Chart lists for album sales (56), physical albums (54) record store chart (38) independent albums (25) and Scottish album chart (64) on its week of release.

## CELEBRATE—LIVE AT THE SSE HYDRO GLASGOW

UK: May 2014 (deluxe 2CD+2DVD), July 2014 (2CD+1DVD, Blu-ray), April 2015 (2LP)
Duration: 115 minutes (deluxe 2CD+2DVD), 90 minutes (2CD+1DVD, Blu-ray, 2LP)
Produced by: Olivier Gerard
Chart position: UK: -; US: -

**Track listing**

'Intro'
'Waterfront'
'Broken Glass Park'
'I Travel'
'Once Upon a Time (deluxe only)'
'All the Things She Said'
'Hunter and the Hunted (deluxe only)'
'Promised You a Miracle'
'Glittering Prize'
'Theme for Great Cities'
'Mandela Day'
'Someone Somewhere in Summertime'
'This Fear of Gods (deluxe only)'
'The American'
'Love Song'
'See the Lights'
'Don't You (Forget About Me)'
'Let It All Come Down (deluxe only)'
'New Gold Dream (81-82-83-84)'
'Speed Your Love to Me (Electro) (deluxe only)'
'Big Music'
'Sanctify Yourself'
'Alive and Kicking'

A recording of the concert that took place at the then newly opened SSE Hydro near the River Clyde in Glasgow. The concert took place on 27 November 2013, coincidentally on Charlie Burchill's 54th birthday. It was also filmed for release on DVD and Blu-ray. For those who enjoy interesting pieces of trivia, Jim Kerr's son, James, was credited as camera operator in the liner notes of the DVD.

The deluxe edition 2CD+2DVD package was available to pre-order from one week prior to the concert. Those who pre-ordered before 31 December 2013 also received an exclusive individually numbered 4-track CD titled 'LIVE EP FEATURING BIG MUSIC'. It featured 'Speed Your Love to Me', 'Mandela Day', 'Big Music' and 'Sanctify Yourself'. It was dispatched to eligible purchasers in January 2014. These fans received the completed 2CD+2DVD package in May 2014. This deluxe edition comprised of two DVDs; the full concert on disc one, and behind-the-scenes footage, interviews and a photo gallery on disc two. The CDs feature the concert spread over both discs.

In July 2014, a 2CD+1DVD digipak edition was released with an edited version of the concert. This version of the concert was also released on Blu-ray. The original deluxe edition 2CD+2DVD package contained a colour booklet of photos and quotes from the band members as well as a postcard image of the venue signed by all the band members.

A 2LP edition was initially released on limited-edition clear vinyl for Record Store Day on 18 April 2015, with a black vinyl version released on 31 July 2015. *Celebrate* entered UK charts in the Scottish albums (39), physical albums (68), and independent albums (15) sections on its week of release. These chart positions relate to the 2LP black vinyl edition. The 2LP clear vinyl edition spent two weeks in the UK record store chart from its week of release, peaking at No. 23 on 2 May 2015.

## *Simple Minds Live—Big Music Tour 2015*

UK: 14 November 2015 (2CD), 16 April 2016 (2LP)
Duration: 131 minutes (2CD), 68 minutes (2LP)
Produced by: Olivier Gerard
Chart position: UK: -; US: -

**CD track listing**

'Let the Day Begin'
'Blindfolded'
'Stars Will Lead the Way'
'New Gold Dream (81-82-83-84)'
'Stay Visible'
'The American (Acoustic)'
'Home (Acoustic)'
'Real Life'
'Honest Town'
'Rivers of Ice'
'Dolphins'
'Waterfront'
'Don't You (Forget About Me)'
'White Hot Day'
'Book of Brilliant Things'
'East at Easter'
'Speed Your Love to Me'
'Once Upon a Time'
'All the Things She Said'
'Let There Be Love'
'Let It All Come Down'
'Someone Somewhere in Summertime'
'Midnight Walking'
'Big Music'
'Sanctify Yourself'
'Liaison'
'She's a River'
'Riders On the Storm'
'Alive and Kicking'

**LP track listing**

'Let the Day Begin'
'Blindfolded'
'New Gold Dream (81-82-83-84)'
'Honest Town'
'Waterfront'
'Don't You (Forget About Me)'
'All the Things She Said'
'Let There Be Love'
'Someone Somewhere in Summertime'
'Midnight Walking'
'Big Music'
'Sanctify Yourself'
'Alive and Kicking'

Songs featured on these releases were recorded at various locations throughout mainland Europe and the UK during the spring leg of the *Big Music* tour in 2015. Initially released as a limited edition 2CD set and available only through the band's official online store, the album was then issued as a red vinyl 2LP set for Record Store Day 2016 with a shorter list of thirteen tracks. The vinyl edition entered the UK chart in the record store category at No. 29 one week following its release. A further reissue of the vinyl edition, this time available in white coloured vinyl, was released on 24 May 2019.

## *Acoustic In Concert*

UK: 16 June 2017
Duration: 79 minutes
Produced by: Olivier Gerard
Chart position: UK: 5 (video chart)

**Track listing**

'New Gold Dream (81-82-83-84)'
'See the Lights'
'Glittering Prize'
'Stand by Love'
'Waterfront'
'Andy Warhol'
'Chelsea Girl'
'Someone Somewhere in Summertime'
'Dancing Barefoot'
'Speed Your Love to Me'
'Promised You a Miracle'
'Don't You (Forget About Me)'
'Sanctify Yourself'
'Long Black Train'
'Alive and Kicking'
'Make Me Smile (Come Up and See Me)'

A commercial release of the performance for BBC Radio 2's *In Concert* series, recorded at the Hackney Empire on 10 November 2016. Released on DVD, Blu-ray and as a DVD+CD set. The concert was held on the eve of the release of the band's nineteenth studio album, simply titled *Acoustic*.

The concert aired live on BBC Radio 2, as well as being viewable to UK audiences live through the red button service via BBC iPlayer. The Radio 2 coverage was presented by Jo Whiley.

The final song performed on the night was a cover of Steve Harley and Cockney Rebel's 'Make Me Smile (Come Up and See Me)'. This was a surprise for fans attending the show as well as audiences watching and listening at home as Harley joined the band on stage to perform the song for the concert finale.

Upon release, it entered the UK music video chart at No. 7, peaking at No. 5 during an initial eight-week run.

## *Live in the City of Angels*

UK: 4 October 2019
Duration: 131 minutes (2CD, 4LP), 206 minutes (deluxe 4CD)
Produced by: Gavin Goldberg, Andy Wright and Simple Minds
Chart position: UK: 9; US: -

**2CD/4LP track listing**

'The Signal and the Noise'
'Waterfront'
'Love Song'
'Let There Be Love'
'Up on the Catwalk'
'Sense of Discovery'
'Glittering Prize'
'Promised You a Miracle'
'The American'
'Hunter and the Hunted'
'Stand by Love'
'Dirty Old Town'
'Theme for Great Cities'
'She's a River'
'Walk Between Worlds'
'Hypnotised'
'Someone Somewhere in Summertime'
'See the Lights'
'All the Things She Said'
'Dolphins'
'Don't You (Forget About Me)'
'New Gold Dream (81-82-83-84)'
'Once Upon a Time'
'Alive and Kicking'
'Sanctify Yourself'

**Deluxe edition CD 3+4 track listing**

'Book of Brilliant Things'
'I Travel'
'Blindfolded'
'Honest Town'
'In Dreams'
'Stars Will Lead the Way'
'Big Sleep'
'Let the Day Begin'
'Barrowland Star'
'Midnight Walking'
'Summer'
'Big Music'
'Celebrate'
'The Cross'
'Speed Your Love to Me'

In the autumn of 2018, Simple Minds embarked on their most extensive tour of the United States and Canada in over thirty years. Prior to this, tours in 2013, 2002, 1995 and 1991 had not extended beyond a tally of twenty shows in a schedule. During the *Once Upon a Time* tour the band performed more than sixty dates in North America during 1985–86.

From late September until mid-November 2018, Simple Minds played thirty-one dates across North America. Most of the resulting live album was from a recording of their concert at the Orpheum Theatre in Los Angeles (hence the title of the album), apart from 'Glittering Prize' which was recorded at The Fillmore in Miami Beach. The bonus material making up the extra two CDs was recorded in various locations as well as during soundchecks and rehearsals. This 4CD deluxe set was presented in a hardback book package with a centre 32-page booklet.

It was the band's first UK top-ten live album release since its near namesake, *Live in the City of Light*, topped the chart in 1987. It also made the Scottish album chart (2), the album sales chart (3), the album downloads chart (14), the physical albums chart (3), the vinyl albums chart (9) and the record store chart (31).

### *New Gold Dream—Live from Paisley Abbey*

UK: 27 October 2023
Duration: 44 minutes
Produced by: Peter Walsh
Chart Position: Netherlands: 12; UK: 23; US: -

**Track listing**

'Someone Somewhere in Summertime'
'Colours Fly and Catherine Wheel'
'Promised You a Miracle'
'Big Sleep'
'Somebody Up There Likes You'
'New Gold Dream (81-82-83-84)'
'Glittering Prize'
'Hunter and the Hunted'
'King Is White and in the Crowd'

At the beginning of October 2022, just prior to the release of *Direction of the Heart*, recording took place in Paisley Abbey. The performance was filmed for the Sky Arts television channel, as well as being recorded to produce a live album. The band performed at the Abbey over two days.

Some weeks prior, on 13 August 2022, Simple Minds held a concert at Princes Street Gardens in Edinburgh performing the whole of *New Gold Dream* in track list order. The concert was an addition to one held the previous night, also at Princes Street Gardens. All profits of the second concert were donated to Unicef for the Children in Ukraine appeal.

The production for Sky Arts, fully titled *Greatest Albums Live* is a series of concerts that artists perform exclusively for the channel. Simple Minds were asked to record *New Gold Dream* in its entirety for the series. The show premiered on Sky Arts on 21 July 2023.

The album was released as a deluxe digipak CD and on special red marble effect coloured vinyl. Upon release it entered the UK chart at No. 23. It also made the Scottish album chart (4), album sales chart (8), album downloads chart (11), physical albums chart (8), vinyl albums chart (7), and the record store chart (5) during the first week of release.

## Compilations

As with the section on live albums, I have chosen to highlight the most significant and/or commercially successful compilation albums that Simple Minds have released. Again, to list all the compilations that have been officially released would make this section too lengthy.

### *Celebration*

UK: February 1982
Duration: 46 minutes

Chart position: Italy: 25; UK: 45; US: -

**Track listing**

'Life in a Day'
'Chelsea Girl'
'Premonition'
'Factory'
'Calling Your Name'
'I Travel'
'Changeling'
'Celebrate'
'Thirty Frames a Second'
'Kaleidoscope'

The album was released in February 1982. It was a last-ditch effort by the band's former record label to recoup some funds when left with a sizeable debt. Simple Minds had left the label in March 1981 and signed to Virgin Records. A short time after the release of *Celebration*, Virgin acquired the band's back catalogue from former label Arista. Subsequent issues of the album were released under the Virgin label. A Virgin reissue of the album on CD in 1989 led to the erroneous inclusion of 'Kant-Kino', tacked on to the end of 'Thirty Frames a Second' and not listed on the CD.

In an open letter to Jim Kerr printed in the *New Musical Express* on 6 February 1982, Paul Morley wrote a rather cutting review of the compilation. The target was not the band, as Morley was a champion of theirs. Rather, the critique was aimed squarely at Arista for their perceived 'cash-in'. In the letter, Morley is keen to know whether Kerr was aware of the release of 'that pathetically obvious "best of"', and goes on to declare it 'a pretty desperate looking slice of s**t ... put together with only a very tiny fraction of thought'. For some curious reason Morley has some begrudging praise for the second side of the album.

Personally, I think it acted to rectify the disservice done to songs like 'Premonition' and 'Factory', as they were never released as singles when the band were with Arista, unlike 'I Travel', 'Changeling' and 'Celebrate'. To my mind the inclusion of 'Kaleidoscope' was also well thought out. It offered something new to fans that had been won over since the move to the Virgin label, but perhaps not yet ardently enough to have invested in the entire Simple Minds back catalogue. This compilation showcased the band's early output concisely.

To promote the album, Arista also reissued 'I Travel' as a single, using the same cover art (with a different colour scheme) as the *Celebration* album. The 7-inch single contained a live recording of 'Thirty Frames a Second' on its B-side. The 12-inch single contained both the live version of 'Thirty Frames' as well as a live version of 'I Travel' on its B-side. The reissued single failed to chart. Despite the single's failure, the album conversely managed some minor chart success. It had a six-week run in the top 100, peaking at No. 45.

## *Glittering Prize 81/92*

Europe: 12 October 1992
Duration: 73 minutes (Europe CD/MC), 63 minutes (Australia CD/LP, Europe LP), 55 minutes (US CD/MC)

Chart position: UK: 1; US: -

**Australia CD/MC/LP, Europe LP track listing**

'Waterfront'
'Don't You (Forget About Me)'
'Alive and Kicking'
'Sanctify Yourself'
'Love Song'
'Someone Somewhere in Summertime'
'See the Lights'
'Belfast Child'
'The American'
'All the Things She Said'
'Promised You a Miracle'
'Ghost Dancing'
'Speed Your Love to Me' (Europe CD/MC only)
'Glittering Prize'
'Let There Be Love'
'Mandela Day' (Europe CD/MC only)

**US CD/MC track listing**

'Alive and Kicking'
'See the Lights'
'Don't You (Forget About Me)'
'Promised You a Miracle'
'Sanctify Yourself'
'Belfast Child'
'Stand by Love'
'Up on the Catwalk'
'Let There Be Love'
'All the Things She Said'
'Someone Somewhere in Summertime'
'Waterfront'

The first compilation that was a true 'hits' package, as it featured a total of thirteen UK top-twenty hit singles on the 16-track UK CD and cassette versions. Of the list of sixteen tracks on the UK CD and cassette, 'Someone Somewhere in Summertime,' 'Love Song' and 'The American' charted outside of the top twenty at Nos 36, 47 and 59 respectively. The liner notes for all for formats contained a brief biographical history of the band written by Brian Hogg.

The album became the band's fifth UK No. 1, reaching the top spot one week after its release. It held the No. 1 spot for a total of three weeks. It spent a total of twenty-one consecutive weeks in the top 100 from its release, and a further twenty-six weeks sporadically from 1993–96. A single featuring a remix edit of 'Love Song' mixed by Gregg Jackman and the original single edit version of 'Alive and Kicking' was released on 7-inch vinyl and cassette two weeks prior to the release of the album. There were also two CD EPs produced. The first CD contained the remix edit of 'Love Song' and the album version of 'Alive and Kicking', as well as the instrumental of 'Alive and Kicking' and an extended version of the Gregg Jackman remix of 'Love Song'. The second CD, which would be released the following week (in the digipak along with the first CD) contained four live tracks recorded at the Barrowland Ballroom in Glasgow on 13 August 1991: 'Love Song', 'Travelling Man', 'Oh Jungleland' and 'Alive and Kicking'. The single spent a total of six weeks on the UK chart, peaking at No. 6.

The American version of *Glittering Prize 81/92* released on A&M Records features just twelve tracks in a different order and includes 'Stand by Love,' and 'Up on the Catwalk'. These two tracks only feature on the American release.

## *The Best of Simple Minds*

UK: 5 November 2001 (2CD), April 2002 (SACD), November 2007 (2CD+1DVD)
Duration: 150 minutes (2CD/SACD), 123 minutes (DVD)
Chart position: Netherlands: 11; UK: 34; US: -

**CD/SACD track listing**

| | |
|---|---|
| 'Don't You (Forget About Me)' | 'I Travel' |
| 'Promised You a Miracle' | 'Let There Be Love' |
| 'Waterfront' | 'This is Your Land' |
| 'Alive and Kicking' | 'Kick It In' |
| 'Glittering Prize' | 'Let It All Come Down' |
| 'All the Things She Said' | 'See the Lights' |
| 'Sanctify Yourself' | 'Stand by Love' |
| 'Someone Somewhere in Summertime' | 'Real Life' |
| 'Ghost Dancing' | 'She's a River' |
| 'Up on the Catwalk' | 'Hypnotised' |
| 'Speed Your Love to Me' | 'Glitterball' |
| 'Theme for Great Cities' | 'War Babies' |
| 'Love Song' | 'Mandela Day' |
| 'The American' | 'Biko' |
| 'Sweat in Bullet' | 'Belfast Child' |
| 'Life in a Day' | 'The Real Life (Raven Maize)' |

**DVD: *Live in Verona (14-15/09/89)* track listing**

| | |
|---|---|
| 'Theme for Great Cities '90 Remix' | 'Kick It In' |
| 'Street Fighting Years' | 'Ghost Dancing' |
| 'Let It All Come Down' | 'Belfast Child' |
| 'Mandela Day' | 'Sanctify Yourself' |
| 'Waterfront' | 'East at Easter' |
| 'This is Your Land' | 'Alive and Kicking' |
| 'Don't You (Forget About Me)' | 'Let It All Come Down (credits)' |
| 'Gaelic Melody' | |

***Late Night in Concert*—Recording from the concert at City Hall, Newcastle, England, 20/11/82 track listing**

| | |
|---|---|
| 'Hunter and the Hunted' | 'The American' |
| 'Glittering Prize' | 'Big Sleep' |
| 'Someone Somewhere in Summertime' | 'New Gold Dream (81-82-83-84)' |

Originally released as a double CD containing some previously unreleased mixes of certain tracks as well as the Raven Maize track 'The Real Life', which was a remix of the original 1988 Corporation of One track of the same title that had sampled 'Theme for Great Cities' and Queen's 'Bohemian Rhapsody' to become a late-nineties dance classic. Upon release, the album spent six weeks in the UK chart, peaking at No. 34. The album also reached the top forty charts in several other European countries.

As a double CD comprising thirty-two tracks, it is a broader showcase of the band's history than its predecessor, *Glittering Prize 81/92*. All the tracks had been digitally remastered for the release. In April 2002, *Best of* was released on SACD format. In 2007, the original 2CD set was repackaged to incorporate the addition of a DVD and was presented in a fold-out digipak. The CDs were identical to the 2001 version of the *Best Of* discs while the DVD featured material that was on the second disc of *Seen the Lights—A Visual History*, released in 2003. This second disc was subsequently released as a single DVD titled *Seen the Lights—Live in Verona*.

Upon its original release in 2001, *Best of* entered the UK chart in the top forty, peaking at No. 34 during a six-week run. In November 2003 when *Seen the Lights—A Visual History* was released, it entered the official UK music video chart at No. 18.

## *Early Gold*

UK: 30 June 2003
Duration: 70 minutes
Chart position: UK: -; US: -

**Track listing**

'Life in a Day'
'Chelsea Girl'
'Changeling'
'Factory'
'Premonition'
'I Travel'
'Celebrate'
'Thirty Frames a Second'
'The American'
'Love Song'
'Sweat in Bullet'
'Promised You a Miracle'
'Glittering Prize'
'Someone Somewhere in Summertime'
'New Gold Dream (81-82-83-84)'

This single CD release was issued by Virgin less than two years after the more comprehensive *Best of* double CD in 2001. A few months after the release of *Early Gold*, Virgin released the first Simple Minds official DVD, the two-disc *Seen the Lights—A Visual History* set. The thinking behind this release was perhaps to offer a concise single CD compilation of the band's early history from 1979–82. The liner notes for the album contained a brief passage by Jim Kerr, recalling the 'exciting blur' the band experienced in those early years. The text ends with the sentence, 'This is the sound of those times, and these songs are our Early Gold'. The track listing of the CD was compiled by the band. All the tracks were released as singles except for 'Factory', 'Premonition' and 'Thirty Frames a Second'. All the tracks are the original full-length album versions.

## CELEBRATE—THE GREATEST HITS+

UK: 25 March 2013
US: May 2013
Duration: 150 minutes (2CD), 216 minutes (3CD), 79 minutes (US)
Chart position: UK: 19; US: -

**2CD track listing**

'Life in a Day'
'Chelsea Girl'
'Changeling'
'I Travel'
'Celebrate'
'The American'
'Love Song'
'Promised You a Miracle'
'Glittering Prize'
'Someone Somewhere in Summertime'
'Waterfront'
'Speed Your Love to Me'
'Up on the Catwalk'
'Don't You (Forget About Me)'
'Alive and Kicking'
'Sanctify Yourself'
'All the Things She Said'
'Ghost Dancing'
'Belfast Child'
'This is Your Land'
'Kick It In'
'Let There Be Love'
'See The Lights'
'Stand by Love'
'She's a River'
'Hypnotised'
'Glitterball'
'War Babies'
'Space'
'Cry'
'Spaceface'
'Home'
'Rockets'
'Stars Will Lead the Way'
'Blood Diamonds'
'Broken Glass Park'

**3CD track listing**

*1979–1984*

'Life in a Day'
'Chelsea Girl'
'Changeling'
'I Travel'
'Celebrate'
'The American'
'Love Song'
'Sweat in Bullet'
'Theme for Great Cities'
'Promised You a Miracle'
'Glittering Prize'
'Someone Somewhere in Summertime'
'New Gold Dream (81-82-83-84)'
'Waterfront'
'Speed Your Love to Me'
'Up on the Catwalk'

*1985–91*

'Don't You (Forget About Me)'
'Alive and Kicking'
'Sanctify Yourself'
'All the Things She Said'
'Biko'
'This is Your Land'
'Kick It In'
'Let It All Come Down'

'Ghost Dancing'
'Promised You a Miracle' (Live)
'Belfast Child'
'Mandela Day'
'Let There Be Love'
'See the Lights'
'Stand by Love'
Real Life'

*1995–2013*
'She's a River'
'Hypnotised'
'Glitterball'
'War Babies'
'Space'
'Jeweller to the Stars'
'Dancing Barefoot'
'Cry'
'Spaceface'
'One Step Closer'
'Home'
'Stranger'
'Stay Visible'
'Rockets'
'Stars Will Lead the Way'
'Stagefright'
'Blood Diamonds'
'Broken Glass Park'

**US track listing**
'I Travel'
'The American'
'Love Song'
'Promised You a Miracle'
'Glittering Prize'
'Someone Somewhere in Summertime'
'Waterfront'
'Speed Your Love to Me'
'Up on the Catwalk'
'Don't You (Forget About Me)'
'Alive and Kicking'
'Sanctify Yourself'
'All the Things She Said'
'Belfast Child'
'See The Lights'
'She's a River'
'Glitterball'
'Blood Diamonds'
'Broken Glass Park'

Released as a 2CD and 3CD set in Europe on 25 March 2013, both the 2CD and 3CD editions included new material—two previously unreleased tracks in the form of 'Blood Diamonds' and 'Broken Glass Park', which would subsequently be rerecorded for *Big Music* released in 2014. The 3CD set also contains the track 'Stagefright', which had previously only been released as a free limited download track made available to fans through either the Simple Minds Facebook page or via the members area of the Simple Minds website. Several weeks later a single CD version of *Celebrate* was released in the US and Canada.

## *40: The Best of 1979–2019*

UK: 1 November 2019
Duration: 73 minutes (CD, 2LP), 169 minutes (3CD)
Chart position: UK: 27; US: -

**CD track listing**

'Waterfront'
'Love Song'
'I Travel'
'Glittering Prize'
'Sense of Discovery'
'Someone Somewhere in Summertime'
'See the Lights'
'Belfast Child'
'Promised You a Miracle'
'Honest Town'
'Don't You (Forget About Me)'
'Chelsea Girl'
'Hypnotised'
'Stars Will Lead the Way'
'For One Night Only'
'Sanctify Yourself'
'Mandela Day'
'Alive and Kicking'

**2LP track listing**

'Chelsea Girl'
'I Travel'
'Love Song'
'Promised You a Miracle'
'Glittering Prize'
'Someone Somewhere in Summertime'
'Waterfront'
'Don't You (Forget About Me)'
'Alive and Kicking'
'Sanctify Yourself'
'Belfast Child'
'Mandela Day'
'See the Lights'
'Hypnotised'
'Stars Will Lead the Way'
'Honest Town'
'Sense of Discovery'
'For One Night Only'

**3CD track listing**

'Waterfront'
'Love Song'
'I Travel'
'Glittering Prize'
'Sense of Discovery'
'The American'
'Up on the Catwalk'
'She's a River'
'Someone Somewhere in Summertime'
'See the Lights'
'Jeweller to the Stars'
'War Babies'
'Belfast Child'
'Home'
'Magic'
'Promised You a Miracle'
'This is Your Land'
'Honest Town'
'Glittering Prize' (Acoustic)
'Waterfront' (Acoustic)
'See the Lights' (Acoustic)
'Let There Be Love'
'New Gold Dream (81-82-83-84)'
'All the Things She Said'
'Once Upon a Time'
'Don't You (Forget About Me)'
'Chelsea Girl'
'Cry'
'Hypnotised'
'Stars Will Lead the Way'
'For One Night Only'
'Theme for Great Cities'
'Life in a Day'
'Changeling'
'Celebrate'
'Blindfolded'
'Sanctify Yourself'
'Mandela Day'
'Speed Your Love to Me'
'Alive and Kicking'

A very heavily edited *Best of* compilation that tried to do too much with the amount of space it was given, except with respect to the 3CD set which had the opposite result (plenty of space left unused). It was ostensibly a plug for one 'new' song—a cover of King Creosote's 'For One Night Only'—and push for a similarly titled tour that would follow the release, beginning in February 2020. The tour was halted ten days after its start due to the outbreak of Covid-19. Available in a single CD, 2LP and 3CD formats. All sets featured 'For One Night Only', which was also released as a digital download single on streaming platforms to promote the compilation. The decision for the 3CD set to retain the edited versions of the songs rather than full-length versions is quite inexplicable.

## Box sets

I have chosen to highlight the most significant and/or commercially successful box sets. Those omitted include the super deluxe editions of *Sparkle in the Rain* and *Once Upon a Time* released in 2015, *New Gold Dream (81-82-83-84)* released in 2016, and *Street Fighting Years* released in 2020.

### *Themes*

UK: September and October 1990 (Volumes 1-4), 23 June 2008 (Volume 5, 1-5 box set)
Duration: 497 minutes
Chart position: UK: -; US: -

**Volume 1: March '79–April '82**
Duration: 88 minutes
Theme 1-5

'I Travel'
'Celebrate'
'Film Theme'
'The American'
'League of Nations'
'Sound in 70 Cities'
'Love Song'
'This Earth That You Walk Upon'
'Life in a Day'
'Sweat in Bullet'
'20th Century Promised Land'
'League of Nations'
'In Trance as Mission'
'Promised You a Miracle'
'Theme for Great Cities'
'Seeing Out the Angel'

**Volume 2: August '82–April '85**
Duration: 88 minutes
Theme 6-10

'Glittering Prize (Club Mix)'
'New Gold Dream (81-82-83-84)' (German 12-inch Mix)
'Glittering Prize' (Theme)
'Someone Somewhere in Summertime'
'King Is White and in the Crowd'
'Soundtrack for Every Heaven'
'Waterfront'
'Hunter and the Hunted'
'"C" Moon Cry Like a Baby'
'Speed Your Love to Me' (Extended Mix)
'Speed Your Love to Me'
'Bass Line'
'Don't You (Forget About Me)'
'Up on the Catwalk'
'A Brass Band in African Chimes'

**Volume 3: September '85–June '87**
Duration: 109 minutes
Theme 11-15
'Alive and Kicking'
'Alive and Kicking' (Instrumental)
'Up on the Catwalk' (Live)
'Sanctify Yourself' (Extended Mix)
'Sanctify Yourself' (Dub)
'Love Song' (Live)
'Street Hassle' (Live)
'All the Things She Said' (Extended)
'Promised You a Miracle' (US Remix)
'Don't You (Forget About Me)'
'Ghost Dancing' (12-inch)
'Ghost Dancing' (Instrumental)
'Oh Jungleland' (12-inch)
'Oh Jungleland' (Instrumental)
'Promised You a Miracle'
'Book of Brilliant Things'
'Glittering Prize'
'Celebrate'

**Volume 4: February '89–May '90**
Duration: 106 minutes
Theme 16-20
'Belfast Child' (Full Length Version)
'Mandela Day'
'Biko'
'This is Your Land' (Full Length Version)
'Saturday Girl'
'Year of the Dragon'
'Kick It In' (LP Version)
'Waterfront' (89 Remix)
'Big Sleep' (Live)
'Kick It In' (Unauthorised Mix)
'Sign O' the Times'
'Let It All Come Down'
'Sign O' the Times' (CJ Mackintosh Mix)
'Jerusalem'
'Street Fighting Years'
'Mandela Day'
'Kick It In'

**Volume 5: March '91–September '92**
Duration: 106 minutes
Theme 21-25
'Let There Be Love' (Extended Mix)
'Goodnight'
'Let There Be Love' (7-inch Mix)
'Let There Be Love' (Live)
'Real Life' (Edit)
'See the Lights' (Live)

'Alive and Kicking' (Live)
'See the Lights' (Julian Mendelsohn Extended Remix)
'Theme for Great Cities '91' (Extended Version)
'Theme for Great Cities '91' (Edit)
'Soul Crying Out' (Live)
'Stand by Love'
'King Is White and in the Crowd' (Live)
'Belfast Child' (Live)
'Love Song' (Extended Version)
'Love Song' (Live)
'Travelling Man' (Live)
'Oh Jungleland' (Live)
'Alive and Kicking' (Live)

A rather innovative package idea from Virgin, one that would become quite the financial drain for ardent fans and purist collectors alike. Each volume contained five CDs consisting of various 7-inch and 12-inch versions of singles, as well as other extended mixes and B-sides from the Simple Minds catalogue from 1979–1992. Each CD featured either three or four tracks, except for *Theme 25* which has five tracks. The first four volumes were released at two-week intervals in September and October 1990.

In 1991, *Themes* was reissued as nineteen CDs and released as individual single discs in slimline cases. *Theme 20*, the *Verona* EP, was omitted from sale. These nineteen *Themes* were also released as cassette singles.

In 2008 the four original *Themes* volumes were repackaged into a square box set, complete with the addition of a fifth volume. Volume 5 was also made available on its own for those who had previously invested in volumes 1–4.

## *Silver Box*

UK: 18 October 2004
Duration: 318 minutes
Chart position: UK: -; US: -

**CD1—1979–1981**

'Life in a Day'
'Chelsea Girl'
'Here Comes the Fool'
'Changeling'
'Premonition'
'Citizen (Dance of Youth)'
'Room'
'I Travel'
'Celebrate'
'Thirty Frames a Second'
'Twist/Run/Repulsion'
'Capital City'
'New Warm Skin'
'Constantinople Line'
'Careful in Career'

**CD2—1981–1985**

'The American'
'Life in Oils'
'Glittering Prize'
'Hunter and the Hunted'

'Sweat in Bullet'
'Love Song'
'Promised You a Miracle'
'In Trance as Mission'
'Someone Somewhere in Summertime'
'The Kick Inside of Me'
'New Gold Dream (81-82-83-84)'
'Take Me to the River'
'Light My Fire'
'Don't You (Forget About Me)'

**CD3—1985–1991**
'Waterfront'
'Ghost Dancing'
'Book of Brilliant Things'
'Once Upon a Time'
'All the Things She Said'
'Alive and Kicking'
'Sanctify Yourself'
'Mandela Day'
'Real Life'
'See the Lights'

**CD4—1991–1995**
'Travelling Man'
'East at Easter'
'Bangin' on the Door'
'Stand by Love'
'Oh Jungleland'
'King is White and in the Crowd'
'Big Sleep'
'Let There Be Love'
'Ghost Rider'
'Belfast Child'
'She's a River'
'Up on the Catwalk'
'Hypnotised'

**CD5: *Our Secrets Are the Same* (see studio album entry for track list and song details)**
NB: 'Life in a Day,' 'Chelsea Girl,' and 'Here Comes the Fool' were recorded live from the Paris Theatre in London on 8 August 1979. 'Changeling,' 'Premonition,' 'Citizen (Dance of Youth),' and 'Room' were recorded for John Peel Sessions on 19 December 1979. The remaining tracks on disc one are demo recordings. On disc two, the first four tracks are demo recordings from 1981. 'Promised You a Miracle,' 'In Trance as Mission' (11 February 1982) 'Someone Somewhere in Summertime', 'Glittering Prize', 'Hunter and the Hunted' (13 August 1982) and 'The Kick Inside of Me' (11 September 1983) were all recorded for David Jensen Sessions on the dates shown. 'New Gold Dream (81-82-83-84)/Take Me to the River/Light My Fire' was recorded live at Barrowlands on 5 January 1985. 'Don't You (Forget About Me)' was a live recording from a rehearsal for Live Aid on 10 July 1985. On disc three, all songs were recorded live from Ahoy in Rotterdam on 3 December 1985, apart from 'Mandela Day', which was recorded live at Wembley Stadium on 11 June 1988, 'Real Life' and 'See the Lights', which were recorded live at Barrowlands on 13 August 1991. On disc four, all songs were recorded live from Barrowlands on 13 August 1991, apart from 'She's a River', 'Up on the Catwalk' and 'Hypnotised', which were recorded live in Glasgow on 10 September 1995.

This 5CD box set is now considered a prized possession among those fans fortunate enough to own a copy. It remains the only official release of *Our Secrets Are the Same*, which had initially been set for release in early 2000 but was side-lined by the band's then record company and subsequently shelved. Virgin decided to include *Our Secrets Are the Same* in this package.

The first four discs serve as an anthology of the band's formative years, celebrating their early creative *tour de force* through a selection of live concert recordings, radio sessions and demo recordings. Many of the recordings were previously unreleased.

The CDs were presented in a long, slim silver digipack (hence the title *Silver Box*) which contained a 76-page booklet filled with archival photos, a concise band history written by Alfred Bos and liner notes on *Our Secrets Are the Same* by Jim Kerr.

A review of the box set in the 28 August 2004 issue of *NME* features a review under 'Box-Set of the Week' yet it is rather slated by reviewer Rob Fitzpatrick with a suggestion on how to approach each of the five CDs as follows, 'So, devour disc one, check out two, throw away three and four and burn five. Lesson learned'. It's curious what is said about disc five as Fitzpatrick had earlier in the review described it as being 'almost wank-free'. Yet here he is suggesting that it should be 'burned'. Does he mean 'burn' in the 'making an illegal copy' sense? Either way, the review praises the early content up until the mid-1980s on disc three.

## *X5*

UK: 20 February 2012
Duration: 358 minutes
Chart position: UK: 28; US: -

**Bonus material on each disc**

1: 'Special View'/'Garden of Hate'
2: 'Kaleidoscope'/'Film Theme Dub'/'Premonition' (Live at Hurrah's Club, New York: 24/10/79)
3: 'New Warm Skin'/'I Travel' (Extended)/'Celebrate' (Extended)
4A: 'Sweat in Bullet' (Extended Remix)/'In Trance as Mission' (Live at Hammersmith Odeon, London: 25/9/81)/'This Earth That You Walk Upon' (Instrumental)
4B: 'The American' (Extended)/'League of Nations' (Live at Hammersmith Odeon, London: 25/9/81)
5: 'Promised You a Miracle' (Extended)/'Glittering Prize' (Club Mix)/'Someone Somewhere in Summertime' (Extended)/'Soundtrack for Every Heaven'/'New Gold Dream' (German 12-inch Remix)/ 'In Every Heaven'

Discounting the 2004 live and rarefied anthology that was *Silver Box*, and the fabulously bloated number of CDs used for the otherwise finely repackaged

*Themes* set released in 2008, a reissue of Simple Minds albums hadn't happened for a decade.

In 2002, Virgin had digitally remastered the Simple Minds back catalogue and released the albums as individual remasters, or in smaller double sets. There had not yet been a definitive album set—until now.

*X5*—not wanting to be pedantic but I feel it should have been titled *X6*—saw the band's first six albums repackaged into a 6CD set. *Life in a Day*, *Real to Real Cacophony*, *Empires and Dance*, *Sons and Fascination*, *Sister Feelings Call* and *New Gold Dream (81-82-83-84)* were all included in the set with original artwork printed on the cardboard inlays for each of the CDs. *Sons and Fascination/Sister Feelings Call* were packaged in a special gatefold card inlay with the artwork for the albums printed on the outer and inner folds respectively. The discs had the original vinyl label artwork printed on them.

As well as the whole albums in their original track running order, there was bonus material added to each CD relevant to the album. These bonuses are listed above.

The album release coincided with the *5x5 Live* tour which had been announced on the band's website on 22 November 2011. This tour saw the band play sixteen dates in Europe and the UK with a setlist of twenty-five songs from their back catalogue up to and including *New Gold Dream (81-82-83-84)*. Upon release *X5* entered the UK top forty chart at No. 28 and remained within the top 100 for a further week.

## *Rejuvenation: 2001–2014*

UK: 7 December 2018 (6LP), 29 March 2019 (7CD+DVD)
Duration: 245 minutes (6LP), 511 minutes (7CD+DVD)
Chart position: UK: -; US: -

CD1: *Neon Lights* plus: 'Being Boiled'/'Love Will Tear Us Apart'/'The Man Who Sold the World' (White Spaces Main Mix)/'Homosapien' (Vince Clarke Mix)'
CD2: *Cry* plus: 'Lead the Blind'/'For What It's Worth'/'The Garden'/'New Sunrise'/'Where is the Max?'
CD3: *Black and White 050505* plus: 'Too Much Television'/'Bird on a Wire'/'Mighty Joe Moon'
CD4: *Graffiti Soul* plus: 'Shadows and Light'
CD5: *Searching for the Lost Boys* (as featured in the deluxe edition of *Graffiti Soul*) plus: 'Children of the Revolution'
CD6: *Big Music* plus: 'Blindfolded (Reprise)'
CD7: *Big Music* deluxe bonuses and extras: 'Swimming Towards the Sun'/'Bittersweet'/'Liaison'/'Riders on the Storm'/'Dancing Barefoot'/'(Get A) Grip (On Yourself)' with The Stranglers/'Blindfolded' (Johnson Somerset Remix)/'Midnight Walking' (Johnson Somerset Remix)/'Honest Town' (Johnson Somerset Remix)/'Big Music' (Johnson Somerset Remix)

DVD: 'Dancing Barefoot'/'Cry'/'Home'/'Rockets'/'Stars Will Lead the Way'/'This Is It' (clip)/'Blindfolded'/'Honest Town'/'Let the Day Begin'/'Midnight Walking'/ *Neon Lights* EPK/*Black and White 050505* EPK/*Black and White 050505* Interview/*Graffiti Soul* EPK/*Big Music*: Behind the scenes/*Big Music*: Band interviews/*Big Music* clip medley: 'Human'/'Let the Day Begin'/'Midnight Walking'

This retrospective of Simple Minds' musical output from 2001–14 was titled *Rejuvenation* as the band appeared to go through a renaissance in popularity and critical acclaim.

The set was released in two formats. Firstly, as a 6LP set comprising the albums *Neon Lights*, *Cry*, *Black and White 050505*, *Graffiti Soul* and *Big Music* (as a 2LP edition) in December 2018. Secondly, as a 7CD+DVD set which included all bonus material from each of the album recordings, as well as the Johnson Somerset remixes from *Big Music* and the single release of '(Get A) Grip (On Yourself),' the band's collaborative recording with The Stranglers. The DVD featured promotional videos, EPKs, interviews and other behind-the-scenes footage as detailed. On the LP set, *Neon Lights* includes 'Being Boiled' and 'Love Will Tear Us Apart' as bonus tracks, *Black and White 050505* includes 'Too Much Television' as a bonus track. Apart from these bonus tracks, the LP versions of the albums are the standard editions.

# Bibliography

## Books


Forbes, D., *A Very Simple Mind: On Tour* (Jedburgh: McNidder & Grace, 2023)

Thomson, G., *Themes for Great Cities: A New History of Simple Minds* (London: Constable, 2022)


## Music magazines


Burke, D., 'Piece of Minds', *Vox*, Issue 28, pp. 42-44 (London: IPC Media 1993)

Butcher, B., 'Taking Kerr of Business', *New Musical Express*, 3 September 1983, pp. 22-23 (London: IPC Magazines 1983)

Cooper, M., 'Simple Minds: Professional Pupils', *Record Mirror*, Vol. 28 No. 38, 26 September 1981, p. 18 (London: Spotlight Publications 1981)

Cooper, M., 'In the Flesh: New Gold Dreams', *Number One*, Issue 17, 27 August 1983, pp. 14-15 (London: IPC Magazines 1983)

Cooper, M., 'Singing in the Rain: The Simple Minds manifesto', *Number One*, Issue 40, 4 February 1984, pp. 36-37 (London: IPC Magazines 1984)

Cranna, I., 'Simple Minds', *Smash Hits*, Vol. 3 No. 19, pp. 20-21 (Peterborough: EMAP National Publications 1981)

Gill, J., 'It's Time We Got Our Crown', *Sounds*, 19 September 1981, pp. 18-19, 44 (London: Spotlight Publications 1981)

Hanna, L., 'Only New Gold Dreamers Move Mountains', *New Musical Express*, 4 December 1982, pp. 28-29, 32, 55 (London: IPC Magazines 1982)

Lester, P., 'Classic Album: Once Upon a Time, Simple Minds', *Classic Pop*, Issue 20, pp. 54-59 (Bath: Anthem Publishing 2015)

Morley, P., 'Life in a Mind', *New Musical Express*, 3 October 1981, pp. 25-26 (London: IPC Magazines 1981)

Page, B., 'Dark Horses Turn Gold', *Noise*, Vol. 9: 2-15 September 1982, pp. 13-15, 39 (London: Spotlight Publications 1982)

Rimmer, D., 'A Bit of a Dreamer', *Smash Hits*, Vol. 4 No. 19, pp. 12-13 (Peterborough: EMAP National Publications 1982)

Sinclair, M., 'The Water Baby', *Sounds*, 3 December 1983, pp. 20-21 (London: Spotlight Publications 1983)

Snow, M., 'Do Not Disturb', *Q*, Issue 33, pp. 52-58 (London: EMAP Metro 1989)

Soave, D., 'A Gift from Heaven', *Record Mirror*, 1 May 1982, pp. 40-41 (London: United Newspapers 1982)

Stafford, P., 'A Change of Skin', *RAM*, 20 January 1984, p. 14 (Sydney: Newspress 1984)

Sutherland, S., 'The Impossible Dream', *Melody Maker*, Vol. 56 Issue 38, p. 8 (London: IPC Magazines 1981)

Sweeting, A., 'Tourists in Heaven', *Melody Maker*, Vol. 57 Issue 13, pp. 15-16, 45 (London: IPC Magazines 1982)

Sweeting, A., 'Subtle as a Flying Mallet', Melody Maker, Vol. 57 Issue 30, pp. 10-11 (London: IPC Magazines 1982)

Taylor, S., 'The Star-crossed Progress of Simple Minds', *The Face*, No. 18: October 1981, pp. 16-19 (London: Wasted Talent Media 1981)

Thrills, A., 'Simple Minds: The New Europeans? Whatever happened to the old ones then?', *New Musical Express*, 21 March 1981, pp. 21-22 (London: IPC Magazines 1981)

## Websites

https://www.billboard.com/artist/simple-minds/chart-history/tlp/, accessed 28 February 2025

https://www.billboard.com/artist/simple-minds/chart-history/hsi/, accessed 5 March 2025

https://www.discogs.com/artist/18547-Simple-Minds, accessed 17 March 2025

https://www.facebook.com/simpleminds, accessed 26 March 2025

https://www.officialcharts.com/artist/28243/simple-minds/, accessed 14 March 2025

https://priptonaweird.co.uk, accessed 31 March 2025

https://www.simpleminds.com, accessed 26 March 2025

http://simpleminds.org, accessed 28 March 2025

https://www.youtube.com/results?search_query=simple+minds, accessed 26 March 2025

https://en.wikipedia.org/wiki/Simple_Minds, accessed 20 March 2025